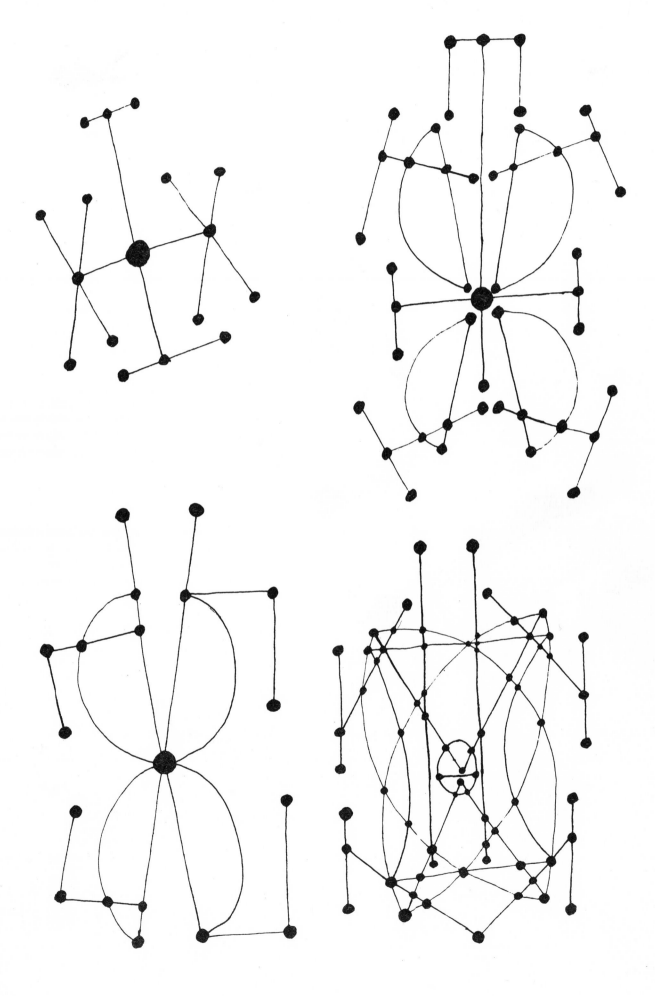

*Je Suis le Cahier*

*Je Suis le Cahier*

# JE SUIS LE CAHIER
# THE SKETCHBO

# KS OF PICASSO

Edited by Arnold Glimcher
and Marc Glimcher

May 2–August 1, 1986

The Pace Gallery
32 East 57 Street, NYC

Limited Collector's Edition

This volume is one of 4,000 printed especially for The Pace Gallery to serve
as a catalogue for its exhibition of the sketchbooks of Picasso.

Library of Congress Cataloging-in-Publication Data

Picasso, Pablo, 1881–1973.
  Je suis le cahier.

  Catalog of an exhibition held at the Pace Gallery, New York, May 2–
Aug. 1, 1986.
  Bibliography: p.
  1. Picasso, Pablo, 1881–1973 — Exhibitions.
I. Glimcher, Arnold. II. Glimcher, Marc. III. Pace Gallery. IV. Title.
N6853.P5A4   1986        741.944         86-47536
ISBN 0-87113-082-3 (lim. collector's ed.)

Endpapers: four pages from sketchbook No. 84, drawn in Juan-les-Pins,
France, in 1924, related to the endpaper designs for *Le Chef-d'oeuvre inconnu*
by Honoré de Balzac (Paris: Ambroise Vollard, 1931)

Designed by Alessandro Franchini Design, Inc., New York City

Set in type by The Typecrafters Inc., New York City

Printed in Italy by Arnaldo Mondadori Editore, Verona

# Contents

*Je Suis le Cahier*
# The Sketchbooks of Picasso

# Preface
by Arnold Glimcher

*"When I worked at the painting* War and Peace *and the series of these drawings, I picked up my sketchbooks daily, saying to myself: 'What will I learn of myself that I didn't know?' And when it isn't me anymore who is talking but the drawings I made, and when they escape and mock me, then I know I've achieved my goal."*

Picasso considered all of his works to be entries in his diary; he excluded nothing. The sketchbooks are generic chapters inextricable from his oeuvre. In Picasso's paintings the spontaneity of gesture is deceptive since the manner in which he leaves his tracks visible superficially suggests minimal preparation. Although most of Picasso's solutions appear to be immediately worked out on the canvas, this was far from the fact. Many paintings sprang fully formed as the fulfillment of preconscious models, but very often others were the product of the process of trial solution and discovery through drawing. There are eight sketchbooks for *Les Demoiselles d'Avignon*, five for the saltimbanques, four for the *Luncheon on the Grass* series, and two for *The Rape of the Sabines*. In sketchbook No. 171, Picasso inscribed: "La peinture est plus forte que moi elle me fait faire ce qu'elle veut" ("Painting is stronger than I am; it makes me do what it wants"). The sketchbook itself is the statement's validation.

"I am the sketchbook"—"Je suis le cahier"—appears in Picasso's own hand on the cover of sketchbook No. 40, and also serves as the title and cover of this book. That assertion of identity is crucial to an understanding of the sketchbooks as vital and interdependent parts of the development of Picasso's work. Conversely, we might say the sketchbooks are Picasso. They are the legacy by which we may decipher the process of Picasso's creativity and understand the cohesive totality of his lifework.

Some of the sketchbooks are small enough to have been carried in Picasso's pocket to cafés, bullfights, and on outings, to record events, responses to the environment, and interpretations of what he saw. Larger sketchbooks, sewn or spiral-bound, were used in his studio; these are volumes of preparatory and intermediary drawings in the service of picture-making as well as statements complete in themselves. Often they contain aftersketches based upon completed paintings and sculptures, such as sketchbook No. 140, which has images of the sculpture *The Bathers*. On occasion there are depictions of paintings that appear to be records of completed works functioning like inventory photographs of pieces that may have been lent to exhibitions. This kind of image exists in sketchbooks No. 96 and No. 99.

When the drawings within the sketchbooks are not preparatory studies for specific paintings, they are often used to work out solutions to problems inherent in the painting process itself. In Henri-Georges Clouzot's 1955 film *Le Mystère Picasso*, Picasso is photographed at work drawing. The sequence in which the drawings develop is a wonderment—Picasso becomes a magician materializing objects from thin air. He starts drawings in totally unexpected places, both on the page and in the anatomy of the figure. A squiggle in the center of the page evolves from an embryonic mystery to a hand that eventually grows a body, more vegetal than animal in the process. In the development of the painting *La Garoupe*, drawings construct and deconstruct each layer of the work. After painting and scrubbing away successive solutions, Picasso sticks paper to the wet paint and draws a series of new solutions that result in the finished work while allowing the viewer to comprehend the process.

The sequence of drawings within a given notebook is important to an understanding of the creative process. It is, therefore, crucial that these sketchbooks remain intact. Unfortunately, some have been dismantled since Picasso's death, and, in at least one instance (sketchbook No. 24), the pages have been sold separately. Occasionally, serial images, each so obsessively similar to the others that they might have been traced, are interrupted by a drawing that, at first, appears anachronistic (for example, sketchbook No. 59, p. 12). Sometimes the relationship is clarified later in the series, but often the drawing appears to have functioned as an oasis for refreshment before Picasso continued his analytical investigation through the end of a series.

There are 175 known sketchbooks, created between 1894 and 1967. Picasso kept most of them intact, occasionally removing a page to be released as a single drawing. After 1964, however, Picasso sold complete sketchbooks of drawings to his dealer Kahnweiler at the Galerie Louise Leiris, where, with Picasso's agreement, they were dismantled and the pages exhibited as separate drawings. In these particular sketchbooks, though, the drawings were most often conceived as individual works, elaborate in color and complexity.

This book is an attempt to document Picasso's development through his sketchbooks and to provide a reference book for scholars. It is the direct result of five years of planning and research that culminated in the first exhibition of Picasso's sketchbooks, held at the Pace Gallery in New York, May 2 to August 1, 1986, with this book as its accompanying catalogue.

After conceiving the idea of the exhibition and volume, I proposed it to Claude Picasso, whose enthusiasm and tireless assistance have made it a reality, and together we have been curators of the exhibition. He worked with me and my staff on every aspect of the project and it could not have been realized without him. Paloma Picasso was consistently encouraging, generous, and helpful, and Bernard Picasso's enthusiasm and assistance to Marc Glimcher were vital. The cooperation of Christine Picasso, Marina Picasso, Maya Picasso, and Jan Krugier is also greatly appreciated.

I am indebted to Matthew Marks, whose excellent research and devotion to the project resulted in the catalogue raisonné, and to Marc Glimcher, whose indefatigable spirit, attention to detail, and research and organization in coediting this volume were invaluable.

I am honored and grateful that E. A. Carmean, Sam Hunter, Rosalind Krauss, Theodore Reff, Robert Rosenblum, and Gert Schiff agreed to write about the notebooks, and set aside other commitments to meet the deadline. Margi Conrads did the photographic research relating to those texts, for which I express my thanks. I would also like to thank Mildred Glimcher; Michèle Archambault Dulman; Sydney Picasso; Rafael Lopez-Sanchez; Laura Ruiz-Picasso; S.P.A.D.E.M.; Martine Guigaz; Marie Teresa Ocaña; Dominique Bozo; Morton Janklow; the staff of The Pace Gallery; the Musée Picasso, Paris; and the Museo Picasso, Barcelona.

# Foreword
by Claude Picasso

It has been raining all day, so we children have been in Cannes at the movies. It is late afternoon now and as we drive up the winding road to Villa la Californie, the lights are already on in people's homes. When it rains on the Côte d'Azur all is grim and awkward. We cannot go to the beach or play among the eucalyptus, mimosas, and tall palm trees on our pirate treasure hunts, or float away on a raft in a six-by-six-foot pool two feet deep, or ride a bicycle to the bullfight with the goat or hunt for snakes to tie around the kitchen faucet to terrorize the maid. No, on rainy days we have to be quiet, as quiet as our own image. We have to remain indoors, shackled wild ones. One last turn on avenue Costebelle and Jeannot, the chauffeur, will honk twice, and Lucette, the *gardienne*, will open the elaborate but blind wrought-iron gate and we will be home, and will run into the atelier through the enormous rococo glass and wood door and tell the latest adventures of Jerry Lewis and Dean Martin in that other Californie.

But, as unusual as the rain in the south of France, the atelier is dark. We tiptoe upstairs and walk into Jacqueline's sitting room. She puts a finger on her mouth: silence! I creep back and around through the bathroom to the bedroom. My father is sitting in darkness except for the twenty-five-watt bulb in the night-light above his head, clipped to the painting on wood paneling, face to the wall, that is the headboard. Resting on his raised leg is a big spiral-bound notebook opened to a page of writing in red pencil. His left hand is wrapped around his bald head to touch the right ear as it often is when he is thinking. I do not say anything, I caress the fur blanket. I do not even dare read what is written. I am ten or eleven and used to my father's drawing in notebooks and working in his studio at night with strong electric lights, but this is odd.

In September 1974, almost a year and a half after my father had died, we started making a proper inventory of his belongings and embarked on research about his work that is not complete yet. Before we started sifting through works and objects one by one, we sampled problems to come by walking through the rooms thinking up categories. Soon all the tens of thousands of objects would become numbers, would be dated, measured, photographed, tagged, and matched to existing catalogues such as Zervos, Bloch, and Geiser. Those catalogues in turn would be annotated with our verifications and corrections. The headboard of my father's bed would return to being Zervos XV, 237, *Françoise Reading* of January 29, 1953, 114 x 146 cms, and then MP207 in the Picasso Museum in Paris. The spiral notebook with the red writing in it, the manuscript for the *El Entierro del Conde de Orgaz* published in 1969 by Ediciones la Cometa, would become No. 146 in the Cramer catalogue.

But so much more was brought to light. For the first time I could roam freely through the house, at first shyly because of the historical responsibility of upsetting this organized disorder, then hungrily—finding again paintings, sculptures, familiar objects, old toys, favorite shoes and hats; discovering in leather satchels notepads, photos, circus tickets, Apollinaire drawings, Max Jacob's notebooks with drawings by both Jacob and Picasso. Out of this chaotic jumble came the sketchbooks—a "live" testimony to my father's thought processes.

Imagine the work of every period just laid against a wall according to size. Every room is filled with memories and the smell of paint. Every room is brimming with collectors' dreams, with museum curators' show material, with historians' missing links, with blank paper and sharp pencils and even sharper gouges for engraving. And here we go straightening all this out. At least the sketchbooks need not be organized. They are, from one page to the next, from cover to cover, an adventure—a diary of the painter, the layers of paint, thin or heavy-brooding or jolly on a canvas. They are the notes working up to something or bouncing off something else, perhaps a sculpture onto a painting and back. The pages of the notebooks are the sketches for paintings but they are also often the afterwords. Sometimes they stand as elaborate works on their own. Picasso's notebooks are stepping-stones to trampolines for somersaults. Some notebooks no longer exist. They were taken apart and sold as individual drawings in the later years. Sadly, then, the magic is lost. Very often, however, no one had known them as notebooks, because they appeared in Zervos in separate parts, not one page after another as you would expect but scattered through one volume, maybe two, and sometimes not in chronological order.

This fortunate circumstance means that today we can all discover the notebooks of Pablo Picasso and share the excitement and intimacy of unraveling the enigma of painting, writing, sculpturing, and drawing the twentieth century.

# I. Six Complete Sketchbooks

*Picasso, 1904*

# The *Saltimbanques* Sketchbook No. 35, 1905

by E. A. Carmean, Jr.

*Figure 1. Picasso* Family of Saltimbanques *oil on canvas, 1904–1905. National Gallery of Art, Washington. Chester Dale Collection*

"Chronologically we are entering the unknown," wrote Pierre Daix and Georges Boudaille of Picasso's rose period, in their classic volume of the artist's early years, published in 1966.[1] And with good reason. These eighteen months, from the end of 1904 until May of 1906, not only gather Picasso's saltimbanque and circus themes, they also mark the transition from the youthful blue-period works to the classicizing and abstracting pictures made at Gosol, works created, so to speak, near the border of cubism. Furthermore, this period embraces Picasso's first clearly major undertaking, in the central painting of this period: the *Family of Saltimbanques*, the very large picture now at the National Gallery of Art, Washington (figure 1).

In 1980, the rose period gained some new clarity. In that year, I requested the conservation laboratory of the National Gallery to make a complete x-radiographic record of the *Family of Saltimbanques*.[2] The resultant photographic images (figure 2), combined with other, subsequent laboratory examinations and an extensive review of the rose-period works and the accompanying art historical literature, showed that the *Family of Saltimbanques* had evolved through three very different stages, and that key elements of the initial two were still extant beneath the final surface. Almost like archaeological strata, these successive layers in the painting recorded the developments in Picasso's art during this period. Moreover, as each layered work was very different in imagery, composition, and feeling, they create a trio of artistic magnetic poles, and around one or another, many of the other rose-period works can be clustered.

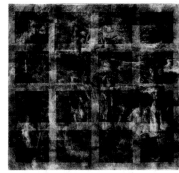

*Figure 2. Composite x-radiograph of* Family of Saltimbanques

Now other works from this key transitional period have emerged. These are the drawings and notes contained in three Picasso sketchbooks of 1904–1906, No. 33, No. 35, and No. 36. Together, they further clarify Picasso's evolution of the *Family of Saltimbanques* and add new insights into his pictorial thinking during this crucial time. And, as always seems to be the case when unknown works of Picasso come to light, we find revealed in these notebooks further evidence of the depth and richness of the artist's imagination.

### A History of the Painting

A grand composition of six nearly life-size figures, the *Family of Saltimbanques* was Picasso's first truly major work. Probably beginning the painting in late 1904, Picasso continued revising it for over a year. His financial investment in this large canvas was also considerable, given that he was living at the time in near poverty—a fact that gives the creation of the painting further impact. As Daix and Boudaille wrote: "*Family of Saltimbanques* was not commissioned. Picasso undertook this enormous painting for his own pleasure, a very costly one so far as canvas, stretcher and paints were concerned: it is about 2.12 by 2.30 meters. This gives some indication of the importance it had for him."[3] Furthermore, this unprecedented expense accounts for the three repaintings of the work revealed in the 1980 x-radiograph; Picasso could not afford to begin each composition on a new canvas.

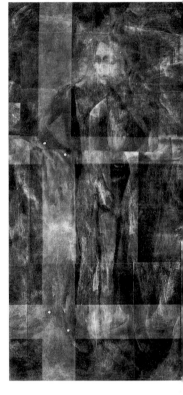

Even before the discoveries were made from laboratory evidence, there were clues that this layering existed. In her 1933 autobiography, Fernande Olivier—Picasso's mistress during this period—wrote, "Picasso had progressed, and the 'Blue Period' gave way to the *Saltimbanque*. The first of these was a large canvas: a group of actors on a plain, some are resting, the others working. A child is trying to balance on a large ball. If I remember correctly, this canvas was repainted several times."[4] Olivier's description, as we will see, is of the initial state of the large painting; it also corresponds to a gouache now in the Baltimore Museum that, along with a drypoint variant from Picasso's 1904–1905 suite of prints known as *Les Saltimbanques* and pages in sketchbook No. 35, served as studies for this first layer (figures 3 and 4). Unfortunately, art historians misread Olivier's remarks, and assumed that the large, repainted work she discussed was "lost," rather than connecting it with the *Family of Saltimbanques*.[5]

*Figure 3. Picasso* Circus Family *ink and gouache on board, 1904–1905. The Baltimore Museum of Art. The Cone Collection, formed by Dr. Claribel Cone and Miss Etta Cone of Baltimore, Maryland*

*Figure 4. Picasso* Circus Family: Les Saltimbanques *drypoint, 1904–1905. National Gallery of Art, Washington. Ailsa Mellon Bruce Fund*

An even earlier discussion of the painting had identified the existence of both the first and second states below the final composition. In his 1928 book on Picasso, André Level, who was part of an investment group that owned the *Family of Saltimbanques* between 1909 and 1914, wrote: "A famous painting [the *Family of Saltimbanques* was] superimposed over . . . two other compositions as important."[6] Curiously, Level's observations were completely overlooked in the art historical literature. This middle state remained unseen until the development of the x-radiographic evidence and the emergence of sketchbook No. 35.

Despite these two earlier "clues," it was only with the 1980 studies that a clearer profile of the creation of the large painting, and thus of the rose period, emerged. Using the successive states of the large painting as focal points, it became possible to cluster other works around each, creating three separate galaxies of saltimbanque imagery. In the course of this, a fourth—and separate—cluster also

*Figure 5. Details showing the harlequin in the x-radiograph and* Circus Family *drypoint*

Figure 6. Details showing the child at right in the x-radiograph and Circus Family drypoint

Figure 7. Picasso Two Acrobats with a Dog gouache on cardboard, 1905. Mr. and Mrs. A. M. Burden, New York

became apparent; the role of this independent group of drawings is now further identified in sketchbook No. 33. Finally, the present composition evolved through two stages in itself, steps clarified further in sketchbook No. 36. Before turning to sketchbook No. 35, and aspects of the other two, let us review our present understanding of this work as well as all the steps in the creative history of the *Family of Saltimbanques*.

### State One

Picasso began the *Family of Saltimbanques* with the scene described by Fernande Olivier. This composition, called here the "Circus Family," shows ten figures engaged in various activities in a barren landscape (see figures 3 and 4).

X-radiography reveals that several traces of this composition are still evident in the larger canvas. The bent arms and torso of the standing harlequin, and the head of the small child at the right, are most clearly discernible (figures 5 and 6). Less readily apparent, but still present, are elements of the girl on the ball, the horse in the center, and the ladder at the left margin.

In making the large painting, Picasso used the drypoint print, whose format more closely corresponds to the near-square proportions of the canvas. Indeed, after the 1980 discoveries were made in the laboratory, but before publication, an unknown earlier state of the drypoint came onto the market. This apparently unique work is missing a number of minor details (such as the wheel's spokes), but more important, it was lightly scored with fifteen vertical and horizontal lines. This grid was superimposed over the imagery to facilitate its transfer to the larger canvas.[7]

### State Two

Sometime in early 1905, Picasso painted out the "Circus Family" composition, and replaced it with one showing two young acrobats in the empty countryside. Again, x-radiographs show the two figures, the most prominent being a small boy on the right. This second composition, which I call "Two Acrobats," relates directly—in reverse—to a known painting, where a related image shows two boys with a dog, placed before a bleak building in the distant background (figures 7, 8, and 9).

### "Circus Portrait": An Interim

During construction of the galaxies of works around the three states of the *Family of Saltimbanques*, a fourth group emerged. This I call the "Circus Portrait," due to its penultimate drawing (figure 10), where the figures are arranged to create a formal portrait, in contrast to the earlier images of figures at work, at rest, or in isolation.[8] Interestingly, we still find in the "Circus Portrait" the harlequin of the "Circus Family," with bent arm and hat. Harlequin is now seen standing beside a new character—a seated fat jester, a figure Picasso based upon an actual

Figure 8. Photographic reversal of figure 7

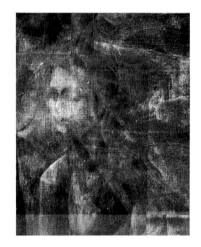

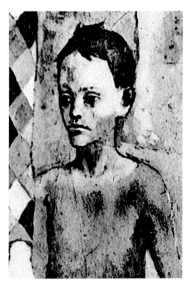

Figure 9. Details showing the head of the younger acrobat in the x-radiograph and in figure 8

11

*Figure 10. Picasso* Circus Portrait *ink and gouache on paper, 1905*

*Figure 11. Picasso* El tío Pepe don José *ink on paper, 1905. Lee A. Ault, New York*

*Figure 12. Picasso* Jester *ink on paper, 1905. National Gallery of Art, Washington. Ailsa Mellon Bruce Fund*

performer named El tío Pepe don José, as so identified in a separate sheet (figure 11). This jester was very popular with Picasso at this time, and appears in many other works (figure 12). Also repeatedly appearing in this "Circus Portrait" grouping is a young woman who is seated on the ground before the jester, often engaged in feeding a small pet.

### State Three, First Phase
In 1980, I proposed that the first phase of state three began when Picasso paired a standing acrobat with the fat jester, now also standing. This pair was then combined with the two figures already in the larger painting from state two, although these extant acrobats were then reduced in size. By this stage, the composition had evolved to look something like one seen in a study now at the Pushkin Museum in Moscow (figure 13), where a small girl has joined the male quartet and a horse race fills the background. X-radiographic searches failed to reveal any remaining traces of the horse race in the background of the large painting. However, even mere surface examination of the *Family of Saltimbanques* indicates that the present harlequin did originally wear the hat and coat shown in the Pushkin Museum study. In a similar way, the surface of the Washington picture also shows that the small boy originally wore tights like his companion, as in the study, and that the young girl initially petted a small dog—in this instance as shown in a separate study (figure 14)—rather than touching a basket, as she does in the final composition.

### State Three, Second Phase
In the final working of the painting, Picasso changed the costumes of the harlequin and the young acrobat, replaced the dog with the basket, and added the woman and the pottery vase at the left. This figure derives from another work now in the Pushkin, the so-called *Woman of Majorca* (figure 15). She appears to be painted over a stone cube at the lower right; this underimage could not be directly connected with any earlier state. Also, and presumably at this final state, the barren landscape—which was previously blue in tonality—was repainted in terra-cotta passages.[9]

In summary, the *Family of Saltimbanques* evolved from the ten-figure "Circus Family" through the "Two Acrobats" to the final six-figure *Family of Saltimbanques*; this last composition evolved in part from the interim "Circus Portrait" drawings, and went through at least two phases within this creative journey, where Picasso's art moved from a scene of anecdotal character to one of poetic resolve and implied meaning.

### Sketchbook No. 35
The three notebooks of this period, which have now emerged, do not contradict the pictorial itinerary I proposed in 1980. Certain drawings in these books, however, do tend to show more clearly how some stages did take place.

*Figure 13. Picasso* Study for "Family of Saltimbanques" *gouache on cardboard, 1905. The Pushkin Museum of Fine Arts, Moscow*

*Figure 14. Picasso* Young Girl with a Dog *pastel and gouache on paper, 1905*

Perhaps the most exciting is sketchbook No. 35, where the young Picasso recorded the beginning of his first grand painting.

No. 35 is a very small sketchbook—actually more of a pocket notebook in size, measuring only 14.5 by 9 cms, or approximately 3½ by 5¾ inches. With a total of fifty-one pages, it contains thirty separate drawings. The remaining pages are given to various notes and other written passages, including two laundry lists. This latter material, in addition to its notebook size, suggests that Picasso carried sketchbook No. 35 around outside the studio, using it for practical as well as artistic purposes.

Of course, in sketchbook No. 35, as well as in the other two sketchbooks, we cannot say with certainty that the sequence of drawings from front to back is the order in which Picasso actually created them; but the extant chronological ordering we do already have from other works suggests that such a first-to-last-page sequencing is indeed the case, and it is followed here in the discussion of the drawings.

*Figure 15. Picasso* Woman of Majorca *gouache on cardboard, 1905. The Pushkin Museum of Fine Arts, Moscow*

### Seated Figures

Sketchbook No. 35 begins with a set of six drawings in pen and ink of a seated boy. Nude and placed on a stone cube, this figure is studied in right profile, two back views, left profile, a frontal placement, and finally in a three-quarters position. Such a series suggests that Picasso was working with an actual model, rather than his imagination. This observation, in turn, suggests that Picasso had a stone cube in his studio for posing such models.

The seated figure comes as something of a surprise at the beginning of this first saltimbanque sketchbook. However, it does provide a transition—among Picasso's lost blue-period works in Paris in the fall of 1904 is the watercolor *Old Man with a Child*, where the elderly figure is shown seated on a similar cube.[10]

*Figure 16. Picasso* Young Acrobat on a Ball *oil on canvas, 1904–1905. The Pushkin Museum of Fine Arts, Moscow*

The theme of the figure seated on the stone cube, and occasionally the representation of just the cube itself, appears throughout this period. Its most fully realized form is in the sizable painting *Young Acrobat on a Ball*, now in the Soviet Union (figure 16). This composition—also known in a related drawing (figure 17)—shows a male figure seated on the cube (or upon a drum in the study) watching the young girl on the ball in the near background. Interestingly, in this drawing (location unknown) Picasso appears to have a suggestion of possible color on the male's costume. Such a testing accords with the passage of brownish red Picasso has washed over the seated boy in the first of the six notebook studies.

*Figure 17. Picasso* Study for "Young Acrobat on a Ball" *ink on paper, 1904–1905*

### Four Girls

The next four drawings are a sequence of "portraits" of four different girls. Unrelated to anything in the saltimbanque

13

imagery, these four works appear to be taken from observations made outside of the studio, especially the last drawing, a charming study of a young girl in a school uniform, shown holding a hoop.

### *"Circus Family"*

Characters from the first state of the grand *Family of Saltimbanques* make their first sketchbook appearance on pages 17, 18, and 19. The first of these is the standing harlequin, shown with his diamond-pattern costume and hat. Staring downward with his left hand on his hip, he introduces the central figure of the first composition.

We can assume this is an early image, for in the Baltimore gouache, in the drypoint, and in the traces shown in the radiograph of the large canvas, the harlequin position is consistent in formulation, and different from this study. In these other versions, his right leg falls straight from the hip, rather than having the pronounced bend shown in the sketchbook images. Even more decisive, in all three other images, he stands with both hands on hips, and elbows outward, whereas in sketchbook No. 35, his right arm falls across his waist. Nevertheless, despite these differences, the figure clearly belongs to the "Circus Family" composition, especially as his downward stare implies the presence of the girl on the ball whom he watches in the three other versions of this image.

Page 18 shows a woman and small child walking in a landscape, while page 19 contains a pair of detailed drawings of their faces. Again, there is reason to assign them an early date. The woman and child also come from the first state of the *Family of Saltimbanques*, and like the harlequin, appear in the gouache, the drypoint, and the x-radiograph (figure 16). But, again, the position of the pair in these three versions of the "Circus Family" composition differs from that shown in sketchbook No. 35. In the other works, the child is shown on the woman's left, in contrast to the notebook, where the child walks at her right. Interestingly, the two faces on page 19, studies for the figures on page 18, are more detailed than those in the final images in the gouache and the print, where the woman's face is further blocked by her bundle.

In creating the woman and child in the sketchbook, Picasso first drew them in pen and ink, outlining the figures in firm, summary lines. Details of shading are present in a pattern of long, looping lines, especially on the right side of the child. Similar lines are used to indicate the piles of firewood carried by each figure.

Over this pen and ink drawing, Picasso has added touches of blue watercolor, particularly for the woman. Then, using only the blue, he has added the landscape elements in the background; the horizon line also accords with the landscape employed in the later works. This blue tonality,

which is a hallmark of the earlier blue period, can still
be seen in the blue tonality that pervades the *Family of
Saltimbanques* as an underlayer beneath its present
ocher surface.

## Acrobats

The figures from the "Circus Family" are followed by
several pages related to more general saltimbanque themes.
Page 20 presents the profile of a young boy, possibly the
same model who posed for six studies of the seated figure,
given that the drawings share a general resemblance. Filled
in with solid black, it calls to mind Picasso's frequent usage
of a direct profile in numerous works during the rose
period, culminating with the *Woman with a Fan*, of 1905.

Pages 21 and 22 introduce the subject of the young
male acrobat, shown nude on the first sheet and in costume
on the second. Close variants of each other, these figures
stand hands on hips, recalling the pose of the
harlequin, although in these drawings this acrobat is seen
from the back. In each image, Picasso introduces color.

In the nude study, light markings in blue indicate modeling
on the head, across the back, and on the extended right
leg. The clothed acrobat is more fully developed in color,
and is on one of the two most realized sheets contained in
sketchbook No. 35. Here, the costume of red shirt and tights
is combined with dense black shorts. More delicate tones
are used to model the acrobat's body, and to articulate his
neck and head.

*Figure 18. Picasso* The Harlequin's Family
*ink and gouache on paper, 1904–1905. Mr.
and Mrs. Julius Eisenstein*

Perhaps the most important aspect of this second acrobat
drawing is Picasso's addition of a background, a loosely
brushed-in empty floor and wall. This closed space
—the figure is near the back plane—contributes the sense
of a restricted environment, one that Picasso made the
theme of numerous other saltimbanque works at this time,
showing circus performers backstage.

## Seven Nudes

Pages 23 through 29 form a sequence of seven nude female
studies, divided into two standing images, four seated
figures, and one profile study. On all seven pages Picasso
again appears to have used the same model. And, like earlier
studies of the boy on the stone cube, certain of the nude
images contain small highlights of color.

For the saltimbanque theme, the most important of
the seven nudes is the last one, on page 29. Here the figure
is seen seated and attending to her hair, using a mirror that
is only suggested in the background. In the lower left
corner, a cat observes this figure. This theme of vanity also
appears in saltimbanque works, including *The Harlequin's
Family*, where the male figure watches his nude wife adjust
her coiffure (figure 18). In a similar manner, the cat
introduces another backstage theme found throughout the

15

saltimbanque pieces: that of the "Circus Family" together with animals, including monkeys, dogs, and squirrels.

### *Toby Jug and Sambo*

We are used to finding unexpected images in Picasso works, and sketchbook No. 35 contains two of them. On page 30, we discover a standing figure based on a toby jug—a beer or ale mug in the form of a human figure. On page 46, we find a filled-in figure standing in a tropical setting, an image suggestive of "Little Black Sambo," the Helen Bannerman story published in 1900. Both images are divorced from the saltimbanques, although the toby jug figure does indirectly recall certain humorous drawings Picasso made of Guillaume Apollinaire during this period.

### *234 x 222*

Pages 32, 33, and 34 present a surprise of a different sort. On page 32, beneath a listing of colors, Picasso has boldly written "3 de Mayo / 1905," and enclosed it with an outline not unlike that of a heraldic shield. Clearly meant to be of some importance, this date might refer to the appearance of Apollinaire's review of Picasso's March 1905 saltimbanque exhibition at Galerie Serrurier, an extensive discussion that the poet published in the journal *La Plume*, dated May 15, 1905.

Even more intriguing is the idea that this May 3, 1905, inscription might refer to the following two pages. These sheets contain various jottings of numbers, including addition sums, as well as the words "61 francs." It is the final numbers—noted as "234 x 222" and *underlined* three times—that reveal what these pages disclose. Picasso's grand painting of the *Family of Saltimbanques* today measures 212.8 by 229.6 cm, and we know this size is a reduction from its original measure.[11] Indeed, when it sold in 1914, the size was listed as 225 by 235. The closeness of these numbers to those in Picasso's underscored addition implies that the figures on pages 33 and 34 record Picasso's working out of the potential size of a painting he was buying, a purchase of used canvas, which had some unpainted areas folded behind the stretcher, areas of canvas he could add to the total surface. Furthermore, it suggests that this used canvas cost sixty-one francs, as noted at the top of page 34—sixty-one francs at a time when the journal *La Plume* with Apollinaire's review sold for seventy-five centimes.

In my 1980 study of the *Family of Saltimbanques*, I suggested that Picasso had abandoned the first state of the large painting, the "Circus Family," largely because no reference is made to its existence in any contemporary discussion of the saltimbanque works. Pages 32 to 39 offer the intriguing possibility that he had not yet begun the painting in 1905.[12]

Figure 19. Picasso Seated Saltimbanque
with Boy *watercolor, pastel, and charcoal
on paper, 1905. The Baltimore Museum of
Art. The Cone Collection, formed by
Dr. Claribel Cone and Miss Etta Cone of
Baltimore, Maryland*

### Jester

One of the most familiar members of the saltimbanque cast
makes his appearance on page 35—the fat jester. This
figure is one of the six in the final state of the *Family
of Saltimbanques*, but as sketchbook No. 35 records, he
is introduced much earlier in the development of the large
painting. The particular image shown in the notebook
relates to several gouaches and drawings (figure 19). Its most
direct counterpart, however, is another drypoint, *The
Seated Saltimbanque*, of 1905 (figure 20). Like the young
acrobat on page 22, the jester is fully colored, with a red
costume and a pink face, and is seated on a black box.

### Circus Family II

On pages 43 and 45 we return to the world of the "Circus
Family" of state one of the *Family of Saltimbanques*. Here
Picasso debuts a bent-over figure engaged in washing or
sewing, with a garment of some kind across the figure's legs.
A similar image is found in the "Circus Family," where an
old woman washes dishes next to the standing harlequin.
Again, this variation from the first state suggests that even
the initial composition had not been resolved at this point
in the keeping of sketchbook No. 35.

### Acrobat

The final drawing, page 47, in sketchbook No. 35
is especially intriguing. Here, Picasso studies another nude
figure of a young male, with attention to his muscles and
overall physique. But this figure is not part of the "Circus
Family" (first state). Rather, this drawing marks the debut of
the smaller acrobat who will appear in the "Two Acrobats"
(second) state of the painting; the acrobat who will
eventually join his colleague, the fat jester from page 35,
also in sketchbook No. 35, in the final composition. But that
union, which may have taken over a year to effect, involved
many more changes from the initial concept recorded in the
pages of this sketchbook.

### Epilogue

Sketchbook No. 35 contains the seeds of all three states of
the *Family of Saltimbanques*, as well as recording Picasso's
purchase of the canvas. Two other sketchbooks, No. 33 and
No. 36, hold studies that further explain the creative journey
of this work.

Sketchbook No. 33 records a potential state only suggested
in my earlier study of the Washington painting. As noted
above, within the vast panoply of saltimbanque
images, four galaxies of themes seem to be defined, three
of them eventually becoming states in the *Family of
Saltimbanques*. The fourth of these, the "Circus Portrait,"
appears to be independent of the large canvas, existing
instead as a kind of interim idea.

Sketchbook No. 33 has drawings that belong to this "Circus
Portrait" theme. Two of them, on pages 17 and 18, show

Figure 20. Picasso The Seated
Saltimbanque *drypoint, 1905. National
Gallery of Art, Washington. Rosenwald
Collection*

several of its key components: the tightly organized grouping composed of the standing harlequin with hands on hips, the seated jester (still in red, as noted on page 18), and the kneeling woman playing with a small pet (figure 21).

Page 35, however, introduces an unexpected concept (figure 22). Here, in a composition in the format of the *Family of Saltimbanques*, Picasso combines the "Circus Portrait" at the left with the right-hand portion—the harlequin and the girl on the ball—of the already extant first state. Such a pairing brings the "Circus Portrait" much closer to the initial "Circus Family" than had earlier been proposed. Out of this connection emerges something puzzling: no traces of the "Circus Portrait" central grouping exist in the x-radiograph of the paintings. However, the x-radiograph does record the clear presence of a standing figure at the left margin, one called "unidentified" in my 1980 study. Here, location, scale, and possible costume can be directly connected with the similar figure standing at the left on page 35 of sketchbook No. 33.

Sketchbook No. 36 brings us to the beginning of the final state. On page 5, three of the central figures—the jester and the two acrobats—at last join up, although their striding movements are different from their held positions in the final composition (figure 23). Earlier, on page 4, we find a sketch for the horse race shown in the Pushkin Museum study but not in the final painting (figure 24).

Other saltimbanque images are also essayed in sketchbook No. 36, works related to known compositions. But on page 38 of this sketchbook, we suddenly enter the world of the Gosol themes, images identified as coming from the summer of 1906 (figure 25). Chief among them is a set of drawings for another, unknown composition again in the format of the large Washington painting, showing two riding figures and one walking, with a dog, in a barren landscape (figure 26). Does this represent yet another possible state for this canvas? And does this account for the final change in the painting's tonality to ocher—and the addition of the vase—the two aspects of the *Family of Saltimbanques* that belong to the Gosol period, not to the rose? Indeed, it is possible that Picasso labored on his large painting for almost two years.[13]

*Figure 21. Picasso Sketchbook No. 33, p. 18 ink and crayon on paper, 1905*

*Figure 22. Picasso Sketchbook No. 33, p. 35 ink on paper, 1905*

*Figure 23. Picasso Sketchbook No. 36, p. 5 pencil on paper, 1905–1906*

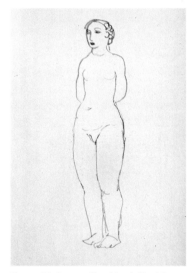

*Figure 25. Picasso Sketchbook No. 36, p. 38 pencil on paper, 1905–1906*

*Figure 26. Picasso Sketchbook No. 36, p. 61 pencil on paper, 1905–1906*

# Notes

1. Pierre Daix and George Boudaille, *Picasso: The Blue and Rose Periods* (Greenwich: New York Graphic Society, 1966), p. 67.

2. See E. A. Carmean, Jr., *Picasso: The Family of Saltimbanques* (exhibition catalogue, National Gallery, Washington, D.C., 1980).

3. Daix and Boudaille, *Picasso*, p. 74.

4. Carmean, *Picasso*, p. 17.

5. *Ibid.*, p. 60, n. 1. Vollard acquired fourteen of Picasso's 1904–1905 plates in 1913, and after steel-facing them, he and Louis Fort published editions of the series, entitled *Les Saltimbanques*.

6. Carmean, *Picasso*, p. 17.

7. Although Picasso used a fifteen-by-fifteen grid, he numbered only fourteen in each direction, eliminating the left margin and upper register; these are exactly those areas missing from the x-radiographic image.

8. Theodore Reff has called attention to the relationship between these drawings and photographs of circus families; see Carmean, *Picasso*, p. 42.

9. See Carmean, *Picasso*, pp. 37 and 61, n. 50.

10. See Daix and Boudaille, p. 248, D.XI.3.

11. This reduction is apparent just in looking at the painting today, as the signature is now folded over the stretcher. See Carmean, *Picasso*, p. 74.

12. On dating the painting, see Carmean, *Picasso*, p. 49.

13. The relationship between the saltimbanques and the Gosol works still needs to be explored. For example, we know that Picasso's composition *The Peasants*, from August 1906 (Barnes Collection), was painted *after* Gosol, but based on works done there. The Marina Picasso collection contains a version of this composition that not only shows the Eiffel Tower in the background, but a striding harlequin next to the dominant couple—a harlequin in August 1906.

Antiquario

16 rue Victor Masse

1

2

3

4

5

6

7

8

9

10

11

Avenue
Tudine
31 fundidor

12

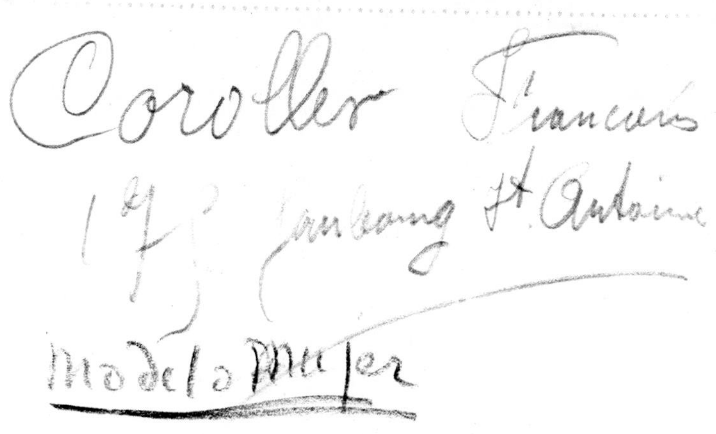

Coroller Francois
17 fauboug St. Antoine

Modelo Mujer

13

28

14

15

16

17

18

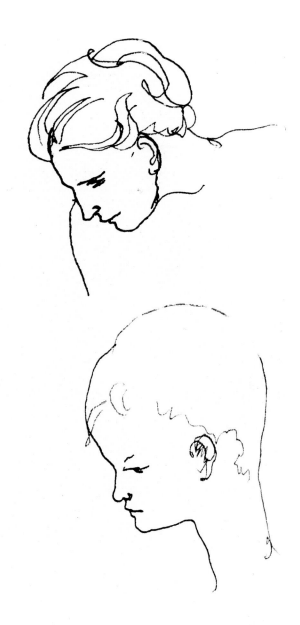

19

20

21

22

25

23

24

26

27

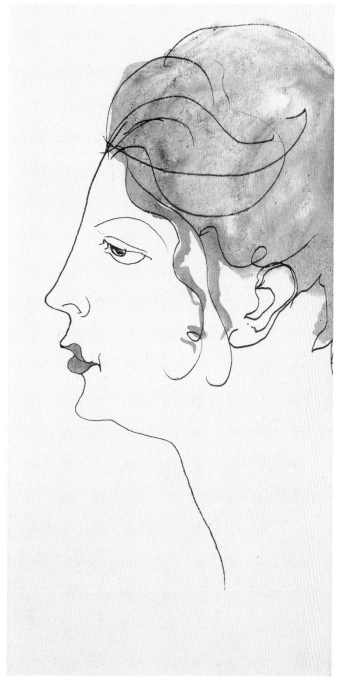

28

29

30

Sorrel
33 av. du Maine

Toen un azul de
prusia mate un
2.ra palido

3 de Mayo
1905

31
32

2 recas y 17
208
14
222

2·x   15   3.
3 4   14
    5
35·5  14

33

61 francs
104 : 4 = 26
208   El Sabado
26
234

234 x 222

34

42

35

sabanas 2
camisetas #5
calzoncillos 4
camisas 4
una camisa de Dormir
toallas 3
servilletas 1
almoadas 1
pañuelos 8
calcetines 3 pares

38

Ricardo
Casals
18 calle Boria
Quincalleria

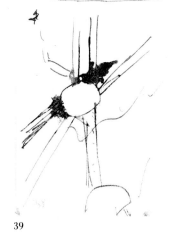

39

Guirald. S. quan camarad

36

Rojas hizo prologo
ó introduccion
lo demas
Rodrigo de Cota
Toledano
Rojas de Puebla d
Montalvan

utribuida á
Juan de Mena
y hoy quien dice
que s parece à obra de
d Pero Diaz
de Pulgar

37

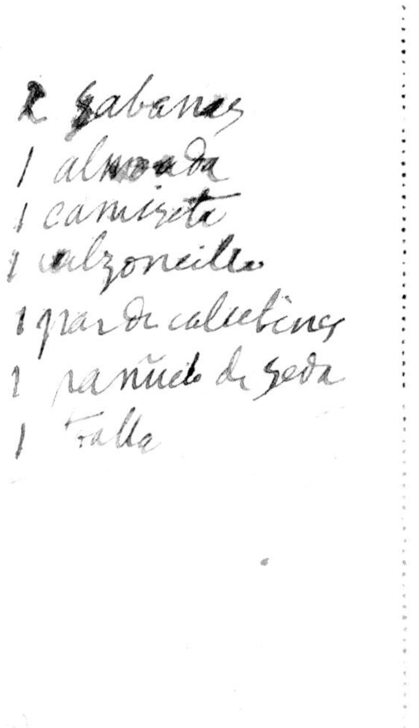

2 sabanas
1 almoada
1 camiseta
1 calzoncillos
1 par de calcetines
1 pañuelo de seda
1 Talla

40

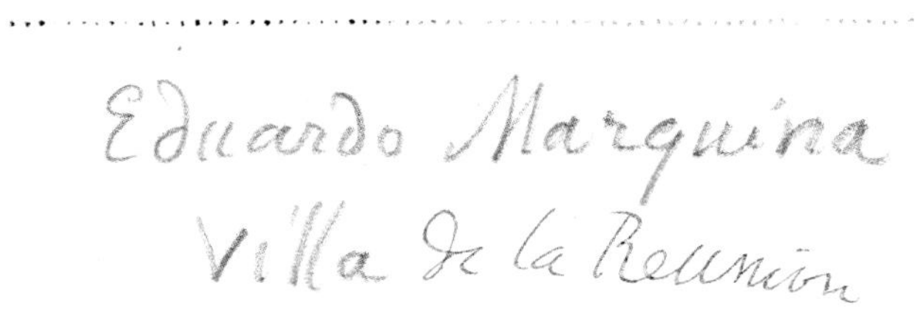

Eduardo Marquina
Villa de la Reunión

41

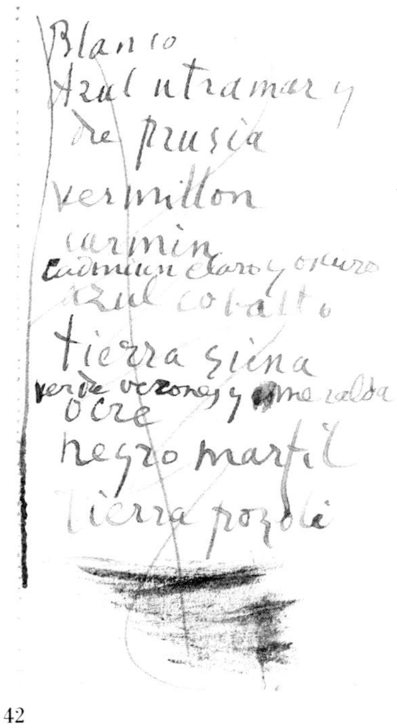

Blanco
Azul ultramar y
de Prusia
vermillon
carmin
cadmium claro y oscuro
azul cobalto
tierra siena
verde veronés y esmeralda
ocre
negro marfil
tierra pozole

42

45

43

44

45

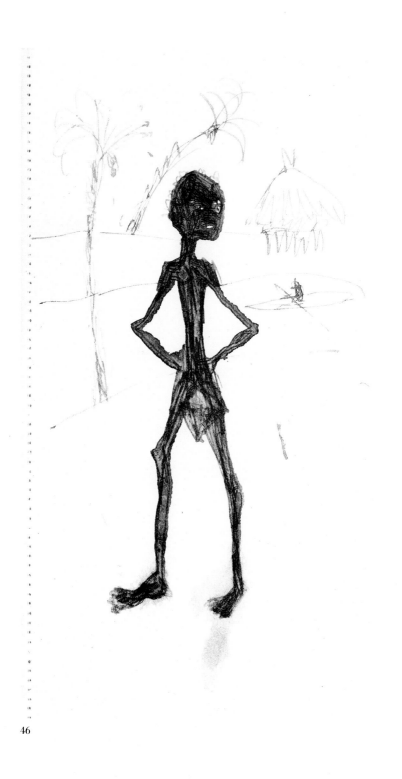

46

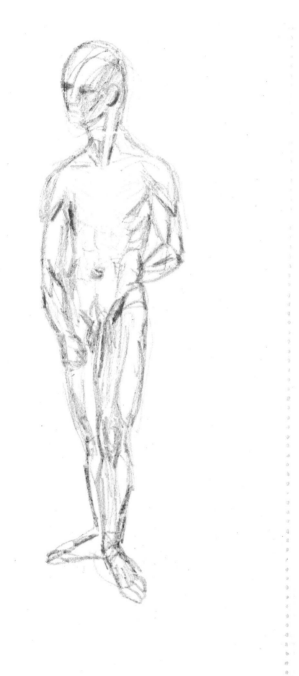

47

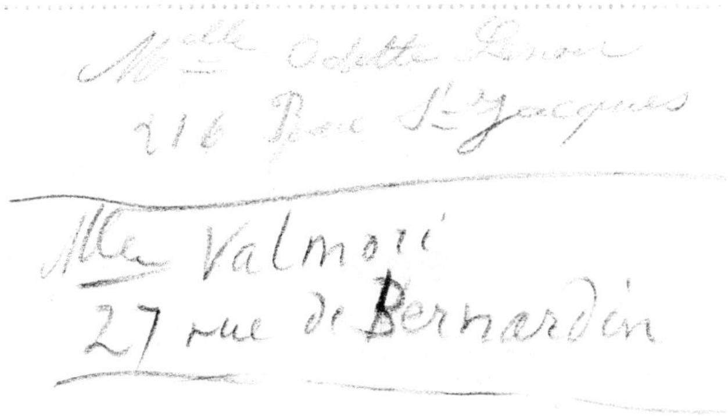

Mlle Odette Gros
216 Rue St-Jacques

Mme Valmori
27 rue de Bernardin

50

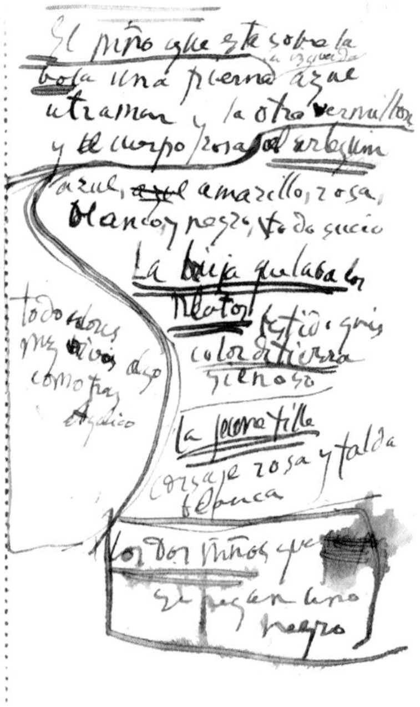

El niño que está sobre la
bola una pierna azul
ultramar y la otra bermellón
y el cuerpo rosa verbellín
azul, amarillo, rosa,
blanco y negro, y toda sucia
La bola que lababa los
platos teñida gris
color de tierra
cielo oso
la pecaratille
corsaje rosa y falda
blanca
los dos niños que
se juegan uno
negro

48

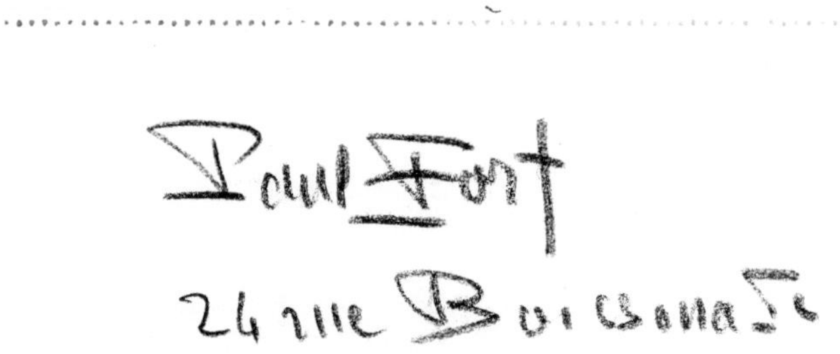

Paul Fort
24 rue Boissonade

51

49

*Picasso, 1906*

# The *Demoiselles*
## Sketchbook No. 42, 1907

by Robert Rosenblum

It was appropriate to the most superstitious of twentieth-century artists that I myself harbored an utterly silly superstition about Picasso, which was brusquely shattered on April 8, 1973. On that day, some six and a half months before what would have been his ninety-second birthday, he unbelievably revealed his mortality by dying, whereas I had always had a crazy hunch that if anybody in the history of the human species might forever outwit Death by a truly supernatural creative energy, it would be that diabolic Spaniard. Of course, I was wrong, but only partly. Since 1973, Picasso has gone on living the afterlife of a canny pharaoh, whose buried tomb treasures, one by one, are turning up in the form of an unending succession of unknown paintings, sculptures, and drawings that oblige us to think about him not in the past but in the present and future tenses. From his teens to his nineties, he still seems to be making art posthumously, and everything we thought we knew about him remains tentative and alive, subject to the changes effected by the next disclosure of this or that startlingly unfamiliar work or by a flurry of smaller bits of new visual and documentary evidence that may either underscore or subtly alter some moment or some masterpiece of his eight decades of frenetic productivity.

It is in the latter category that this fresh rain of Picasso sketchbooks falls, a group of highly individualized *carnets* that, as exhibited and presented here, may set off yet a whole new sequence of interpretative events in the never-ending career of Picasso. The year of the sketchbook of pencil drawings I am introducing, 1907, is the most epochal of his first maturity; and the specific season is apparently the spring months, from about March to May, when he was involved in the early phases of *Les Demoiselles d'Avignon*. The sketchbook offers a variety of visual and written evidence to enforce and to expand our knowledge of Picasso's ever more breathtaking inventiveness in creating a strange new human race that would soon be shattered in the pictorial earthquake of the *Demoiselles*.

One drawing alone is off this figurative track, a Cézannesque landscape fragment (page H) that records, with an Impressionist sense of nuance, the webbed and forking branches of a trunkless, gravity-defiant tree. It may well be the perceived origin of a series of more abstracted gouache and watercolor landscapes (figure 1) associated with an outdoor scene of toiling peasants, *The Harvesters*, a painting that also occupied Picasso in the spring of 1907.[1] Primarily, however, the sketchbook is populated with studies of the female nude, an open-ended exercise generating a humanoid species that regressed to some archaic form of anatomical imagery and of regained magical powers. Here, the Darwinian evolution of a nineteenth-century realist art —which had attained, by the time Picasso was born, an infinite virtuosity in making painted and sculptured facsimiles of the human body in motion—is reversed, with the master pushing backward to imaginary origins that may glimmer, in passing, in figures such as those on pages F and G, who evoke an archaic Mediterranean world where women, like caryatids or peasants, carry baskets on their head or stride forward with ritualistic vases in hand. But such figures, which hark back to an abundance of similarly archaizing motifs painted largely during Picasso's sojourn in spring and summer, 1906, at the Catalan hill town of Gosol, can revert to even more elementary distillations of form, as if a primeval vocabulary were being invented for the making of new idols to serve a religion still to be codified. Pages A and B, for example, appear to be the same goddess seen both head-on and from behind in an image of absolute frontality associated with exotic tribal arts or with the origins of Western sculpture in Egypt or archaic Greece. Moreover, this austere and rigid creature will serve as a model for other paintings of the period (figure 2). Other pages, such as 19 and 20, demonstrate more informal variations on this manufacture of hieratic icons, with the former offering frontal and dorsal views and the latter, two lateral elevations of a deity cut from the same symmetrical mold.

*Figure 1. Picasso* Landscape Associated with The Harvesters *watercolor on paper, 1907*

It is, of course, appropriate to think about such idol-making in terms of a modern tradition in which the sophisticated geniuses of Western art, beginning with Gauguin, confront the anonymous craftsmen of what would earlier in this century have been called "primitive" art from such remote places as the Marquesas Islands or the Ivory Coast. By now, thanks especially to the exhaustive research behind the Museum of Modern Art's exhibition and catalogue "'Primitivism' in Twentieth-Century Art," this story has been precisely documented for modern art in general and for Picasso in particular. But certainly one of the lessons of this confrontation most relevant to Picasso's relation to tribal art in 1907 is, as William Rubin emphasizes,[2] that the master's art converged with these exotic idols not so much as a result of direct influence but rather through an internal evolution that finally seemed to duplicate the emotional and structural characteristics of much tribal art. Indeed, the most "primitive" of the figural fantasies in this sketchbook might at first appear to be paraphrases of a variety of African sculpture (from Dogon, Baga, Kota, and so on),

*Figure 2. Picasso* Petit nu de dos aux bras levés *oil on board, 1907. Musée Picasso, Paris*

whereas Picasso, at the time, was ignorant of such works. Here it might be useful to recall that Picasso's efforts in early 1907 to create figures appropriate to a new kind of cult worship—severely symmetrical, static, and geometrically schematized—can also be seen in the broader context of a longer modern tradition that transcends the account of the specific impact of tribal art on the West from the 1890s on. Already in the late eighteenth century, John Flaxman, in his engraved illustrations of Homer (1793), Aeschylus (1795), and others in the style of Greek vase painting, had prompted a regression to a solemn, archaic world where figures, like the Theban maidens who pray to the statue of Ares (figure 3), approach an alignment of rigorous profile and frontal views and where the "primitive" geometric patterns of an early phase of art become the elementary components of anatomical description.

*Figure 3. John Flaxman* The Supplication of the Theban Women (from The Tragedies of Aeschylus, Plate 14) *engraving by Thomas Piroli, 1795*

This willfully archaizing mode of hierarchic symmetry and elemental order was often resurrected by the symbolist generation that dominated art at the turn of the century in both the Barcelona and the Paris of Picasso's youth. As a characteristic example, *Truth* (figure 4), a painting of 1903 by the internationally renowned Swiss master Ferdinand Hodler (who, like Picasso, exhibited at the Paris world's fair of 1900), offers, within the restrictions of a vocabulary whose sources in academic realism are still overt, one of these iconic goddesses. With the timeless purity of her nude body, fixed eternally on an axis of rigid symmetry, she confronts us head-on in a heraldic posture. Like a magical deity from some primitive religion, she can dispel, with upraised hands, the symmetrical sextet of evil male spirits, whose more complex anatomical contortions and foreshortenings seem to relegate them to a more timebound, terrestrial realm.

*Figure 4. Ferdinand Hodler* Truth (II) *oil on canvas, 1903. Kunsthaus, Zurich*

Picasso's figural inventions in this sketchbook belong, in fact, as fully to Hodler's archaizing mode as they do to the more often told story of the sequence of Polynesian, Iberian, and African influences upon his work of 1906–1907. As in the case of the stylistic regression in Hodler's painting from more sophisticated postures of almost Michelangelesque torsion to the central statement of immutable and fearful symmetry, Picasso, too, as revealed in this sketchbook, alternates between what appear to be simplifications of academic studies from the nude model, in which muscular strain and movement are implied, and emblematic abstractions of these figures that freeze and codify their anatomies into the timeless stasis of idols. We can see this process at work in, for instance, pages 2–8, where what seem to be the direct perceptions of a standing model are metamorphosed into a cult goddess, whose upraised arms, with hands behind head, and exposed and silhouetted genitalia make her the remote ancestor (or the modern descendant) of a genealogical table of love goddesses, ranging from the standing, newborn Venus (as re-created in Ingres's *Venus Anadyomene*) to a host of nineteenth-century supine women of charged sexual availability, such as Goya's *Naked Maja* and Ingres's odalisques. But this path from the observed to the abstracted, or back from the remote to the immediate, is constantly fluid and reversible in Picasso's work; and it is fascinating to see, in this sketchbook, how this obsessive image can be transformed into the ferociously direct sexual confrontations that reached fruition in *Les Demoiselles d'Avignon*, whose compositional ideas are also adumbrated here. Most memorable is the sequence on pages 22–25, which culminates in a monster whose brazen erotic voltage, delineated with a crackle of splintered hatchings, makes her almost the double of many de Kooning drawings of the 1950s (figure 5) related to that demonic series of *femmes fatales* known bluntly as *Women*.

*Figure 5. Willem de Kooning* Study of Woman *charcoal on paper, 1952. Private collection*

Indeed, within the context of the sketchbook, this image of aggressive female sexuality becomes a kind of Galatea to Picasso's Pygmalion, a creature who can shift from the role of a timeless, immutable idol to that of a shrill modern harlot and who provides, so to speak, a rehearsal for the major drama of the *Demoiselles*. It is no surprise, then, to find interspersed in these pages two studies for that scene in a brothel parlor that began with a kind of stage setting in which a sailor draws back a curtain to enter the inner sanctum of what the French call a *maison close* and that ended, in July 1907, with that quintet of furies who confront the spectator head-on as if to draw him into their tumultuous theater of sexuality (figure 6).

In the first of these compositional studies (page I), the cast of characters is the most reduced of all the related preparatory drawings for the *Demoiselles*.[3] Here, the constant motif of the lone sailor entering the scene behind the curtain is repeated, but he now confronts only two whores, instead of the usual four or five. These two are also recurrent in the later sketches, the one above bursting forward through the parted curtains of the secondary inner sanctum of the bordello, and the one below, her back to us, spreading her thighs shamelessly to expose her sex to the new customer. In the center foreground, a triangular shape provides a forceful and, if one wishes, phallic thrust from the outside to the inside of the picture,[4] a wedge that in the final painting will become the unstable base for a tumultuously erotic still life of a slice of melon that presses upward toward the whores' flesh and a bunch of grapes and pair of round and pear-shaped fruits that tumble downward. Here, however, it is a rudimentary triangle, inexplicable as an object without knowledge of the later evolution of the painting. Far more perplexing in this reduced version of the *Demoiselles*—a cast of three—is the large object on the left curtain, which eludes my ability to identify it, but which must be something specific, composed of what looks like a dumbbell shape surrounded and clasped by a kind of ring. Its cruciform, geometric format evokes at once a magic symbol, a sort of hex sign, as well as a piece of utilitarian hardware like a window lock or a door knocker, perhaps

*Figure 6. Picasso* Les Demoiselles d'Avignon *oil on canvas, 1907. The Museum of Modern Art, New York. Acquired through the Lillie P. Bliss bequest*

appropriate to our penetration from the street outside to the clandestine domain behind the facade. But surely, as in the case of other undecipherable objects in Picasso's work, this one will eventually be decoded and, like the others, fall into logical place.

No less baffling on this page are the inscriptions in a meticulous cursive handwriting, almost like the schoolboy exercises in penmanship found among the juvenilia at the Museo Picasso, Barcelona, such as signature variants practiced in Latin books of 1891–1892. Especially vis-à-vis the scene of prostitution above, these words become an ironic throwback to childhood education, calligraphic homework in a primer. *Aurais*, as isolated here, suggests the study of the French conditional verb form; *Germinal* might be a reference to Zola's novel or, more likely, to the name of the month associated with spring (March 21 to April 19) in the French revolutionary calendar, which might correspond to the actual date of the drawing; and *Crurs*, perhaps some misspelled schoolboy Latin variant of *crus* and *cruris*, the singular and plural forms for "leg." But these are only guesses about a verbal and calligraphic doodle that may someday be explained more coherently.

The other page (J) that proposes a set for the drama of the *Demoiselles* conforms more closely to several dozen related studies[5] in which the brothel parlor is now populated by two more whores at the left and another sailor in lower center has already joined the bawdy players. The thrusting triangular wedge now bears a cylindrical vase of faintly sketched flowers, whose uppermost crescents appear to have metamorphosed into a separate still life of paired melon slices presumably supported by a more distant plane. As for the two new whores at the left, the central upper one now utilizes the posture of the single standing love goddess who, arms raised above and behind her head, appears throughout the pages of this sketchbook as well as in several small oil paintings of these months (see figure 2).[6] In this context, her frontal, near-symmetrical posture at the apex of this scene and her primitive geometries of right-angled elbows and wrists virtually proclaim her a kind of Gauguinesque idol, the abstraction of an erotic muse who eternally dominates the temporal commotion below and the oblique displays, viewed from front and back, of sexual merchandise.

The other new whore at the left, sloping downward against a nichelike frame, suggests a reclining figure, thighs parted, leaning backward against a bed or sofa, who, like a figure in a pop-up book, might spring forward to greet the new client,[7] much as the whore squatting at the right, exposing her sexual wares, seems paired (in the shape of the head, as well) with the sailor at center stage. This sexual polarity may even involve a biological double image, for the rear view of the exhibitionist whore creates in the egg-shaped head and pigtailed hair a spermatic form that recalls the prevalence of such imagery in the work of Edvard Munch,[8] who loomed so large in the formation of the young Picasso. In the Norwegian master's *Ashes* (figure 7), for example, sperm cells, as the fateful biological carriers of human behavior and destiny, appear both in the margin and, as a subliminal pun, on the pattern of the unbuttoned dress of the temptress whose posture of sexual availability again corresponds to the type that obsessed Picasso in these months. The overriding sense in Munch's work that sexual consummation is lethal for the male of the species is also part of the fearful subplot of the *Demoiselles*, which, as many recent studies have emphasized, would fuse the power of sexual attraction with the terror of a fatal venereal disease.

*Figure 7. Edvard Munch* Ashes *oil and tempera on canvas, 1894. Nasjonalgalleriet, Oslo*

As for further nineteenth-century background to the *Demoiselles* that glimmers in this sketchbook, there remains perhaps another link to be explored. On page 1 and the inside back cover, the name Eugène Rouart appears, first with his address at Bagnole-de-Grenade in the Haute-Garonne, and second, with what appears to be a Thursday noon appointment (*jueves a las 12*) at the Restaurant Fogot. Preliminary research has disclosed that this man is the son of Henri Rouart, a member of the famous Rouart family who were closely connected with Degas as friends and patrons, one descendant of whom, Denis, would publish in 1948 the monotypes of Degas. Included in these prints is a remarkable series of Parisian brothel scenes, related to naturalistic fiction by the Goncourts, Maupassant, and Huysmans;[9] and in 1958, when a group of these monotypes was put on the London art market, Picasso himself was one of the major buyers.[10] It would seem highly likely that Picasso knew these clandestine prints over the decades (some were published by his dealer Ambroise Vollard in 1935 to illustrate Maupassant's *Maison Tellier*), and it is tempting to speculate that he was first introduced to them by the Eugène Rouart in question here at perhaps the very time, 1907, when he was gestating the *Demoiselles*. Indeed, in a characteristic monotype from the series, and one that ended up in Picasso's personal collection, we see exactly the same kind of scene in which a dressed male client enters from the side to face the *patronne* as well as a bawdy display of spread thighs and supine bodies ready to be covered by the prospective buyer (figure 8).

*Figure 8. Edgar Degas* Au salon *monotype, 1879. Musée Picasso, Paris*

Still another motif in the sketchbook evokes a different kind of speculative scenario that may soon be supported or toppled, and that is the sequence of drawings, pages 27–36, which now seem to represent a nude male emerging through a parted curtain. It is a motif that transsexualizes the persistent theme in the *Demoiselles* of the whore who shrilly pulls aside the curtains at the upper right and enters the scene breasts first. The undulant, almost art nouveau rhythms of the enclosures in these drawings suggest something sexual and fetal, a return to womblike experience; and indeed, the naked creature who is born from these organic shapes appears to regress to a kind of homunculus, infant, or embryo. On pages 31 and 33, the sudden specificity of the head, with its staring, almond-shaped eye and strongly contoured arc of an ear, is quickly associated with Picasso's self-portraiture of 1906–1907, as if the artist had become fully identified with this initiation into the bordello's sexual rites. And is there not some adumbration here, too, of those biological cycles of erotic awakening and fetal development that the artist would bring to masterful fruition in the 1932 *Girl before a Mirror*? As always, the master's imagery, even when glimpsed in the most modest and casual drawing, sets up unexpected vibrations with other works that may lie decades away.

As a postscript to the sexual motifs that control this sketchbook, Picasso, in the very last drawing (page 40), provided a perfect coda. Abstracted, almost like a logo, from the squatting whore in the *Demoiselles* studies, this figure has now lost her head to become all sexualized body. Splayed out symmetrically before us, in almost a monogrammatic emblem, she reveals her back to our outer eye but her front to our erotic imagination, an archetype of arousal that seems to close and symbolize the entire *carnet*.

Last, there are several other sketchbook pages that need mentioning, for they are provocative in quite different ways. On page 41, a partly legible scribble tells us that "Stein estará en su casa toda la semana próxima . . . ?? el martes" (Stein will be at home all of next week . . . Tuesday), a handwritten memento of Picasso's friendship with Gertrude Stein, which began in the fall of 1905. But above this scrawl is another statement, "Escribir à Braque" (write to Braque) —Picasso has accented the *a* in the French rather than the Spanish manner—and on the inside back cover, next to the note about the appointment with Rouart, Picasso has written "Braque, el viernes" (Braque, Friday). Presumably, Picasso and Braque did not meet until sometime in October–November 1907, through the intermediary of Apollinaire; but if, in fact, this sketchbook dates, as it must, from the spring before the completion of the *Demoiselles* in July 1907, could this be evidence that the meeting of these two great artists, which would result in the most extraordinary partnership in the history of art, had actually occurred some six months earlier? If the first perusal of this little sketchbook can raise such questions, think how much more lies in store for us as the resurrected Picasso continues to reveal one work after another.

# Notes

1. For *The Harvesters*, and the related landscape studies, see Pierre Daix and Joan Rosselet, *Picasso: The Cubist Years, 1907–1916* (Boston: New York Graphic Society, 1979), cat. nos. 55–63.

2. William Rubin, ed., *'Primitivism' in Twentieth-Century Art*, 2 vols. (Boston: New York Graphic Society, 1984), vol. I, pp. 260ff.

3. For the fullest coverage now of the preparatory studies for the *Demoiselles*, see Josep Palau i Fabre, *Picasso: The Early Years, 1881–1907* (New York: Rizzoli, 1981), figs. 1469–1557.

4. This wedge is more amply discussed in the first ground-breaking study of the *Demoiselles* to inaugurate a whole series of new interpretations: Leo Steinberg, "The Philosophical Brothel, Part 1," *ARTnews*, Sept. 1972, pp. 22–23.

5. See Palau i Fabre, *Picasso*, figs. 1509–1511, 1515–1548.

6. See Daix and Rosselet, *Picasso*, cat. nos. 16–19.

7. This transformation from a supine to an upright figure is fully and incisively discussed in Steinberg, "The Philosophical Brothel," pp. 24–25.

8. For other examples of spermatic imagery in Munch, see the color prints *Madonna* (1895–1902) and *Meeting in Infinity* (1899).

9. On these monotypes and their probable source in Huysmans, see Theodore Reff, *Degas: The Artist's Mind* (London: Thames and Hudson, 1976), pp. 180–182.

10. For details of the provenance of these monotypes, see Eugenia Parry Janis, *Degas Monotypes* (Cambridge: Fogg Art Museum, 1968), nos. 62ff.

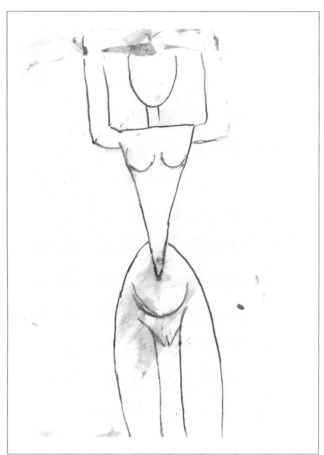
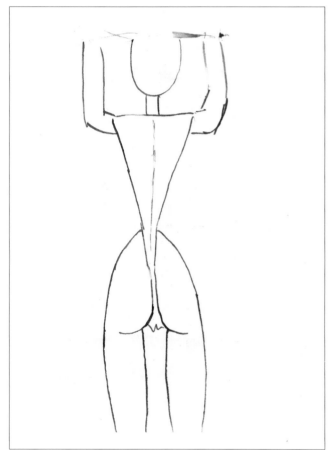

A; the first ten drawings are loose pages kept in the front of the sketchbook    B

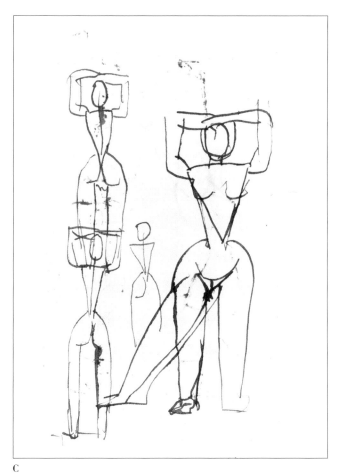

C

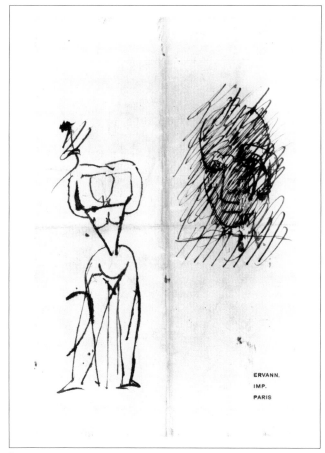

D

ERVANN.
IMP.
PARIS

63

E

F

64

G

H

K; this drawing is on the verso of the bottom half of the reconstituted previous page

Eugène Rouart
Bagnols-de-Grenade
par St Jory
Haute Garonne

adresse Télégraphique
Rouart—Capy St Jory

Salle 11

mardi et mercredi

1

2

68

3

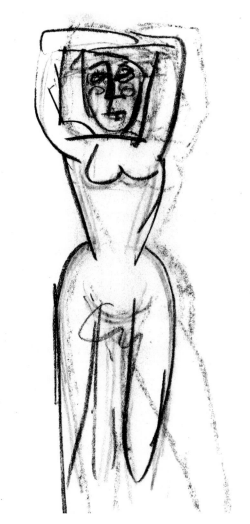

4

5

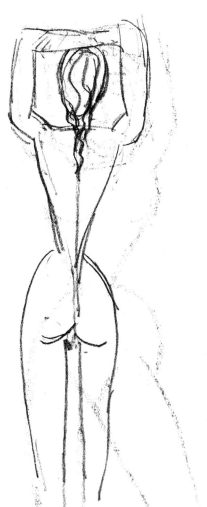

6

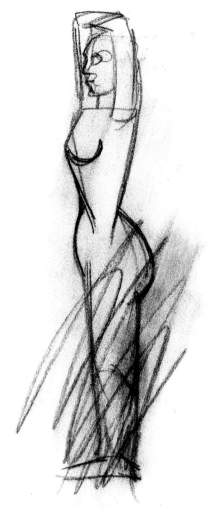

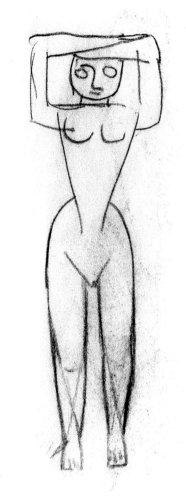

7

8

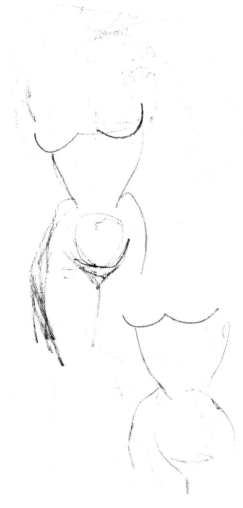

9

10

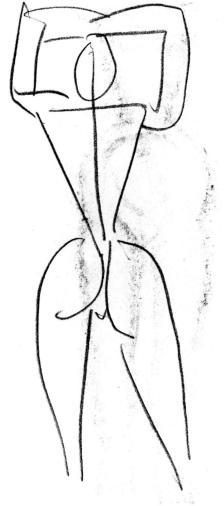

11

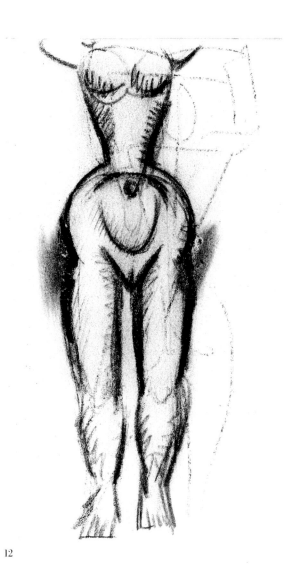

12

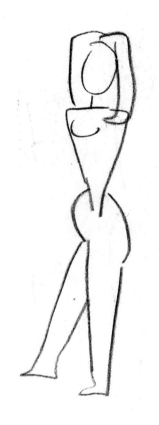

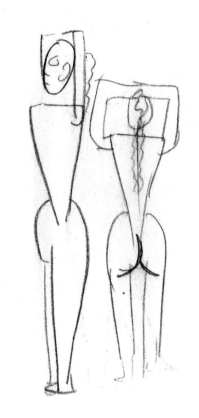

13

14

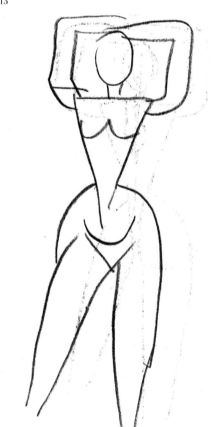

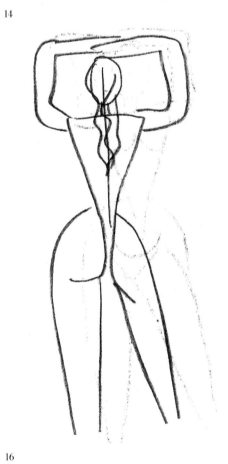

15

16

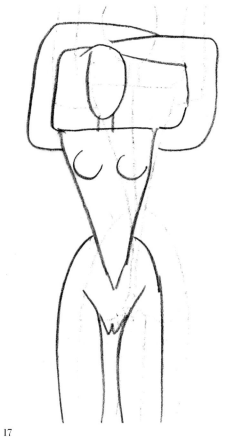

17

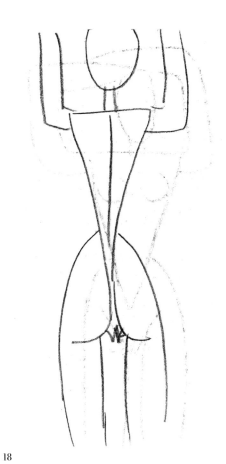

18

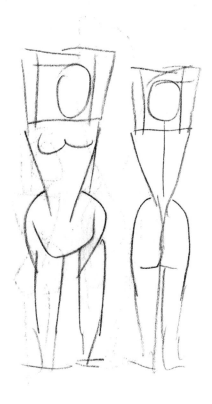

19

20

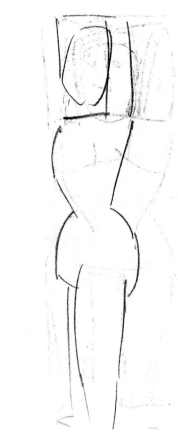

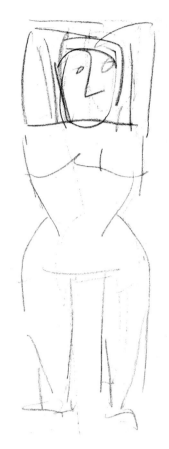

21

22

23

24

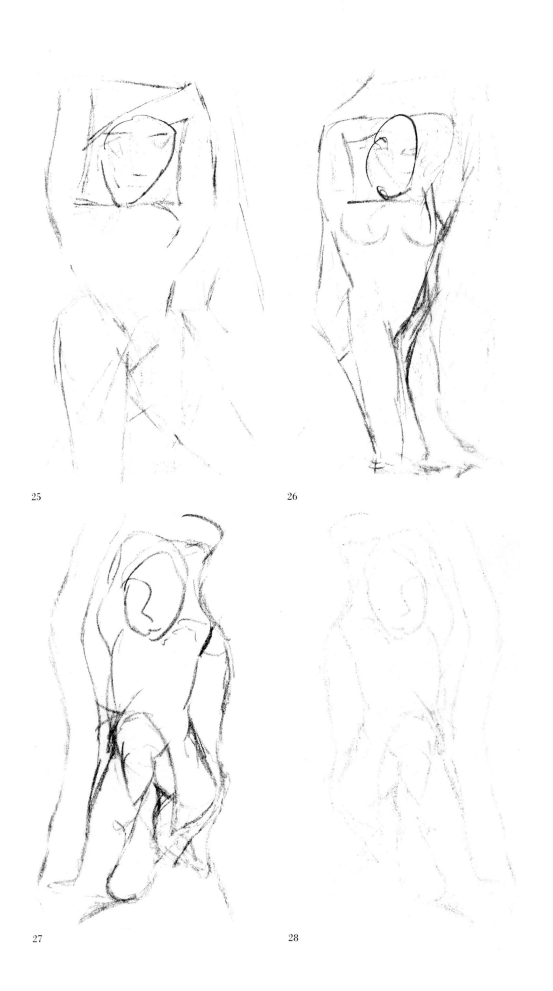

25

26

27

28

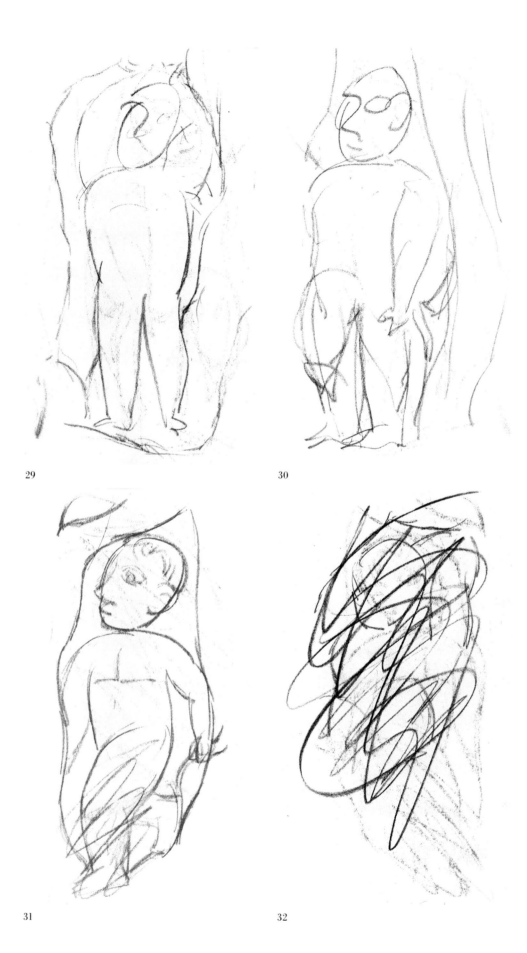

29

30

31

32

33

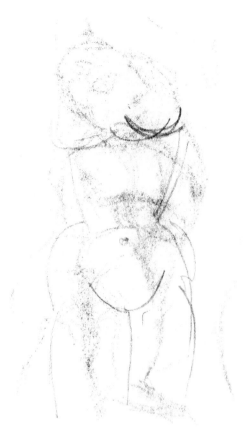

34

35

36

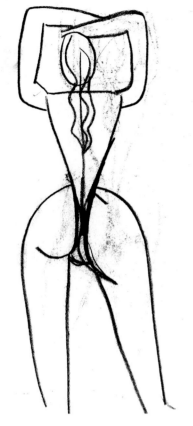

37

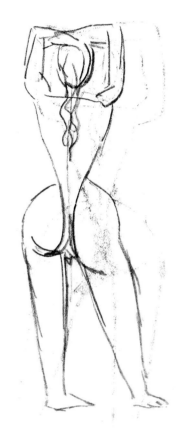

38

39

40

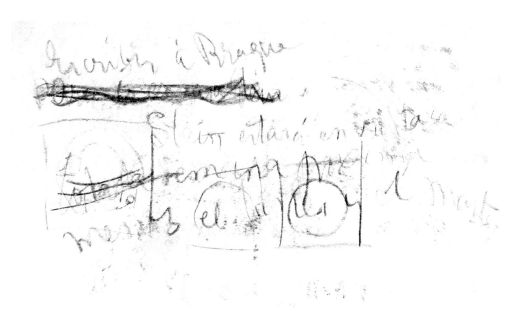

41

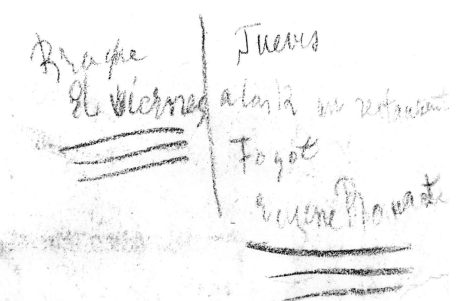

inside back cover

*Picasso, 1915*

# Picasso at the Crossroads
## Sketchbook No. 59, 1916

by Theodore Reff

Initially, it is through the quality of its drawings that
Picasso's sketchbook of 1916 exerts its fascination.
They project forms of a monumental power and scale with
a boldness of vision altogether exceptional for an object of
this kind. Over nine inches wide and twelve high, this is the
largest of the ten sketchbooks Picasso used in the years of
the First World War; but more important, most of its pages
are filled to the edges with a single image, giving it an
expansive power well beyond its actual size. The larger
format evidently also encouraged Picasso to work more
deliberately, for there are many signs of revision and of
reworking in another medium—in black chalk or soft pencil
over the harder pencil he began with—yet no signs of a
softening or blurring of that fierce clarity which is this
sketchbook's essential characteristic. The whole is in fact
in excellent condition, as if it had not been opened in
the seventy years since Picasso last closed it sometime in
1916. Close examination reveals that eight pages have been
removed—the perforations near their inner edges made
it easy to tear them out—and this was most likely done by
Picasso himself, perhaps to give them away. Three of the
missing drawings, two of them signed, are probably among
those published separately in the Zervos oeuvre catalogue
(see Appendix A).

The artistic quality of the individual drawings is matched by
the historical value of the sketchbook as a whole. In its
pages we observe in miniature that simultaneous cultivation
of two opposed styles, cubism and naturalism, which was the
most striking feature of Picasso's art throughout the war
years. The two styles not only coexist here, but are at their
greatest distance apart: the severely rectilinear "crystalline
cubism" of the studies of a seated woman (pages 5–11),
whose flattened, largely abstract forms seem like exercises
in plane geometry, could hardly be more remote stylistically
from the suavely curvilinear "Ingresque naturalism" of the
sketches of a sugar bowl and of the artist's own hand (pages
12, 37), whose foreshortened, fully rounded forms seem like
experiments in perspective projection. Obviously delighted
by his mastery of the two styles, Picasso deliberately
compared them in different drawings of the same subject.
In studies of a seated harlequin playing a guitar, for

example, light, curved strokes describe the skillfully foreshortened forms on one page and dark, rigid lines define the boldly patterned shapes on the next (pages 35, 36). Two drawings of a full-length standing nude, one smoothly outlined and subtly shaded in the Renaissance manner, the other reduced to a system of strongly contrasted lines and planes in the cubist manner (pages 13, 29), provide another example, equally striking if less intentional.

For all their obvious differences, however, the two styles share certain features—perhaps inevitably, as products of the same vision at the same moment in its development. With a few notable exceptions (pages 3, 4, 13, 17, 21), there is little suggestion of local color or modeling in the drawings in this sketchbook; line alone is used to define form and space. And this line is consistently thin and uninflected, without the graceful mannerisms seen in Picasso's drawings of a decade earlier or the nervous intensity of those he made one or two decades later. It is a deliberate, almost impersonal device for creating form, suggesting in most cases an incisive certainty and in others a slight hesitancy as the artist's hand gropes for the right direction. Besides this purely graphic unity, however, there is a unity of vision in the sketchbook that reveals itself in the cubist devices employed in naturalistic images, and vice versa: in the tilting up and flattening of the fruit in a powerfully sculptural still life (pages 2–4), for example, and in the vivid rendering of the table leg and chair in a largely abstract still life (page 21).

*Figure 1. Picasso* The Painter and His Model *oil and crayon on canvas, 1914. Musée Picasso, Paris*

Although Picasso had already been working simultaneously in the two styles since the summer of 1914, he had employed the naturalistic one almost exclusively for drawings, especially for portrait drawings of friends such as Jacob, Vollard, and Apollinaire; the only major example among his paintings, *The Painter and His Model*, begun that summer (figure 1), remained in his studio, unfinished and entirely unknown. In the summer of 1916, the period in which he most likely used this sketchbook (see Appendix B), Picasso was preparing to reveal this recently developed naturalism on a grand public scale in the overture curtain he designed for the Diaghilev company's ballet *Parade* (figure 2). His first thoughts about that project can be found in this very sketchbook, in the many drawings of a harlequin of the type already discussed. Thus, the historical significance of the sketchbook is obvious: in its pages we witness Picasso, not only employing and consciously comparing the two styles that so fascinated him at the time, but also beginning to plot that *coup de théâtre* in which they would be brilliantly juxtaposed in public for the first time.

*Figure 2. Picasso* Overture Curtain for "Parade" *tempera on canvas, 1914. Musée National d'Art Moderne, Centre Georges Pompidou, Paris*

In the summer of 1916 Picasso was indeed at one of the major turning points in his career. His decision to collaborate in the creation of *Parade* had ramifications far beyond the revelation of a heretical naturalism to a dismayed band of orthodox cubist disciples. Through this first venture into the theater, and the others that soon followed, Picasso was able "to go from the public of laborious though friendly exegetes to that of snobs, from Bohemians to society women, from Kahnweiler's narrow shop to the international stage," in short, "to open the doors that the uncompromising austerity of cubism had maintained shut against him."[1] It was in August that he took this momentous decision, which accelerated his movement away from the cubist style he had worked in almost exclusively, at least in painting, for the past nine years. And appropriately, it was in July that he chose for the first time to exhibit *Les Demoiselles d'Avignon*, the revolutionary work in which he had begun to explore that style in the spring of 1907.[2] The two events may not have been associated in Picasso's mind, but in retrospect they seem to symbolize the crossroads at which he found himself that summer. It was not unlike the crossroads at which the young Hercules had found himself in the well-known myth —an analogy made all the more compelling by the famous photographs of Picasso, taken in 1915–1916, showing the compact, muscular artist as a modern Hercules, stripped to the waist or in a workman's overalls.

In stylistic terms, it would be wrong to describe Picasso's art simply as moving from cubism to naturalism in these years. The movement we observe in the sketchbook of 1916 is not a progression from one to the other but an oscillation between them; and as he himself later said, "Different motives inevitably require different modes of expression,"[3] though we have seen that he could treat the same motive in entirely different modes. In psychological terms, however, it would certainly not be wrong to see a progression from the static and hermetic works of the "cold" or "crystalline" cubism of 1915–1916 to the more dynamic and accessible works of the "classical" cubism and naturalism of 1917–1919. As always with Picasso, such a change reflected changes in the circumstances of his life.

The winter of 1915–1916 and the following spring was undoubtedly one of the most difficult periods Picasso ever experienced. In December Eva Gouel, the "Jolie Eva" of his paintings and collages and his mistress for the previous four years, died of tuberculosis; his state of mind is evident in the ominous black background and sinister smile of the harlequin he painted that autumn (figure 3). Many of his former companions—the artists Braque, Derain, and Léger, the writers Apollinaire, Salmon, and Cendrars—were at the front in a war of unprecedented savagery that moreover was going badly for France. His dealer Kahnweiler was in exile and all the works in Kahnweiler's stock were in the hands of the custodian of alien property. He was living alone, for the first time in many years, in a studio whose windows looked out directly on the Montparnasse cemetery; and when he moved, in May or June, it was to the still more isolated and dreary suburb of Montrouge. It is hardly surprising, then, that Picasso's cubist style, which had already been tending

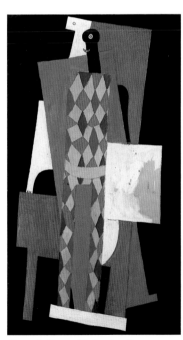

*Figure 3. Picasso* Harlequin *oil on canvas, 1915. The Museum of Modern Art, New York. Acquired through the Lillie P. Bliss bequest*

in this direction since the outbreak of the war, became increasingly austere and impersonal, as in the 1916 paintings of a man seated at a table (Daix 888, 889),[4] where the human figure is reduced to an awesome, monumental architecture. This virtually abstract form of cubism is precisely what we find, on a much smaller scale, in the drawings of a seated woman in the sketchbook of 1916, where the same flattened, geometric forms are combined in endless variations, occasionally enlivened by a witty detail (pages 5–11).

Picasso did not really begin to experience the changes that his collaboration on *Parade* would cause in his life until he went to Rome in February 1917 to begin active work on it; until then he continued to live in relative isolation in wartime Paris. But he had been thinking about the project since the previous spring, and by the fall was already enthusiastically engaged in it with his newest companions, Cocteau and Satie. In Rome his social horizon continued to expand in all directions to include not only Diaghilev, Massine, and other members of their company, but also Stravinsky and some of the Italian futurists. He could also boast to Gertrude Stein: "I have sixty girl dancers. I get to bed very late."[5] One of them, of course, was Olga Koklova, with whom he soon fell in love and whom he continued to court that spring and summer; by the fall of 1917 they were living together in Montrouge. Expanding his cultural horizon, too, he visited Florence, Naples, and Pompeii, and in the spring he accompanied the Ballets Russes to Madrid and Barcelona, where he was received by his former colleagues as a conquering hero. And in Léonce Rosenberg he found a new dealer who could assure once again the promotion and sale of his work. Not surprisingly, all this was reflected in his art, where he achieved a synthesis of cubist structure and naturalistic description that made it much more human and accessible, as in the *Italian Lady* of 1917 (Zervos III, 18); he also found a renewed interest in caricature and popular art, especially that of the *commedia dell'arte*. This development, too, is present in the drawings in the 1916 sketchbook, those showing Harlequin as a robust, self-confident performer, playing the guitar or striding energetically across the stage (pages 34, 35, 38, 40, 44).

Harlequin is indeed the star performer here: half the drawings in the sketchbook show him in one guise or another. In addition to those just mentioned, he appears as a more slender, youthful figure rather wistfully holding his bat and mask (pages 23–28) and as a more mature and stocky figure standing solemnly alone or seeming to menace a seated gentleman with his bat (pages 18, 20, 33). There is even a detailed, half-length portrait of him as an older man with a carefully trimmed mustache over a full, sensuous mouth and featherlike brows over close-set, thoughtful eyes (page 15). This prominence testifies to the important part Harlequin played in Picasso's work from the fall of 1915 on.

After an absence of six years—there had been a painting of 1913 (Daix 618) where he was barely recognizable— he resurfaced in the haunting image inspired by Eva's illness and imminent death and no doubt by feelings of wartime loneliness and privation (figure 3). Shortly afterward he turned up again in a series of equally macabre watercolors, alone as in the painting (Daix 845, 849, 856), or dancing with a female companion (Daix 846), or accompanied for the first time by Pierrot (Daix 850). But in all these works the style is cubist, and often so hermetically cubist that Harlequin can be recognized only by his diamond-patterned costume. The first works that depict him in an easily read naturalistic style—in fact the first since the end of the rose period a decade earlier—are the drawings in the sketchbook of 1916 and those closely related to them (figures 5–7, 11). The question therefore arises, why here and at this moment?

The most obvious answer is that these images emerged quite naturally as Picasso began to visualize the production of *Parade*. Urged on by Cocteau—who visited him in April 1916 wearing a harlequin's costume to please him, and brought Diaghilev from Rome in May to discuss the project —he agreed to participate at the end of August; and by mid-September he was already working, as Satie reported, "on a script of his own . . . which will be dazzling! Prodigious!"[6] Cocteau's script, which Picasso transformed but did not abandon, depicted a circus sideshow; and although none of the performers—a Chinese magician, an American girl, and two acrobats—was in fact a harlequin, Picasso may well have been reminded of that figure by the circus theme, which may have been chosen to attract him in the first place. From the rose period on, he had tended to conflate the acrobats, clowns, and jugglers he saw at the circus and fairground with the traditional types of the *commedia dell'arte*. In the final version of *Parade* he went on to do the same: the overture curtain (figure 2) shows two harlequins among the varied entertainers seated around a table backstage; and the French Manager's costume derives its divided face—inane in frontal view, mysterious in profile —from that of the harlequin painting of late 1915.[7] We may even ask whether the sketchbook drawing of a harlequin approaching a seated gentleman in formal dress reading a paper (page 20)—an intriguing image, never explained—reflects a passing thought about an actor confronting a manager. In any event, the tradition of the acrobat or clown appearing in the guise of Harlequin (or Pierrot) goes back to the circuses and street fairs of the nineteenth century, just as the type of costume worn by the harlequin in the sketchbook drawings, with its close-fitting suit and bicorn hat, goes back to the harlequinades of that period.[8] In these drawings Harlequin is indeed the traditional entertainer, physically robust and elegantly costumed both onstage and off, holding his familiar mask and bat or playing his familiar guitar. It is the first time he appears as such in Picasso's work, rather than as the sensitive, alienated bystander of the early years or the ascetic, melancholy thinker of the cubist period. This, too, suggests a theatrical conception inspired by Picasso's growing involvement with *Parade*.

There is another, less obvious, answer to the question posed earlier about the sudden appearance in the 1916 sketchbook of a naturalistic image of Harlequin: that it reflects Picasso's familiarity with Cézanne's image. Like some of the first harlequins in the sketchbook (pages 23–28), Cézanne's is slender and youthful, unmasked and unsmiling, and wearing a close-fitting costume and crescent-shaped hat. The version illustrated here (figure 4) is one of three that Cézanne painted about 1888 in preparation for a larger picture of Harlequin and Pierrot, which, it is generally agreed, Picasso saw in the fall of 1904 and drew on for the type of tall, enigmatic harlequin he began to paint shortly thereafter. In 1916 that picture was in Moscow, but two of Cézanne's smaller harlequins were evidently in Paris, in the hands of dealers with whom Picasso was well acquainted,[9] and the third must have been available in a reproduction, for in that very year Juan Gris made three drawings after it, along with several others based on reproductions of Cézannes.[10] Since Gris was the most important cubist painter still in Paris, apart from Picasso himself, and since the affinities between their recent works, if not between the two men personally, were particularly strong, the fact that both were attracted to Cézanne's *Harlequin* may be more than a coincidence.

Picasso's Harlequin, unlike Cézanne's, does not wear his usual diamond-patterned costume in any of the naturalistic drawings in the 1916 sketchbook. But in the one cubist drawing (page 36), the diamonds are repeated almost compulsively, though on different scales, on his chest, arms, and legs, echoing in their diagonal lines the longer diagonals that crisscross this dynamic composition. There is indeed a strong resemblance between Harlequin's costume and a cubist picture to begin with: in both cases, the flat, bright colors and boldly geometric patterns fragment and conceal the forms lying beneath them, assimilating them into a surface design of great decorative brilliance. Willette, the popular illustrator of the adventures of Harlequin and Pierrot, acknowledged the resemblance when he wrote in 1919 that even Harlequin was now a painter whose latest success was "the exhibition and sale of a framed fragment of his multicolored costume"—a sly allusion to cubism and probably to Picasso himself.[11]

Since the images of Harlequin in the sketchbook of 1916 tend to occur in clusters, they have the additional interest of forming sequences in which the changes from one to the next enable us to follow the evolution of Picasso's ideas in exceptional detail. This is especially true of those showing a youthful harlequin holding his mask in one hand and brandishing his bat with the other (pages 23–28, 30), which reveal a movement from naturalistic description to cubist patterning and, contrary to what we might expect, a parallel

*Figure 4. Paul Cezanne* Harlequin *oil on canvas, 1888–1890. Mr. and Mrs. Paul Mellon, Upperville, Virginia*

movement from iconic stiffness to expressive action. As this action unfolds, the figure turns from a full-face to a three-quarter view and eventually turns his back entirely; it is almost as if we were viewing the separate frames of a film. After an interlude in which Harlequin appears in other guises and activities, there is a shorter sequence showing him once again with bat and mask in hand, striding energetically toward the left while twisting back to face us (pages 38, 40, 44). The stylistic evolution from description to patterning is equally apparent here, especially if the "missing" drawing (figure 7) is inserted in the sequence, and the evolution of the image toward a greater dynamism is no less so. Picasso's efforts to enhance the latter aspect are poignantly apparent in the countless pentimenti of the last two drawings.

Still another aspect of Picasso's creative process is revealed by the series of studies of a woman seated in a high-backed armchair, all but one of them drawn in the severely rectilinear style of crystalline cubism (pages 5–11). Seeing them for the first time in the correct order, rather than the arbitrary one adopted in the Zervos catalogue, we can follow Picasso's progressive refinement of his design as he increases the variety of its geometric and organic shapes, improves their proportions and relation to the frame, and introduces details that soften the harshness of the whole. The woman's hands, for example, are at first barely hinted at, then sketched as if her arms were crossed, and finally shown clearly clasped together on her walking stick. The stick itself is recognizable only because it appears in the surprising, naturalistic sketch on the next page. In the remaining studies, once again cubist in style, the hands are first hidden from sight, next shown holding a book, and then resting on the stick. Several pages later, the seated woman appears in two more versions, wittily transformed into a younger person with long, wavy hair and a curvaceous figure whose forms are echoed in the elegant curves of her armchair (pages 16, 19); on her lap she holds a cat, which itself is transformed from a docile pussy into a miniature tiger. In the ultimate version, at the end of the sketchbook, the image is reduced to a striking pattern of straight lines, drawn with a soft pencil, far more powerful in effect (page 41).

The three drawings of a bowl of fruit at the beginning of the sketchbook (pages 2–4) illustrate still another kind of sequence, in which the massive yet strongly planar forms reminiscent of early cubism are seen from three points of view, as if Picasso had moved around the bowl or, more likely, turned it around while remaining stationary himself. In the first, seen from the shorter end of the elliptical bowl, the fruits are grouped in a static, symmetrical manner; in the second and third, seen from each of the longer sides, the fruits form more varied and dynamic groups, the bananas seeming to arch over or bear down on the apples beneath them, as if acting out their well-known gender roles. This is especially clear in the third view, the one that presumably satisfied Picasso most, since he stopped there.

### Appendix A: The Missing Pages in the Sketchbook of 1916

Of the eight pages later removed from this sketchbook (pages 1, 22, 32, 33, 39, 42, 43, 45), three can probably be identified among the drawings dated 1916 in the Zervos catalogue. They are interspersed with other works, but so are the sketchbook drawings themselves, which moreover are reproduced out of order.[12] Like the latter, these three are drawn in pencil, in pure outline or with minimal shading, and are approximately 31 by 23 cm. All three depict the type of tall, slender harlequin, wearing a tight-fitting, belted costume and bicorn hat, who appears in many of the sketchbook drawings; and in each case, his action is one that would logically have appeared at the point in a sequence of drawings where one or more are now missing.

*Figure 5. Picasso* Singing Harlequin *pencil on paper, 1916*

The *Singing Harlequin* (figure 5; Zervos VI, 1329) shows not only the same type but the same model as the sketchbook drawings of a harlequin playing a guitar (pages 34, 35), though he is standing rather than seated. It was probably drawn on the page before (page 33), one of those later removed.

The *Standing Harlequin* (figure 6; Zervos VI, 1285) shows the same figure as the previous drawing, cut at the same point above the knees, but with his arms folded rather than holding a guitar. It was probably drawn on the page before that one (page 32), which was also removed. Thus, the sequence of images, beginning with that of Harlequin facing fully to the left, holding his bat and mask (page 31), would have shown him facing front but looking to the left, with his arms folded (figure 6), facing front but looking to the right, playing a guitar (figure 5), and facing partly to the right, seated, and playing a guitar (page 34).

The *Striding Harlequin* (figure 7; Zervos VI, 1323) shows him moving assertively toward the left, his bat raised in one hand, his mask held in the other, as in several sketchbook drawings (pages 38, 40, 44), but his relatively less twisted posture is closest to that in the faint sketch preceding them (page 31). Hence, the *Striding Harlequin* was probably drawn on the first missing page in this part of the sketchbook (page 39), before the more extreme distortions visible in the other drawings were introduced.

*Figure 6. Picasso* Standing Harlequin *pencil on paper, 1916*

*Figure 7. Picasso* Striding Harlequin *pencil on paper, 1916*

### Appendix B: The Dating of the Sketchbook of 1916

The year must be 1915 or 1916, the two years indicated in the Zervos catalogue, where most of the drawings were first published in 1942—a time early enough for the information

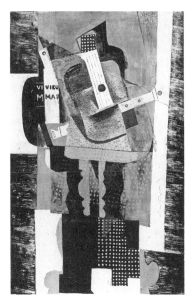

*Figure 8. Picasso* Guitar, Clarinette, and Bottle on a Pedestal Table *oil and sand on canvas, 1916*

*Figure 9. Picasso* Seated Man with Pipe, Reading a Newspaper *watercolor and pencil on paper, 1916. Columbus Museum of Art, Ohio. Gift of Ferdinand Howald, 1931*

to have come from Picasso himself or, what is more likely, from his dealer Kahnweiler.[13] But more precisely, the year must be 1916, since many of the drawings are closely related to paintings or watercolors inscribed with that date:

1. The still life of a guitar on a pedestal table (page 14) has the same subject, vertical format, and severely rectilinear design as two paintings, one dated 1915 by the artist but clearly reworked later (Daix 811), the other inscribed "1916" (figure 8). They remind us also of Cocteau's remark that precisely in those years "a dictatorship existed in Montmartre and Montparnasse: those objects that could fit on a table top, such as a Spanish guitar, were the only allowable pleasures."[14]

2. The equally austere studies of a woman seated in an armchair, her arms folded or holding a book or a cat (pages 5–11, 16, 19), belong to the same series as the watercolors of a seated woman holding a book or a guitar, dated 1915–1916 (Daix 862–869). But the closest parallel, oddly enough, is the watercolor of a seated man reading a newspaper, inscribed "1916" (figure 9); here the wall moldings running askew, the angular planar structure, and the wavy outline of the head and torso all recur. (Although the dimensions of this work are identical to those of the sketchbook drawings, the differences in medium and degree of finish make it unlikely that this is one of the missing pages.)

3. The sketch of a seated harlequin playing a guitar (page 34) corresponds so closely in the figure's posture, gestures, and expression to a painting dated 1916 in the inventory of the Marina Picasso collection (figure 10) that it can be considered a preparatory study for the painting, despite its more naturalistic style.[15]

If the year must be 1916, the season must be the spring and summer, since many of the remaining drawings can be related to works or projects of that period:

1. The drawings of a full-length, youthful harlequin facing us with a bat in his raised right hand and a mask in his left (pages 23–26) closely resemble another drawing—too small, however, to have belonged to this sketchbook—that bears a dedication dated July 14, 1916 (figure 11; Zervos XXIX, 192).

2. Given the sudden appearance of all these images of Harlequin, those just discussed plus a dozen others (pages 15, 18, 20, 27, 28, 30, 31, 38, 40, 44), all represented in a naturalistic style for the first time in Picasso's oeuvre since the end of the rose period a decade earlier, we are surely safe in assuming that they reflect his first ideas for *Parade*, which he discussed with Cocteau in April 1916, with Diaghilev in May, and formally agreed to work on in August.

*Figure 10. Picasso* Harlequin with a Guitar *oil on wood, 1916. Eugene V. Thaw, New York*

*Figure 11. Picasso* Harlequin with a Bat *pencil on paper, 1916*

3. Although the evidence just given concerns only about half the drawings in the sketchbook, it is likely that the remainder also date from the spring and summer of 1916, since Picasso, unlike many other artists, normally filled his sketchbooks quickly, in a relatively short period of time.

## Notes

1. Pierre Cabanne, *Pablo Picasso: His Life and Times*, translated by Harold Salemson (New York: Morrow, 1977), pp. 176–177.

2. Pierre Daix, *La Vie de peintre de Pablo Picasso* (Paris: Seuil, 1977), p. 151.

3. Statement of 1923, cited in Cabanne, *Pablo Picasso*, p. 197.

4. Picasso's cubist works are listed according to the numbers in Pierre Daix and Joan Rosselet, *Le Cubisme de Picasso* (Neuchâtel: Ides et Calendes, 1979).

5. Letter of April 1917, cited in Cabanne, *Pablo Picasso*, p. 186.

6. Letter of September 14, 1917, cited in Cabanne, *Pablo Picasso*, p. 183.

7. See Richard Axsom, *"Parade": Cubism as Theater* (New York: Garland, 1979), p. 79.

8. See Cyril Beaumont, *The History of Harlequin* (London: C. W. Beaumont, 1926), plates opposite pp. 88, 90, 96, 110.

9. See Lionello Venturi, *Cézanne, son art, son oeuvre*, 2 vols. (Paris: Paul Rosenberg, 1936), no. 553 (owned by Paul Rosenberg) and no. 555 (owned by Ambroise Vollard). For further information on their provenances, I am indebted to John Rewald.

10. Venturi, *Cézanne*, no. 554. See *Juan Gris*, exhibition catalogue, Salas Pablo Ruiz Picasso, Madrid, 1985, nos. 134, 135; also pp. 51–52, 99, 310–311.

11. Adolphe Willette, *Feu Pierrot* (Paris: Floury, 1919), p. 128.

12. Christian Zervos, *Pablo Picasso*, vol. 2** (Paris: Cahiers d'Art, 1942), plates (not oeuvre numbers) 372–378, 380–383; two of the sketchbook drawings (pages 37, 38) are not reproduced.

13. See n. 12.

14. Jean Cocteau, memoir of 1923, cited in Cabanne, *Pablo Picasso*, p. 177.

15. *Picasso: Opera dal 1895 al 1971 dalla Collezione Marina Picasso*, exhibition catalogue, Centro di Cultura di Palazzo Grassi, Venice, 1981, no. 129.

2

3

4

5

6

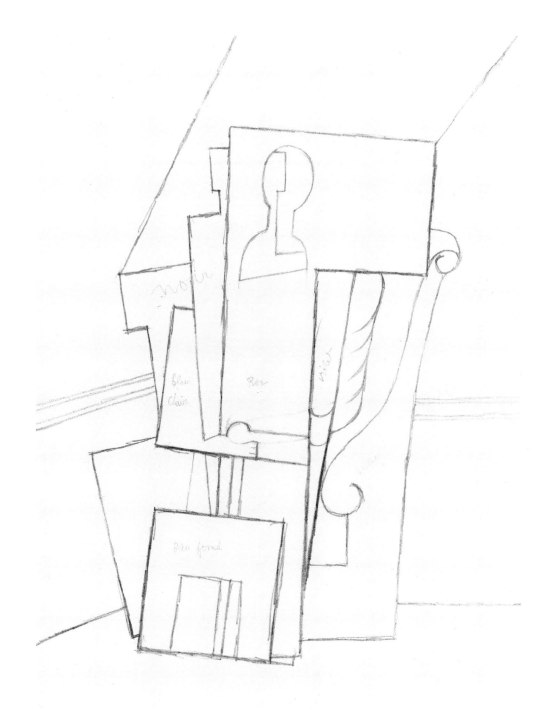

7

95

8

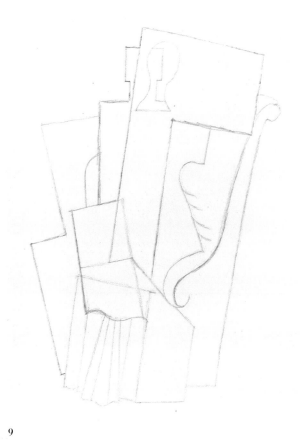

9

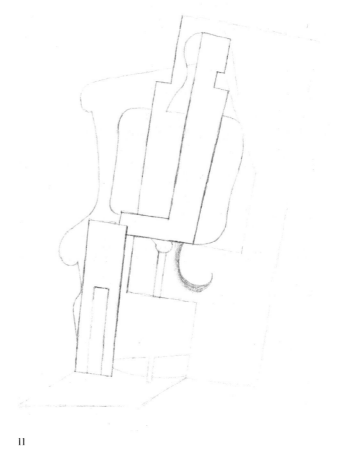

10

11

12

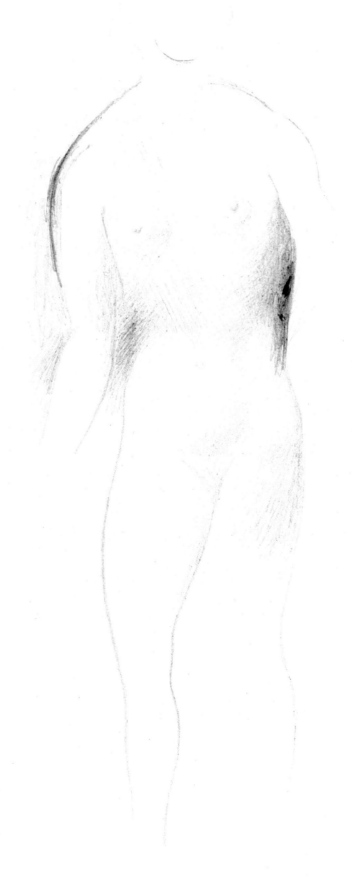

14

15

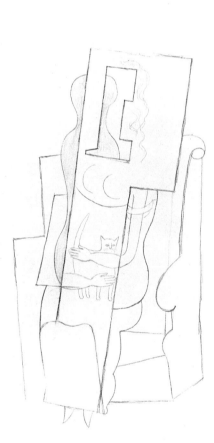

16

17

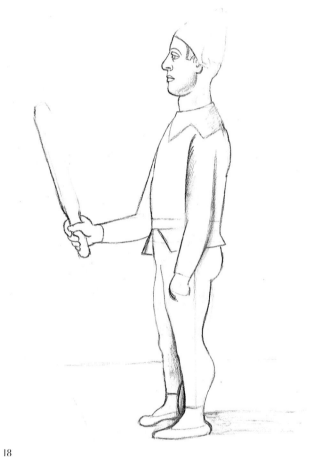

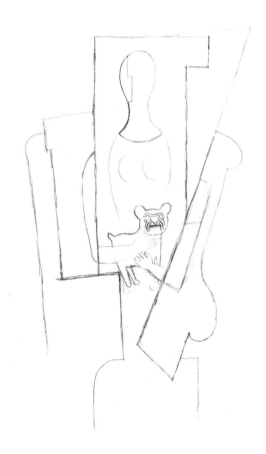

18

19

20

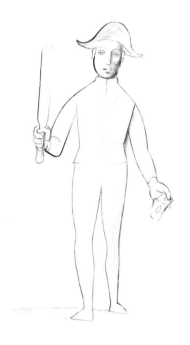

23

24

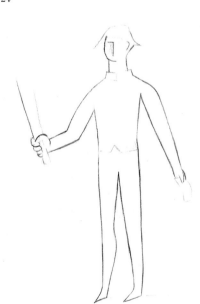

25

26

27

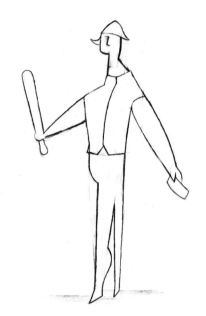

28

29

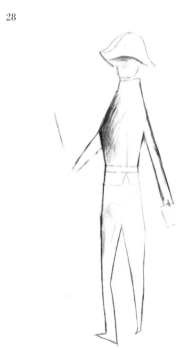

30

31

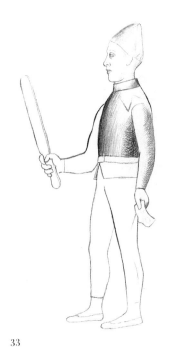

33

34

35

37

38

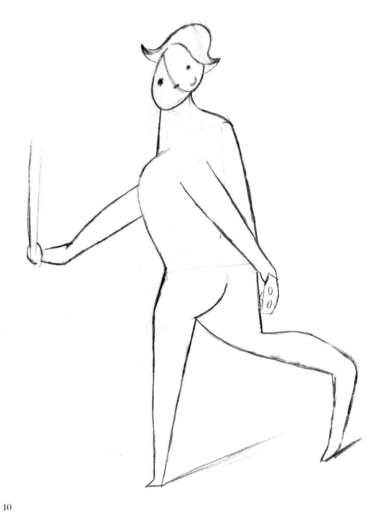

40

41

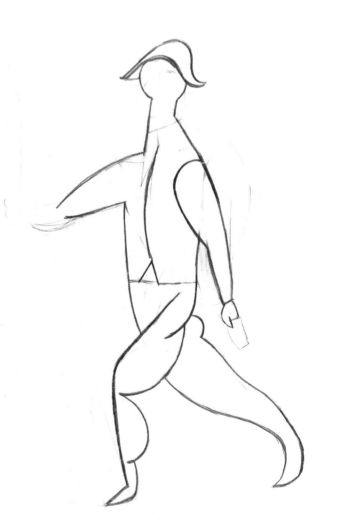

44

46

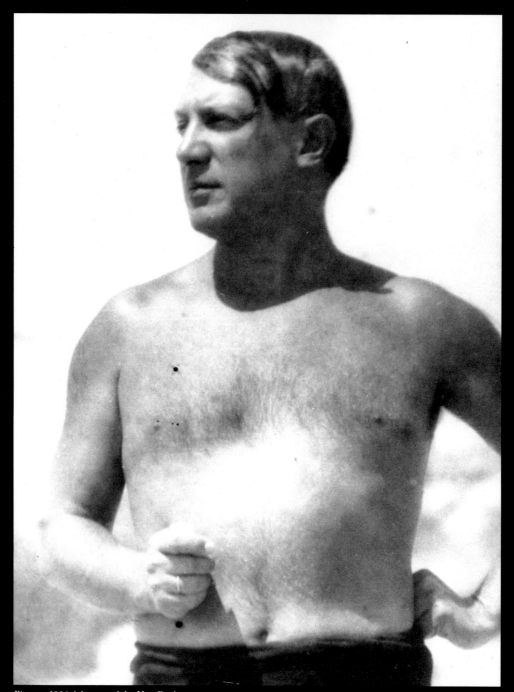

*Picasso, 1926 (photograph by Man Ray)*

# Life with Picasso
# Sketchbook No. 92, 1926

by Rosalind E. Krauss

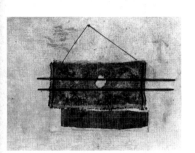

*Figure 1. Picasso Guitare cloth, newspaper, string, and nails on canvas, 1926. Musée Picasso, Paris*

*More than one commentator has already remarked on the important role autobiographical content played in the art of Picasso. His private life constantly showed through his work, either directly as, for example, in the portraits and in many figures, or in a highly allusive manner, and where one would least expect it. . . .*
Michel Leiris[1]

*Jaime Sabartés, Picasso's lifelong friend, quite aware of the autobiographic quality of Picasso's art, suggested that if we could only reconstruct his itinerary step-by-step, "We would discover in his works his spiritual vicissitudes, the blows of fate, the satisfactions and annoyances, his joys and delights, the pain suffered on a certain day or at a certain time of a given year." . . . Indeed, if there were no lacunae in our biographic data about Picasso, there would be no lacunae in our interpretations of his art.*
Mary Mathews Gedo[2]

*Is there any one of us who doesn't share the impression that the poet's volumes are a kind of scenario in which he plays out the story of his life? The poet is the principal character, and subordinate parts are also included; but the performers for these later roles are recruited as the action develops and to the extent that the plot requires them. The plot has been laid out ahead of time right down to the details of the dénouement.*
Roman Jakobson on Mayakovsky[3]

In the massive output of Picasso's production, 1926 was a remarkably lean year. But since, fat years or lean, that production never failed, even in its slacker moments, to generate what other artists might be proud to claim as their triumphs, it is not surprising that this period should nonetheless contain something new: in this case, a striking departure in the conception of collage.

All but abandoning those earlier cubist images of figural ambiguity, Picasso created in March of 1926 two collage *Guitar*s, in which the object's depicted shape is totally at one with the collage material of which it is composed. The rectangular face of one guitar is defined by a swatch of floor rag, with twenty or so nails stuck through its underside, their points projecting outward toward the viewer (figure 1). In the other, an irregular length of the artist's shirttail is sewn to the canvas ground, a border of short, dark, running stitches outlining the instrument's profile (figure 2).[4] The latter was immediately given nearly a page for its

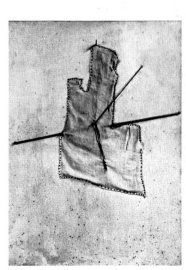

*Figure 2. Picasso Guitare canvas, wood, string, and nails on board, 1926 Musée Picasso, Paris*

reproduction in the sixth number of *La Révolution Surréaliste;* and four years later Louis Aragon did not hesitate to document both these objects in his essay "La Peinture au défi," in which collage—Dada and surrealist collage, that is—is made to announce the end of painting.[5]

Insofar as cubist collage absorbed its varieties of foreign matter into a unified field of visual signs, it could be regarded as continuing to operate within a conception of painting whose language it had radically revised but whose basis—visuality itself—it left intact. Now surrealism, on the contrary, saw the revolutionary potential of collage as an assembly of real things—like the contents of one's pockets emptied onto the dresser at night; as such, it could demonstrate the appearance among these things of that otherwise invisible force, the marvelous. Mocking the grammatically self-evident schoolboy phrase *Le pain est sur la table,* Aragon writes, "No, the bread is no longer on the table, or it's no longer the table, and it certainly isn't bread anymore." And then for his readers he adds a dictionary definition of *marvelous:* "the intervention within the poem of supernatural beings (Larousse)."[6] The logic of this function of the object finally leads Aragon to speak of a magical operation with the things of collage. "One sees here," he writes, "that painters are really setting out to put objects to work as if they were words. The new magicians have reinvented incantation."[7]

Although in Aragon's essay the reference to Picasso's *Guitars* appears only after discussions of the *Fatagagas* of Ernst and Arp, the rayographic assemblages of Man Ray, and the collage paintings of Picabia—it is slipped into one tense paragraph before an appreciation of Miró and Dali— the relationship of Picasso's objects to Aragon's theme of the magical or the incantatory is striking. Dramatically skewered to the surface of the canvas, Picasso's *Guitars* inflict a kind of bodily damage on that very surface, rendering it tactile in a new way, changing the proscenium arch of the pictorial stage into a theater of pain. The nails that pierce, the needles that prick, the barbs that spur, shift the objects on which they operate from the realm of the visual to that of the physical as surely as, say, the later manipulations of Lucio Fontana's knife on the slashed bodies of his canvas fields. And since there is a lexicon of cruelty every bit as conventionalized as that of love, the entry Picasso seems to be invoking here is the one having to do with sympathetic magic—with Congolese nail fetishes, with Haitian voodoo dolls, with all those operations in which representation slides from the visual to the corporeal and from there to death.[8]

It is the presence of these objects amid the sparse production of mid-1925 through 1926 that leads many of the historians of Picasso's work to speak of this moment as the onset of an important connection between the artist and surrealism, agreeing more or less with André Breton's statement that it was in this year—1926—that Picasso "joined" the movement, at least in spirit.[9] Picasso himself would later deny this, specifically refusing to acknowledge surrealist influence in both the 1926 *Guitars* and *The Dance* of 1925, and allowing that designation to rest only for the series of drawings called *An Anatomy*, produced in 1933 and published in *Minotaure*.[10] Yet, few Picasso scholars have followed the master in this demurrer, and Pierre Cabanne speaks for most of them when he characterizes the importance, or more precisely the necessity, of the movement for Picasso at this juncture as

*the revelation by surrealism of an interior world from which Picasso had become alienated and which, thanks to it, he found again. Under its influence, his reawakened, unconscious drives helped him to regain the paths of creativity; they led him to distance himself from the styles of the moment and to transgress the pictorial conformism of this flaccid postwar period by a simplification of his means, at the same time enriching them and giving them a new significance and content. This purification led Pablo to execute forms that figure among the most arbitrary of his entire oeuvre, to approach an unrecognizable reality where the state of trance and of defiance into which he plunged, when pricked by his creative drive, was spurred by deep and unacknowledged instincts.*[11]

*Figure 3. Picasso Collage paper and string on wood, 1926*

In the sketchbook dated Paris, March 21–June 20, 1926, drawings after the two "fetish" *Guitars* (plus another, rather cubist guitar that Zervos identifies as made for a décor, figure 3) place an extremely exact record of the finished collages in the midst of a series of drawings also executed after a recently completed work. This surrounding suite of drawings, occupying nine pages of the sketchbook, does not merely record but rather develops various sections of the very large painting (approximately 5½ by 8 feet) called *The Milliner's Workshop* (figure 4) that Picasso had executed in January of 1926. The interest of the fact of this interruption by the image of the *Guitars* into the otherwise meditative sequence of studies, mainly of female heads and torsos, for the earlier painting is that by tying the ideas set in train by *The Milliner's Workshop* to the ferocity of the collages, the sketchbook tends to confirm Cabanne's characterization of this seemingly late cubist painting as in fact surrealist.[12]

Picasso had been courted by André Breton since the summer of 1923. Breton had defended him against Dada slurs, brought the collector Jacques Doucet to his studio to acquire *Les Demoiselles d'Avignon*, joined with other surrealist poets to buy Picasso's work from Kahnweiler. In the July 1925 issue of *La Révolution Surréaliste*, Breton published the first installment of his essay "Surrealism and Painting." In it, Picasso alone is pictured as the herald of a surrealist vision, an "immense responsibility," in relation

*Figure 4. Picasso The Milliner's Workshop oil on canvas, 1926. Musée National d'Art Moderne, Centre Georges Pompidou, Paris*

to which, Breton solemnly declares, "one failure of nerve on the part of this man and our game would have been at the very least set back, if not lost altogether."[13]

Picasso was not immune to this flattering attention, one proof of which was his acquiescence to being included in a group show of surrealist painting mounted in November of 1925 at the Galerie Pierre.[14] Another sign of his fascination for the surrealist movement, the first important one in his experience to have "developed independently from him and out of the responses of a different and younger generation,"[15] was the attention Picasso gave to the work of Miró—a connection about which Breton was to claim, "One can maintain that the influence of Miró on Picasso has, in large part, been determinant."[16] Indeed, six months before the group show in which Picasso's own paintings hung next to those of Miró, the younger artist had exhibited alone in the same gallery, mounting work like the *Harlequin's Carnival*, in which a weightless web of curving line structures the painting—a notion of visual automatism to which Picasso seems to have turned for the idea of the complex, curvilinear, "quasi automatic" infrastructure of *The Milliner's Workshop*.[17] Undoubtedly, Miró's work was more formally compelling for Picasso than, say, the automatic drawings by Masson that were currently reproduced in *La Révolution Surréaliste*.

However, aside from this question of influence, one other part of the historical record gives a sense of Picasso's experience of *The Milliner's Workshop* having been generated "automatically." It is a statement Picasso made in relation to the death of Juan Gris in May of 1927: "I had made a large black, gray, and white painting. I didn't know what it represented, but I saw Gris on his deathbed, and it was my picture."[18] On one level this claim seems peculiar, since in a literal sense *The Milliner's Workshop* depicts an actual boutique that stood opposite Picasso's apartment on the rue la Boétie and that the artist recorded from the distance of his fourth-floor studio window.[19] But there is another level from which to view this work that gives credence to this "I didn't know what it represented." This includes not only the strange nocturnal effect of the grisaille in which the picture is executed, but the apparent attempt to give way to the unconscious impulses of the hand in forming its compositional network. Not least of all, we must consider the anomalous nature of the work's subject in a long period otherwise entirely barren of anything we could call genre painting. To flip through the Zervos volumes for the years 1922–1927 is to experience the stern limitation of Picasso's subjects, if not his styles. Bathers, dancers, performers, depicted on beaches or in rehearsal halls; mothers and children seen in intimate interiors; still lifes on pedestal tables standing before windows; and, beginning in 1926, the confrontation of artist and model. This is the steady thematic diet of these years, in relation to which the idea of three little shop girls at work in their salesroom, a subject right out of Degas, seems curious to say the least.

The subsequent sketchbook development of the heads and torsos of these girls follows various stylistic protocols. Sometimes the interlocking planes of a synthetic cubist vocabulary establish a jigsaw of contrasting values and textures; sometimes an "automatist" curvilinearity loops back and forth over a mute white page; sometimes a stark black/white opposition lapses into a kind of "deco" cubism; sometimes that opposition moves in the direction of an amoeboid formlessness. But always these drawings elaborate the face in terms of contrast: the conflation of front view and profile that sets in during this year becomes a major structural device of Picasso's work. The experience repeatedly generated by this device is that one is not looking at a single figure, but at two figures, one the double of the other.

There is yet another characteristic of these heads that keeps appearing in these pages: that one of the conflated pair almost invariably possesses a wide, oval face, a Roman nose bridging straight from the forehead, and short, cropped, blond hair. These features, rehearsed again and again in these pages, are the features of Marie-Thérèse Walter (figures 5 and 6).

Figure 5. Marie-Thérèse Walter, circa 1927

Figure 6. Picasso Visage lithograph, 1928. The Museum of Modern Art, New York. Gift of Abby Aldrich Rockefeller

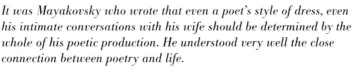

*It was Mayakovsky who wrote that even a poet's style of dress, even his intimate conversations with his wife should be determined by the whole of his poetic production. He understood very well the close connection between poetry and life.*
    Roman Jakobson[20]

Probably more than anything else, it was the revelation in the mid-1930s of the presence of Marie-Thérèse in Picasso's life as the hitherto hidden "source" of the forms and themes that entered his art in 1931–1932 that gave force to the art-as-autobiographical-reading of Picasso's work. At its most painfully literal, that reading is the one projected by Jaime Sabartés, Picasso's amanuensis. If only, Sabartés reasoned, we could reconstruct the itinerary of the master day by day, "We would discover in his works his spiritual vicissitudes, the blows of fate, the satisfactions and annoyances, his joys and delights, the pain suffered on a certain day or at a certain time of a given year." In voicing vigorous agreement with this, another of Picasso's interpreters has made its implications very clear: "Indeed, if there were no lacunae in our biographic data about Picasso, there would be no lacunae in our interpretations of his art."[21]

Assuming this kind of one-to-one relation between life and pictures, it was long thought that Marie-Thérèse's advent into the world of the painter coincided with the upsurge of her image in his work, which is to say, it occurred sometime in 1931. But other testimony has since established that the date of their meeting was in fact January of 1927: she was coming out of the Galeries Lafayette and he was emerging from the Métro; she had just been buying a set of white silk collar and cuffs, a somewhat schoolgirlish purchase, but then, she was only seventeen. It was just one year after completion of *The Milliner's Workshop.*

Marie-Thérèse has recorded what Picasso said as he accosted her in the crowd. "Mademoiselle," he urged, "you have an interesting face. I would like to paint your portrait. I am Picasso."[22]

Picasso had, of course, already painted her face, and with a certain frequency. That somewhat thick, classical blonde appears, for example, in drawings made in the summer of 1923 at Cap d'Antibes, where as a "classical bather" she is bracketed away from real life, a kind of placid aesthetic phantom (Zervos V, 39–43, 98–104). The type, equally abstracted, appears, now turbaned, in 1925 (Zervos V, 369). But it is only in *The Milliner's Workshop*, where, as we are hypothesizing, Picasso consciously surrendered to a certain automatism, painting a large composition about which he could say, "I didn't know what it represented," that this "face" is transported from a land of idyllic abstraction to a place both closer and realer: Paris, rue la Boétie, across the street, a young shop girl with short, thick, blond hair. There is indeed a relationship between art and life, we could say, but it goes in the opposite direction from the one supposed by the naive autobiographical reading of Picasso. Picasso dreamed a type; and then he found her. She was his way of confirming what the poet Mayakovsky had insisted—that art and life are incomparably bound together in the sense that everything a poet says and does, even in his most intimate relationships, will most certainly be a function of his work: determined by it, shaped by it, invented by it.

*The question itself is very clear: do we need the poet's biography in order to understand his work, or do we not?*
"Literature and Biography," Boris Tomashevsky[23]

In the same decade in which surrealism began to rewrite the relationship between the unconscious and the real world, so that fantasy, dream, desire become not the products of that reality but rather its producers, Russian formalist theory was tackling the art/life connection as it perennially confronts literary scholarship in the guise of the artist's biography. In a similar reversal of cause and effect, the formalists came up with conclusions that, from a certain point of view, were not all that different from André Breton's.

Boris Tomashevsky, for example, compares the silence that surrounds the life of Shakespeare—"the 'iron mask' of literature"—with the confessional detail that introduces us to Rousseau, and concludes that at a certain moment (the

118

late eighteenth century) the author-function is born, which is to say that writers begin to produce themselves as biographically present to their readers. Far from leading him to dismiss biography—although the formalists professed disdain for anything "outside" the text—this vision of the historical onset of biography as a poetic invention ("Byron, the poet of sharp-tempered characters, created the canonical biography for a lyrical poet") presents Tomashevsky with one more textual object, one more element of the creative construct that is the "work itself." Therefore if, as he declares, at a certain moment "biography became an element of literature," then the "biographical legend" becomes important to analyze, since it is itself an invention of the artist—"a premise which the author himself took into account during the creative process."[24]

However, we only get a sense of the seriousness with which such theorists took this idea—the *deadly* seriousness, in fact—when we see how it operates in Roman Jakobson's 1930 text "On a Generation That Squandered Its Poets," an essay both triggered by and dedicated to an analysis of Mayakovsky's suicide; for how could one argue that a poet killed himself in order to carry out the dictates, the inner logic, of his art?

Mayakovsky's suicide is an important test case for formalist theory, since common sense would tie it causally to real-world events, most obviously to the poet's increasingly troubled relationship to the Russian revolution. And indeed it is common sense that Jakobson hears chorusing on all sides in 1930, in expressions of shock at this symptom of a sudden breakdown in the relationship between Mayakovsky and the heroic subject of his work. There is universal agreement over the unexpectedness of this occurrence and insistence on its incongruity with "the Mayakovsky we knew." *Pravda* summarizes this conviction by announcing, "His death is just as inconsistent with the life he led as it is unmotivated by his poetry."[25]

*Motivation* is, of course, an interesting word to use here because it is precisely the one—although turned absolutely inside out—that the formalists summoned to describe the relationship of "event" to form. Understanding the goal of the work of art as a kind of perceptual renewal, a revivification of experience, the formalists saw the aesthetic "device" (the specific formal operations) as the work's structural lever on the expectations of its receiver. Therefore, insofar as aesthetic experience is a function of the "device," everything else in the artistic object can be seen as so many ways of staging that formal maneuver. Does a character go on a journey? Does the heroine fall ill? These events do not constitute the point of the narrative so much as they serve as the alibi of its form. Having for their function the "motivation" of the device, they then "cause" or call for the text's real occasion: the serial retardations, the roughened textures, the effects of estrangement that are its real goal, the deepest sources of its pleasure. And what is true of a story's turn of plot is equally true of events in the artist's real life. Those, as well, are produced for the sake of his art; they, like everything else with semantic content, are there to "motivate the device."

Jakobson points out that suicide, far from being unheralded by anything in "the Mayakovsky we knew," was an enduring theme of the poet's work; indeed, "Mayakovsky's most intense poems, 'Man' (1916) and 'About That' (1923), are dedicated to it."[26] Yet if this theme was gripping for the poet—and this is Jakobson's real, formalist point—it was because it was a semantic marker for one of the major poles of the structural opposition that functioned as the dynamic of his art. This opposition was between stasis and motion, between a deadening immobility and a victory over that sameness, in a movement that would overtake, outstrip, transcend time. The figure that is the controlling trope of Mayakovsky's art, sending him racing after the invention of new rhythms, is thus the very figure of the dialectic, and it is this rather than politics that married Mayakovsky to the revolution. The October revolution, Jakobson argues, was simply one more trope for the Mayakovskian system: "Weariness with fixed and narrow confines, the urge to transcend static boundaries—such is Mayakovsky's infinitely varied theme."[27] The revolution, in this sense, motivates the device.

The term Jakobson uses for this hated narrowness and fixity refers to the form it takes in many of the poet's verses, in which the Russian word *byt* repeatedly surfaces. Literally meaning quotidian or everyday, *byt* functioned for Mayakovsky in something of the same way that *spleen* operated for Baudelaire. It seemed to him an immutable present, something inertial, stagnating, stifling. "It is the poet's primordial enemy," Jakobson tells us, "and he never tired of returning to this theme. 'Motionless *byt*.'. . . 'Slits of *byt* are filled with fat and coagulate, quiet and wide.' "[28] *Byt* was Mayakovsky's enemy, the personification of the congealing of time, the equivalent of poetic failure, the figure of rhythmic implosion, of stale, fetid verse. Even in his earliest work, Mayakovsky thought of the possible triumph of *byt*: "Mama! / Tell my sisters, Ljuda and Olja, / That there's no way out." And from this earliest scenario, the theme—structural and symbolic—advanced. What followed, for Jakobson, was that

*gradually the idea that "there's no way out" lost its purely literary character. From the poetic passage it found its way into prose, and "there's no way out" turned up as an author's remark in the margin of the manuscript for "About That." And from that prose context the same idea made its way into the poet's life: in his suicide note he said: "Mama, sisters, comrades, forgive me. This is not a good method (I don't recommend it to others), but for me there's no other way out."*[29]

120

The idea of suicide had long motivated the device of temporal dynamism for Mayakovsky; eventually it became the only way to "write" paralysis.

*You know, I've always been haunted by a certain few faces and yours is one of them.*
          Picasso[30]

For those who really knew Picasso, it was certainly no secret that his tastes had first and foremost been formed in the crucible that was his art. We have only to attend to Françoise Gilot's reflections on why the master had been attracted to her, why he had, as she figured it, even *seen* her:

*I must admit I wondered more than once whether, if he had met me alone, he would even have noticed me. Meeting me with Geneviève, he saw a theme that runs throughout his entire work and was particularly marked during the 1930s: two women together, one fair and the other dark, the one all curves and the other externalizing her internal conflicts, with a personality that goes beyond the pictorial; one, the kind of woman who has a purely aesthetic and plastic life with him, the other, the type whose nature is reflected in dramatic expression. When he saw the two of us that morning, he saw in Geneviève a version of formal perfection, and in me, who lacked that formal perfection, a quality of unquiet which was actually an echo of his own nature. That created an image for him, I'm sure. He even said, "I'm meeting beings I painted twenty years ago." It was certainly one of the original causes of the interest he showed.[31]*

The contrasting couple—two women, one fair, the other dark; one placid, the other tense—is described by Gilot as a consistent "theme" of Picasso's work. And it is indeed a theme, which is to say a semantic variant on what a formalist or a structuralist (as Jakobson was to become) would see as an underlying oppositional pair that worked consistently to structure what Picasso did.

Elsewhere, for example, I have spoken of Picasso's handling of collage as a new way of operating the system of formal oppositions that lie at the heart of the code of painting.[32] These oppositions—the most crucial being that of figure/ ground—multiply into the great stylistic markers, like linear/ painterly, planar/recessional, haptic/optic. The ingenious strategy of Picasso's collage was to have manipulated one and the same pictorial element so that it would signify from within these oppositional pairs by oscillating between both poles, representing now one, now the other half of the couple. A reserved area of blank page is now figure—the guitar's frontal face; now ground—the surface against which a strip of wood-grained paper rests. A newspaper shape is now read as atmospheric surround (optic), now as an object's sharply cut edge (haptic). The great lesson of

121

collage was therefore not only that meaning is produced from within a system of oppositions, but also that those oppositions are structural in kind—that they are not the product of a theme or given bit of content, but are instead the producers of such content, and can thus become the theme of a vast array of material.

The opposition that is simultaneously real (either this thing or the other) and symbolic (now this, now that) seems to have been the one that drew Picasso. Aside from the collage example just adumbrated, we might think of the way he explored the theme of artist and model, where the oppositional pair is inevitably complicated through a chiasmatic exchange in which the watcher becomes watched and the passive, active.

Although the pairing of two women, one fair and one dark, does indeed become particularly insistent in his work of the 1930s, it would seem that it was urged into the artist's aesthetic experience somewhat earlier, in relation to the surrealist influence and its opening onto the theme of desire. We see it arrive, that is, around the automatist birth of Marie-Thérèse within the field of the formal doppelgänger —now black, now white—of 1926. This I would say is what the sketchbook at hand has to teach us.

Picasso's relationship to the structuring terms of his art —for example, to the way they surface in the oscillations of style, now cubist, now neoclassic, into which he settled after 1918—would, if really analyzed, have more to contribute to the interpretation of his work than further filling-in of biographical "lacunae." The question, as Jakobson has already elaborated it, is not *how* the artist authors his own biography, but to what end.

## Notes

1. Roland Penrose and John Golding, eds., *Picasso in Retrospect* (New York: Harper and Row, 1980), p. 161.

2. Mary Mathews Gedo, *Picasso: Art as Autobiography* (Chicago: University of Chicago Press, 1980), p. 253.

3. Roman Jakobson, "On a Generation That Squandered Its Poets," in Jakobson, *Verbal Arts, Verbal Sign, Verbal Time* (Minneapolis: University of Minnesota Press, 1985), p. 124.

4. Although in 1930 Aragon identified the material as a "dirty shirt" (see n. 5), catalogue descriptions of the object since its first exhibition in 1955 have given it as "canvas." A comparison of the photograph of the work as it was reproduced in 1926 and its identical configuration in its present state does not suggest that any changes were made subsequent to the photograph's publication.

5. "La Peinture au défi" was written as the preface to an exhibition of collages at the Galerie Goemans in March 1930. It is reprinted in Louis Aragon, *Les Collages* (Paris: Hermann, 1965).

6. *Ibid.*, p. 36.

7. *Ibid.*, p. 49.

8. The most fulsome development of the incantatory function of these works is by Lydia Gasman in her study on the themes of magic in Picasso's work, in which she devotes a chapter to these objects. See Lydia Gasman, *Mystery, Magic and Love in Picasso, 1925–1938: Picasso and the Surrealist Poets* (Ph.D. dissertation, Columbia University, New York, 1981).

9. Noting that Picasso himself admitted to being influenced by surrealism only in 1933, John Golding nonetheless speaks of the extremely important "release" provided by his contacts with surrealism beginning in the mid-1920s (see "Picasso and Surrealism" in Penrose and

Golding, eds., *Picasso in Retrospect*, p. 50). Pierre Daix speaks of Picasso's entry into relations with the surrealists as undergoing a period of incubation from late 1924 to 1926, culminating in the violent still lifes (Pierre Daix, *La Vie de peinture de Pablo Picasso* [Paris: Seuil, 1977], pp. 198–211).

10. This occurred when Kahnweiler showed Picasso the proofs of the catalogue of his retrospective at the Musée des Arts Décoratifs in 1955. See Pierre Cabanne, *Le Siècle de Picasso*, Vol. I (Paris: Denoël, 1975), p. 404.

11. *Ibid.*

12. *Ibid.*, pp. 407–408.

13. André Breton, *Surrealism and Painting* (New York: Icon Editions, 1972), p. 5.

14. Opinion is varied about the degree of Picasso's participation in this exhibition, due to the fact that the paintings by him that were included were borrowed from collectors. Neither Cabanne, however, nor Penrose feels that this changes what seems to have been a relaxing on Picasso's part of his rule never to appear in group exhibitions.

15. Daix, *La Vie de peinture de Pablo Picasso*, p. 198.

16. Breton, *Surrealism and Painting*, p. 70.

17. Daix, *La Vie de peinture de Pablo Picasso*, p. 216. In addition to the possible presence of an experience of Miró in the curvilinear "automatist" web of sheet 8 in the present notebook, it can be felt as well in the very sparse point-and-line "abstract" drawings of sheets 13 and 16, in which the abstract line drawings of the summer of 1924 (reproduced as engravings in *Le Chef d'oeuvre inconnu* [1931]) are developed in the direction of the extremely spare paintings that Miró made in 1925, such as his variations on the *Head of a Catalan Peasant*.

18. Cabanne, *Le Siècle de Picasso*, Vol. I, p. 421. The reason for assuming that Picasso intended this as a reference to *The Milliner's Workshop*—beyond its being the only candidate to fit his description—focuses on the presence of a male figure entering the door on the right, a figure that can be associated with death since it resembles the black silhouette in *The Dance* of seven months earlier, which Picasso identified as the just-deceased Rámon Pichot (see Roland Penrose, *Picasso, His Life and Work* [New York: Harper and Row, 1973], p. 258).

19. Pierre Daix, *Picasso* (New York: Praeger, 1965), p. 134.

20. Jakobson, *Verbal Arts, Verbal Sign, Verbal Time*, p. 126.

21. See n. 2.

22. See William Rubin, ed., *Pablo Picasso: A Retrospective* (New York: Museum of Modern Art, 1980), p. 253.

23. Ladislav Matejka and Krystyna Pomorska, eds., *Readings in Russian Poetics* (Cambridge: MIT Press, 1971), p. 47.

24. *Ibid.*, p. 52.

25. As cited in Jakobson, *Verbal Arts, Verbal Sign, Verbal Time*, p. 125.

26. *Ibid.*

27. *Ibid.*, p. 126.

28. *Ibid.*, p. 115.

29. *Ibid.*, pp. 124–125.

30. Françoise Gilot and Carlton Lake, *Life with Picasso* (New York: Signet Books, 1965), p. 43.

31. Ibid., p. 23.

32. See my "Re-Presenting Picasso," *Art in America*, LXVIII (December 1980), 91–96; and "In the Name of Picasso" in Krauss, *The Originality of the Avant-Garde and Other Modernist Myths* (Cambridge: MIT Press, 1984).

PARIS
21 mars
1926

inside front cover

1

2

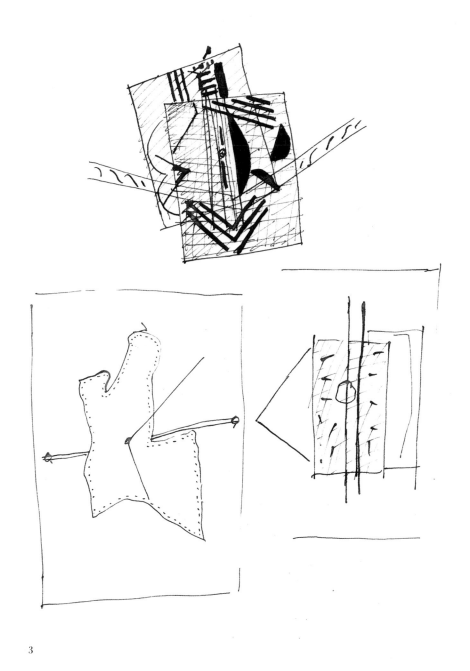

3

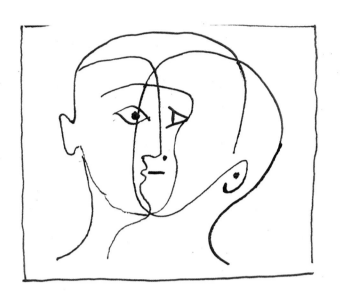

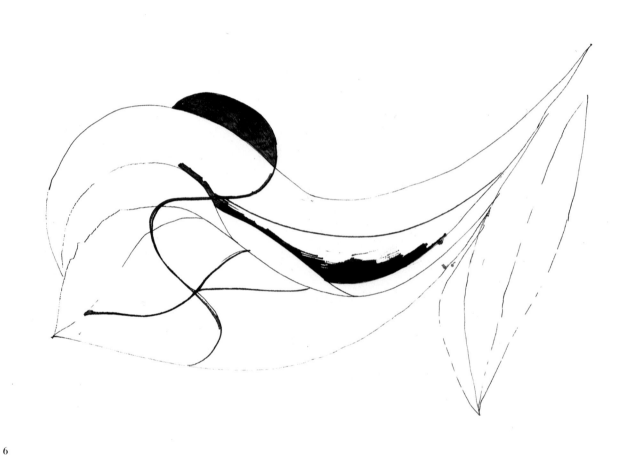

6

7

8

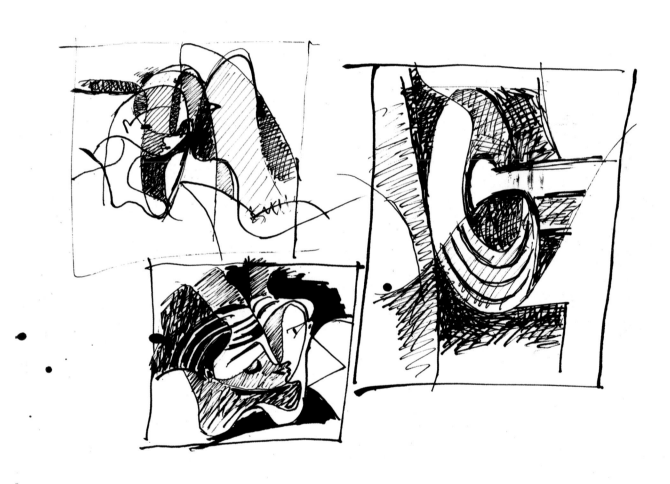

9

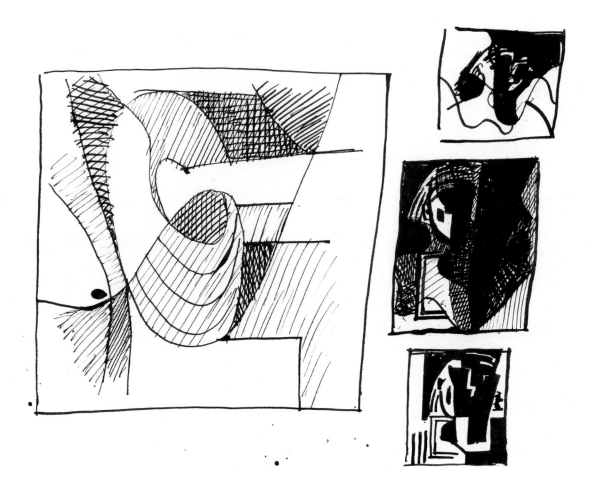

10

11

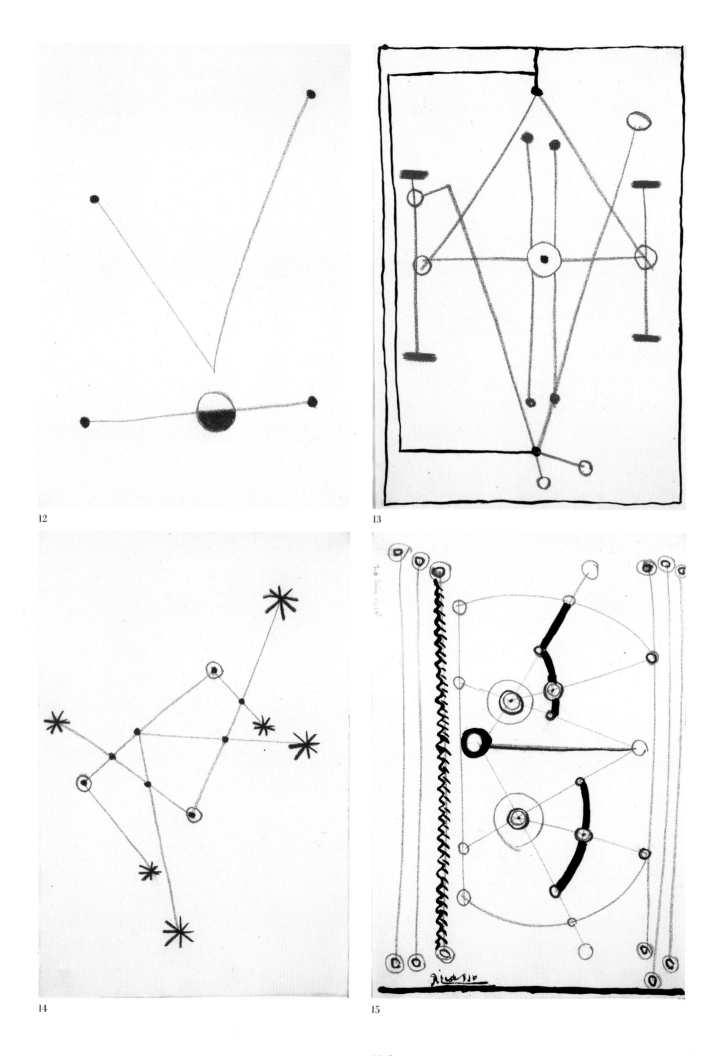

12

13

14

15

136

16

17

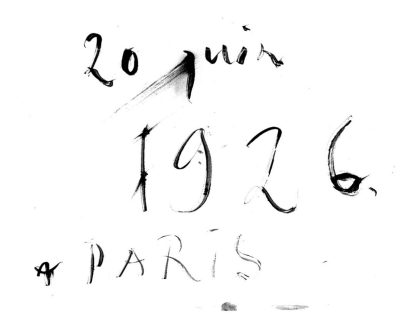

20 juin
1926.
PARIS

inside back cover

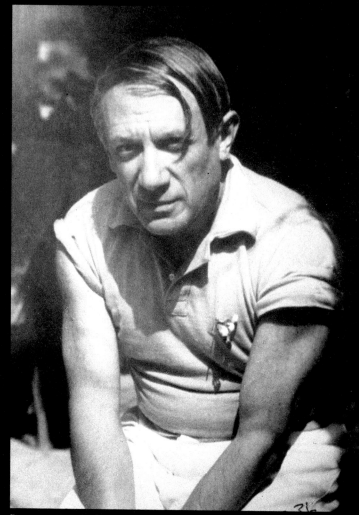

*Picasso, 1935–1936 (photograph by Man Ray)*

# Picasso at War: Royan, 1940
# Sketchbook No. 110, 1940

by Sam Hunter

With the German invasion of Poland in September of 1939, and with the uncertainty and turmoil of the war, Picasso left Paris for Royan on the Atlantic coast near Bordeaux, thus symbolically relinquishing the more seductive ambience of the Riviera and Mougins, the small village above Cannes where he had summered since 1936. He returned to Royan again at the beginning of 1940, after commuting to and from Paris, and installed himself this time on the fourth floor of the Villa les Voiliers, overlooking the town and the sea. He went back and forth restlessly in the spring, and then, on May 16, two weeks before this sketchbook commences with its first ink wash drawing, he returned to Royan, just eluding the German occupation of Paris, and remained there for three continuous months until August 25.

Figure 2. Picasso and Jaime Sabartés in Royan, 1940

According to legend, he met Matisse the day before he went south, and they exchanged ironic compliments on that day, in an apparent mood of artistic disengagement from the drama of events that, of course, was contradicted by the public positions Picasso had courageously taken in such searing indictments of fascism as his *Guernica,* and in the inspired cartoons, *The Dream and Lie of Franco.* Encountering Matisse on his way to his tailor, Picasso was surprised to find the French artist oblivious to the German threat. When he reminded Matisse that the German forces might be in Paris the next day, Matisse is reported to have asked: "But what about our generals, what are they doing?" And to this Picasso responded wryly: "Oh, they're from the Ecole des Beaux-Arts."[1]

Figure 1. Picasso Woman Dressing Her Hair *oil on canvas, 1940. Mrs. Bertram Smith, New York*

In Paris in March, Picasso had filled a sketchbook with drawings for his major painting of 1940, *Woman Dressing Her Hair* (which Zervos published in 1948, under the title *Carnet de dessins de Picasso;* see figures 1 and 2). Three months later, as the German troops entered Paris and Pétain prepared to sign an armistice, Picasso worked in Royan to complete the powerful and rather grim painting, which renews the fantastic inventions of his bone-period monuments and Dinard bathers, but in the context of an actual, rather sharply characterized visage of Dora Maar, surmounting a brutally disjointed nude torso. The stark nude is set in a shallow, partitioned, boxlike space painted in mournful tones of deepest gray and purple, a proscenium space strangely reminiscent of Francis Bacon's later mordant and vacuous cages, imprisoning even more fantastic and hallucinatory lumps of livid human flesh. Picasso's rigid but commanding image in *Woman Dressing Her Hair* is a strange hybrid, mixing moods of grave composure and massive dignity (its rather formal, life-study pose) with the monstrous (its cruel distortions and disorganized anatomy).

When Picasso began to work on the first page of the sketchbook, Paris had fallen, and his humanitarian sentiments, soured by that turn of events, reverted to earlier symbols of poignant martyrdom in the series of weeping women that followed the *Guernica*. These anguished forms express, on a deeply personal and emotional level and with the power of myth, our most disturbing fears and the horrors of war. On the first page, dated May 31, 1940, we find a characteristic Picasso contrast. On a single sheet two gruesome female visages resembling Dora Maar confront us; their bouffant hairstyle and penetrating, rather severe gaze today recall the memorable portrait of her painted on October 9, 1942. Below the grotesque and primeval heads, however, reclines a voluptuous nude, rapidly drawn in the soft curvilinear style reminiscent of the many Marie-Thérèse Walter images of nudes and reading women of the late 1930s. Miss Walter apparently still played a significant role in Picasso's life, although he had publicly taken Dora Maar as his new mistress and installed her in the Royan villa.

With remarkable technical facility Picasso rings the changes on his pictorial preoccupations and explorations of the late 1930s, as he alternates between savage female grotesques and a languorous nude in the classical style. Throughout his career after cubism, Picasso shuttled brilliantly between Greco-Roman tradition and primitive art with its magical imagery; he subsequently included surrealist disjunctions in his image repertory, finding inspiration in the opposition of these dichotomous visions of the human form. The bland, ideal beauty of a classical head might be recaptured in a lithograph; for a ceramic or a bronze, the inspiration might be Cycladic, Etruscan, or African sculpture, passed through the sieve of cubism. Often these contending sources fused in a composite painting or a drawing, establishing that characteristic psychological *frisson* of the civilized outer person confronted by the awareness of subconscious forces that lurk not far beneath the surface. What gave significance to Picasso's erudition and recondite insights, and stabilized a distracted, recapitulative tendency, was pure artistic temperament, not mere technical virtuosity, or an uncanny historical memory.

The second page of the sketchbook produces a handsome, brooding, and rather noble image of Dora Maar, despite its obfuscating chiaroscuro and vague definition. Interestingly, the pose is almost the mirror-image reverse of a portrait of Marie-Thérèse, with her chin propped on the index finger

*Figure 3. Jackson Pollock* War *ink and colored pencil on paper, 1937. The Metropolitan Museum of Art. Gift of Lee Krasner Pollock, in memory of Jackson Pollock, 1982*

of her left hand, now hanging in the new Picasso museum in the Hotel Salé, Paris.[2] The stark schematic line drawings that follow on pages 3–8, all executed on June 6, recapitulate the weeping woman theme, but in a new frontal confrontation, rather than in the accustomed flowing silhouette of its original inspiration. The bobbed hair again suggests the head and visage of Dora Maar, although the image is more archetypal than actual. Jackson Pollock's sketchbook drawings from the late 1930s, which have a common source in the *Guernica* and in the savage imagery of the Franco cartoons, also spring to mind (figure 3).

Most extraordinary is the abrupt and obsessive shift in imagery to variations on a death's-head, between June 11 and June 26. The next ten successive images in the sketchbook, with two exceptions in a more decorative and eclectic manner (pages 10 and 17), are wash drawings that convey the feeling of having been made from an observed skull, although there are occasional startling evocations of Dora Maar's bouffant hair, walleyed gaze, and facial tension even here.

The skulls were repeated in six more variations on June 30 and July 1. Thus, one-third of the images in this entire sketchbook revolve about the death's-head, an isolated, compulsive image whose potency and starkness deny it the role of a conventional *vanitas* symbol, signifying life's transience, and point instead to the obscene menace and human devastation of war. The skulls of these latter dates, interestingly, move toward abstraction and an implicit monumentalism, set as they are like so many of the Dinard bone forms on an arid plain, against a vacant sky.

Perhaps the most astonishing image is that on page 31, whose internal profiles and wash indications for shadow suggest a living creature capable of experiencing pain, and even perhaps of uttering a stifled cry. Ever the undaunted survivor, Picasso defies death and decay. Even extinction cannot prevent the human spirit from communicating the idea of suffering, a contradiction that sits strangely but invites our pity.

The grim constraints of the German occupation had reached into Royan by June 23, and must have weighed heavily upon Picasso. Memento mori of this kind had not appeared explicitly in his art since an early sketch for *Les Demoiselles d'Avignon*. Skulls, with their sense of finality and allegorical charge, were to be embraced unequivocally in finished paintings only in later, isolated works during his Paris years under the German occupation, most notably in *Still Life with Steer's Skull*, 1942, and *Still Life with Skull, Leek, and Pottery*, 1945, and in the magnificent bronze sculpture *Death's Head*, 1943. Picasso's momentary sense of darkness, perhaps even of hopelessness, in Royan was transferred, it would seem, from these sketchbook meditations on mortality into the frozen, contemporaneous grotesquerie of *Woman*

*Dressing Her Hair.* There, the powerfully three-dimensional image is carved out of its dark ground in angular wedges of brilliant illumination and sharply accentuated shadow, to create a similar mood emphasizing the closeness and intimacy of life and death, and also the menace of a base animal condition to the rational human spirit stripped of its defenses. The proximity of life and death, civilized and destructive impulses was undoubtedly driven home by the war and the German presence. Picasso's awesome double-profile image of a monstrous gorgon becomes as intimidating as a two-headed Cerberus guarding the gates of hell. There is also an unintended but nonetheless endorsed comedy in the vanity theme of the female toilet, so grossly caricatured and given such a grim protagonist.

Considering the apparent tensions of Picasso's relationship with Dora Maar, on which many friends and biographers have commented, and in view of her neuroses and self-doubt, it is worth considering at this point certain aspects of the autobiographical content of Picasso's works. "Many of the cruel distortions of the late Thirties and early Forties have their roots in Dora's chronic distress," writes John Richardson, a Picasso intimate and perhaps his most lucid and captivating biographer.[3] One senses an even deeper meaning in Picasso's imagery, however, regarding the obsession with his female companions as models. In this sketchbook, apart from the skull variations, every other image is actually a female figure, seated or standing. Seven made on the dates June 26 and June 27 can be directly associated with the *Woman Dressing Her Hair.* They are somewhat varied in pose, perhaps to avoid the monotony of serial repetition, and they were probably created after the painting was completed. The pictorial rigidities have been sublimated into a new lyrical invention and a more spontaneous, even rudimentary graphic style, as if in recompense for the angularities and stern sculptural planes of the large and impressive painting.

*Figure 4. Willem de Kooning* Two Women in the Country *oil, enamel, and charcoal on canvas, 1954. Hirshhorn Museum and Sculpture Garden, Smithsonian Institution*

The folk cliché in popular criticism of female imagery of this kind, repeated in the early writing on de Kooning's demonic Woman series of the late 1940s (which reached its peak of savagery less than a decade after Picasso's potent image appeared), holds that such brutally distorted visions are steeped in male attitudes and cultural predispositions, which reduce woman to a carnal scapegoat-idol (figure 4). No one has evoked more eloquently the distressing mixture of magical feelings of awe, fear, and sometimes disgust and destructive rage that may possess the mind of man when confronted with woman's fertile and mysterious body than Simone de Beauvoir. "The Earth Mother," she writes in *The Second Sex*, "engulfs the bones of her children . . . Death is a woman." Woman is "night in the entrails of the earth. Man is frightened of this night, the reverse of fecundity, which threatens to swallow him up. . . . In many a legend do we see the hero lost forever as he falls back into the maternal shadows—cave, abyss, hell." Yet at the same time,

"Embracing her, it is all the riches of life that the lover would possess. She is the whole fauna, the whole flora of the earth, gazelle and doe, lilies and roses, downy peach, perfumed berry, she is precious stones, nacre, agate, pearl, silk, the blue of the sky, the cool water of springs, air, flame, land and sea. . . . Nothing lies deeper in the hearts of men than this animism."[4]

Whether or not we must go to such extremes, yielding to the flurry of recent autobiographical and psychoanalytical interpretations of Picasso's imagery, and solemnly condemn him for misogyny, as so many writers have also been quick to do regarding de Kooning's potent female subject matter, is still arguable. The fact remains that Picasso has raised his *particular* imagery to a mythic level as something more, certainly, than a degradation of the generic female, or her investiture with miraculous powers. His art touches a common nerve, transcending questions of sexual politics, or revisionist social history, for it operates most effectively as a powerful indictment of organized societal brutality in a violent time.

Many writers have pointed out the resemblance of drawings of the insane to Picasso's inventions: the disorganized anatomy, the double profile, the compulsive repetition of ornamental pattern. One of the profoundly tragic meanings of the imagery that followed the *Guernica* and its stricken, weeping women has been the projection, through a controlled symbolism, of a kind of mass insanity in the vernacular of psychotic drawing, now made more familiar to us by Dubuffet and others. Goya in his *Caprices* had written an inscription to one of his etchings that "the sleep of reason produces monsters." In his art of the late 1930s and early 1940s, dramatizing the wartime agony of death and senseless destruction, Picasso added an up-to-date, clinical postscript to Goya's vision of man's inhumanity to man in some of the most eloquent and memorable artistic statements of our century. Many of the preliminary studies for this new fund of deeply disturbing, even accusatory imagery originated in Picasso's sketchbook drawings and meditations.

Perhaps the most sober and illuminating commentary on Picasso's capacity to symbolize the human condition, and on his infallible instinct for the human drama, whatever the price paid in unsettling artistic decorum, was made by the art historian George Hamilton. Citing Picasso's well-known statement, "To my misfortune—and probably my delight— I use things as my passions tell me,"[5] Hamilton writes that Picasso

*induces us to look for the meaning of his work within him, and within ourselves. The spaces in which his metamorphoses occur are the spaces of feeling, spaces where the mind reflects on its own experiences as well as*

145

*upon its perceptions of the world without . . . . He does not so much abstract from the actual as make actual what had previously been real only as a passionate apprehension. He makes visual what he has thought and felt . . . . Picasso's work can be read as a continuing and changing dream. But as in dreams . . . there are moments which are hallucinatingly "real," when objects are seen with dazzling and deadly clarity. Picasso is a master of such moments.*[6]

The *ex post facto* wash studies of *Woman Dressing Her Hair* are seven in number, executed on two successive dates, June 26 and 27. These loosely handled drawings, made with a fluent brush, nonetheless convey a sense of psychological acuity and intensity in their invention of painfully repellent, freakish visages. The upper torsos of the forms follow the painting's configuration almost exactly, with the same head pose, arrangement of upraised arms, and violently tipped and skewed breasts. Buttocks and legs, however, have been reversed and defy the painting's *contraposto*, in order to give the figure a stiffly erect attitude, more suitable to its state of incipient calcification. The altogether horrifying changes Picasso has worked on the ideal human form also express a certain nonchalance, despite the ignominy of its visibly eroding humanity so characteristic of the artist's transformation.

The reduction of man, and in this case woman, to his/her id or to a reactive protoplasm, can be linked to both Picasso's personal predilections and his Spanish extremism. His private perspective soon attained a systematic philosophical basis in existentialist thought and in the artistic practices of the immediate postwar period. The half despairing, half comical moods, the deliberate depredations of man's finer nature, the visual inanities, verbal abuse, and irrational, violent imagery and demeaning language of Ionesco's Theater of the Absurd and Antonin Artaud's ritualistic Theater of Cruelty bear witness to the broad social relevance, and cathartic release, of Picasso's rather unflattering vision of contemporary mankind, following its most destructive war.

Picasso himself gave further support to the view that the horrors of modern war directly and deeply affected his art when he wrote in 1941 the play *Desire Caught by the Tail*.[7] Picasso's response to the horror and devastation of the Second World War is encapsulated in the emblematic last lines: "Light the lanterns. Throw flights of doves with all our strength against the bullets and lock securely the house demolished by bombs."

Nonetheless, he himself insisted publicly that the distraught figures and macabre still lifes painted at Royan during the German occupation, and the subsequent turn in his portraiture toward a more gruesome genre of contorted figuration, had no direct reference to the catastrophe. "I have not painted the war," Picasso was quoted as saying in 1944, "because I am not the kind of painter who goes out like a photographer for something to depict. But I have no doubt that the war is in these paintings I have done. Later perhaps the historians will . . . show that my style has changed under the war's influence. Myself, I do not know."[8]

Perhaps the most elaborately finished and self-contained drawings in the sketchbook are three brilliant, formally diverse images of seated women, with color added in a combination of ink wash and reddish brown and blue pastel. Although the images show in abundance the technical facility and assurance that permitted Picasso to express rapidly and with an unsettling immediacy any idea that flitted across his mind, these are also more self-conscious and contrived constructions, each in its different way. Within a matter of days the striking dichotomy and tensions of Picasso's art reasserted themselves within these brilliant variations on a favorite theme, as he integrated side and frontal views, liberally redistributed body parts, and opposed decorative floral and basketry motifs against more rigorous sculptural shapes carved out of light and dark masses.

The first (chronologically) image in the series, dated July 18, installs floral motifs in place of facial detail, as Picasso deliberately embraced the metaphor of the woman-flower, an allusion that continued to fascinate him over the next two decades. He pursued this idea throughout the serpentine, vinelike, and trellis forms, reducing the torso to swags of ropelike creepers, stems, and blossoms. Perhaps more ominously, they also recall the disturbing animism of Picasso's surrealist inventions in his bathing scenes of 1932 at Boisgeloup. Even this intricately ornamental figure reveals Dora Maar's bobbed hair and asymmetrical facial cast; and in the long-nosed profile there is probably a distillate or visual residue of Picasso's Afghan hound, Kasbec. Of Picasso's beloved and companionable dog, Roland Penrose has written: "His profile with its sharp sensitive nose became traceable for several years among the human heads that Picasso invented. In fact, Picasso has told me jokingly that his two most important models in these years before and during the Second World War were Kasbec and Dora Maar."[9]

Of the remaining two images, that of July 25 affects the sculptural monumental style, at least in part, with its angulated mask precariously poised on a plinth made up of a suggestive network of signs for neck and breastbone. The image of August 9 was painted shortly before Picasso tired of Royan and fled the oppressive presence of German troops in the small resort town to resume a less burdened residence in Paris. Disquieting and vertiginous, the image is decoratively overwrought, with its swirling network of curving lines and multicolor dazzle. However, it is also more full-bodied and humanly expressive than the earlier ornamental study of July 18. Each drawing reinstates aspects of the studies of seated and reading women that had begun to obsess Picasso in the late 1930s as a new kind of subject matter that cut across the genres and hierarchies of portraiture, combining the traditional romantic fragment with a purely fantastic invention.

The studies had probably begun in 1937 with such works as the *Woman with a Book* in the Norton Simon Collection, on whose historical roots and cross-cultural currents Robert Rosenblum has expounded in an absorbing and significant article.[10] Another antecedent from the same year was the *Seated Woman (Marie-Thérèse Walter)* in the Musée Picasso, Paris.[11] The formal juxtapositions and psychological content of these two powerful images provided Picasso with "a symbolic vehicle for the revelation of female personality, moving from external to internal worlds," in Rosenblum's discerning commentary, which was, in fact, limited to only the first subject.

Van Gogh and Gauguin had oftentimes painted half-length figures in a similar attitude with their heads resting pensively on a hand or a finger, such as their respective versions of *L'Arlesienne* and Van Gogh's portrait of Dr. Gachet. Van Gogh in several portraits of Mme Roulin, which he called *La Berceuse*, had also created figure studies against a background of assertive decoration that threatened to swallow up the human subject. It is possible, too, that in these examples Picasso found hints not only for the portraits of the late 1930s but also for the drawings in this sketchbook, which set up a precarious balance between the human image and a powerful decorative invention challenging its existence. Whether or not there is also conscious influence from the sixteenth-century Italian mannerist Archimboldo, who made figures of simulated basketry, fruits, and vegetables, Picasso has extracted fantastic elements from his theme and heightened them.

For Picasso, human life becomes, as we have noted, just one among many orders of existence, and there are constant metamorphic transpositions possible to bridge these orders; hence, a chair, a decorative garment, a hat, vegetative nature, and the human figure may engage in a formal dialogue in which each has equal claim as a vital expressive and even humanly meaningful element. His psychology of formal invention was related to surrealist procedures of association and dissociation, which invested even the most banal objects with magical properties and powers. It was part of an outlook that saw change itself as the only permanent aspect of form.

We are also reminded of Picasso's now famous account to André Malraux of his first unsettling encounter with African sculpture in the old Trocadero Museum of Ethnological Art in Paris, just before he repainted the savage masks of *Les Demoiselles d'Avignon*. Picasso contended that the magical powers of these African masks, their role, as he put it, to act ritualistically as *"intercesseurs,"* or mediators, rather than their formal structure, impressed him most deeply and precipitated the violent transformation of the two brutally primitivist figures at the right in this work, his "first exorcism painting."[12] With all his deformations in his scrambled, features-askew portraits, Picasso nevertheless preserves some humanistic allusion in the sketchbook heads, which are a distorted memory of an idealized Greek bust. This allusion presides over the violent transformations —or, better perhaps, endures them—with a sibylic detachment, reminding us that Picasso never entirely lost sight of his antecedents in Mediterranean humanism no matter how radical, fantastic, or primitivistic his inventions.

This sketchbook is crammed with the vital signs and scribbles of Picasso's powerful artistic personality, and it is astonishing, too, for its revelations of an almost dogged ability to home in obsessively on a chosen theme, with a laser-beam intensity. The drawings also vividly persuade us of the artist's limitless depth of understanding for, and curiosity about, the human personality. Finally, the studies we have all too briefly discussed consistently support the view of Picasso as a traditionalist at least as much as a revolutionary innovator, with a profound experience of historical culture, not in the sense of some willful, shallow eclecticism but in the sense of the involuntary, unconscious response of a thoroughly modern spirit.

For Picasso, tradition presents itself as an unlimited panorama of stylistic possibilities existing in a simultaneous present and comprising a new artistic pantheon based on ahistorical, universally valid aesthetic values. He has written, "To me there is no past or future in art. If a work of art cannot live always in the present it must not be considered at all. The art of the Greeks, of the Egyptians, of the great painters who lived in other times, is not an art of the past; perhaps it is more alive today than it ever was."[13] Picasso's dialogue with history has a function similar to his passionate interrogation of himself: they both drive a single, continuous creative impulse whose aim is nothing less than a potent reconstruction of observed reality.

# Notes

1. William Rubin, ed., *Pablo Picasso: A Retrospective*, chronology by Jane Fluegel (New York: Museum of Modern Art, 1980), p. 350.

2. Dominique Bozo, introduction to *Musée Picasso Catalogue sommaire des collections* (Paris: Editions de la Réunion des musées nationaux, 1985), plate 137.

3. John Richardson, *Homage to Picasso for His Ninetieth Birthday*, catalogue for a joint exhibition of paintings and works on paper, 1901–1971, Seidenberg and Marlborough galleries, New York City, October 1971, p. 9.

4. Simone de Beauvoir, *The Second Sex*, cited in Dorothy Dinnerstein, *The Mermaid and the Minotaur: Sexual Arrangements and Human Malaise* (New York: Harper and Row, 1977), pp. 124–125.

5. Christian Zervos, "Conversations avec Picasso," *Cahiers d'Art*, X, 173–178 (1935).

6. George Hamilton, *Modern European Painting and Sculpture, 1880–1940* (Baltimore: Penguin Books, 1967), pp. 305–306.

7. The Picasso play was finished on January 17, 1941, and was first performed in March 1944 to a large gathering at the Leirises' flat, with Albert Camus directing, and with Louise and Michel Leiris, Dora Maar, Simone de Beauvoir, Raymond Queneau, and Jean-Paul Sartre taking parts. It was only recently performed in New York City and on Long Island in an English-language version.

8. Peter D. Whitney, "Picasso Is Safe," *San Francisco Chronicle*, September 3, 1944; cited in A. H. Barr, *Picasso: Fifty Years of His Art* (New York: Museum of Modern Art, 1946), p. 223.

9. Cited in Jean Sutherland Boggs, *Picasso and Man*, exhibition catalogue, The Art Gallery of Toronto, January 17–February 16, 1964, p. 128.

10. Robert Rosenblum, "Picasso's 'Woman with a Book,'" *Arts* magazine, LI, 5 (January 1977), pp. 100-106.

11. Bozo, introduction to *Musée Picasso Catalogue sommaire des collections*, plate 137.

12. André Malraux, *Picasso's Mask*, translated and annotated by June Guicharnaud with Jacques Guicharnaud (from *La Tête d'obsidienne* [Paris: Gallimard, 1974]; New York: Holt, Rinehart and Winston, 1976), pp. 10–11.

13. Statement by the artist made to Marius de Zayas and published in the *Arts*, May 1923, under the title "Picasso Speaks"; cited in Barr, *Picasso*, pp. 270–271.

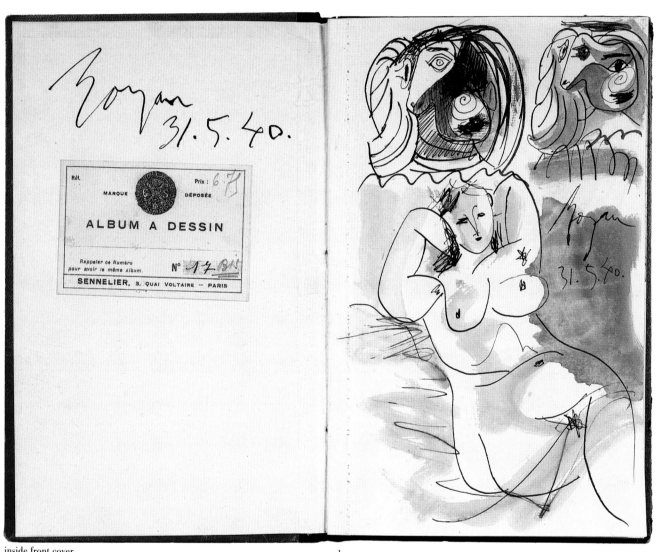

inside front cover

1

2

3

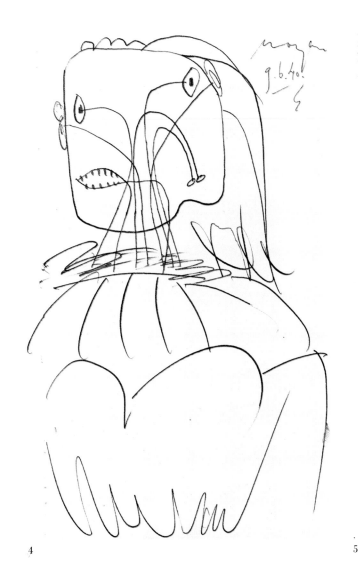

4

5

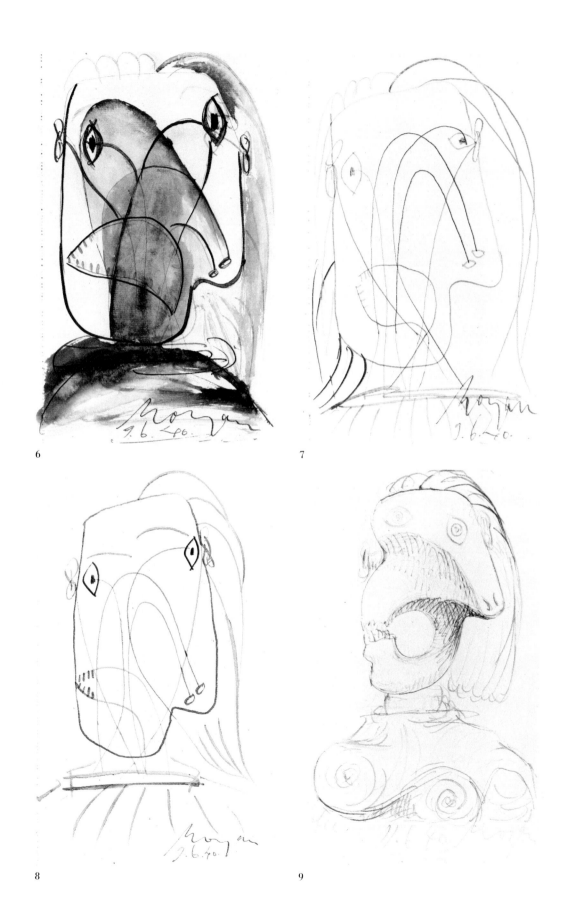

6

7

8

9

10

11

12

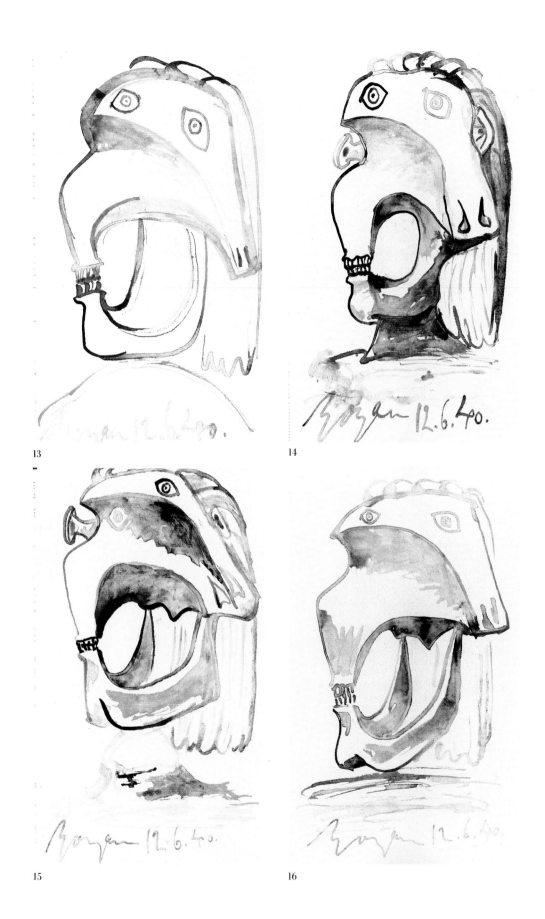

13

14

15

16

20.6.40.

17

18

19

20

21

22

23

24

25

164

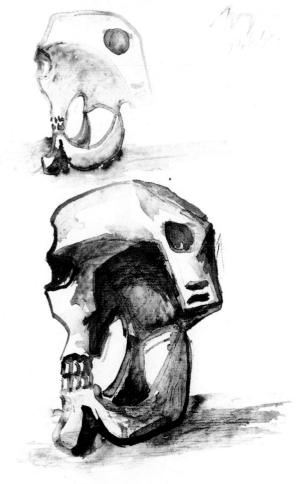

30.6.40.

26

28

1.7.40.

29

1.7.40.

30

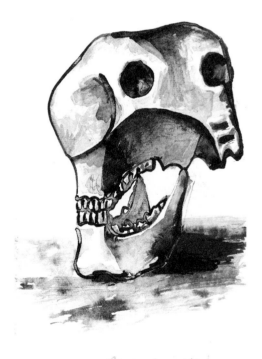

31

32

33

34

35

36

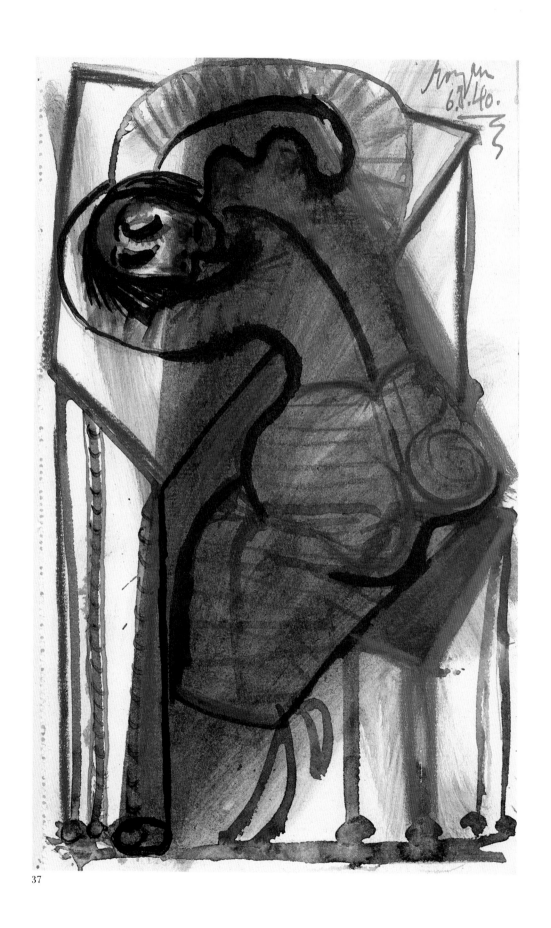

37

39

40

41

42

*Picasso, 1963 (photograph by Edward Quinn)*

# The *Sabines*
## Sketchbook No. 163, 1962
by Gert Schiff

Two notebooks of October–November 1962 elucidate Picasso's work on a series of paintings about war and violence, centered on the old Roman legend of the rape of the Sabines. The drawings make us understand essential features of Picasso's creative imagination. Rooted in myth as well as in intimate private experience, they reflect some of his principal preoccupations as an artist. In addition, they bear witness to his concern about politics.

The series was begun at the end of October 1962, when the Cuban missile crisis threatened to provoke war between the United States and the Soviet Union. Deeply troubled, Picasso responded at first precisely as he had on the eve of the German offensive against France: he depicted the murderous energies of war embodied in animal life. In March 1940, he had turned fish and crustaceans into repellent monsters. Now, he showed the deadly threat mirrored in the greedy eyes of a cat bent over a table with crabs, a flatfish, and a lobster.[1]

*Figure 1. Nicolas Poussin* Massacre of the Innocents *oil on canvas, circa 1628. Musée Condé, Chantilly*

However, Picasso's friend, the painter Edouard Pignon, provided him with more appropriate subject matter for an indictment of war and violence. He invited Picasso to contribute to the 1963 exhibition of the Salon de Mai, traditionally a reunion of veterans of the Resistance and their friends. The old Picasso, isolated by his fame, cherished his participation in the Salon because it offered him once a year the illusion of being a painter among painters. Quite often the organizers proposed a common theme for these exhibitions. This time they suggested that the paintings submitted should be related to Delacroix's *Entry of the Crusaders into Constantinople*, an idea well suited to Picasso's intentions. Yet somehow the *Crusaders* failed to inspire him. Instead, he chose to base his contribution on works by Poussin and David. He asked Pignon and his wife, the writer Hélène Parmelin, to provide him with slides and reproductions of Poussin's *Massacre of the Innocents* (figure 1) and David's *Sabines* (figure 2). Picasso, his wife Jacqueline, and the Pignon-Parmelin couple discussed these paintings inch by inch during a slide session in October 1962, "in a delirium of painterly enthusiasm."[2] Immediately thereafter, Picasso started work

*Figure 2. Jacques-Louis David* Sabines *oil on canvas, 1799. Musée du Louvre, Paris*

on his antiwar series, using the two paintings, together with the Louvre version of Poussin's *Rape of the Sabines* (figure 3), as "raw material." Once more, he pitted himself against two illustrious "ancestors" and translated their achievement into his own, highly idiosyncratic pictorial language.

The first result of this struggle was a painting dated October 24, 1962 (figure 4). Its subject is the rape of the Sabines, yet it conflates motifs from Poussin's version with borrowings from David's work. David's *Sabines*, however, does not depict the rape but its aftermath, in which Hersilia throws herself between the combatants and puts an end to the bloodshed. (This difference between the subjects of the paintings by David and Poussin, often overlooked, has a bearing on Picasso's transformation of these sources.) The small work is a bold improvisation, painted in broad patches of "loamy" color. It is a tightly knit composition of four overlapping groups, of which at least three are clearly legible. The backdrop is an antique town surmounted by hills. To the right, a nude warrior with a raised sword, seen from the back, holds a struggling female with his left arm. The figure is based on David's Romulus, although it retains none of his nobility. To his left, a rider stands up in his stirrups; reaching over his horse's head, he lifts a woman from the ground, her arms spread in lament. This group in its central position, as well as the setting, is derived from Poussin's *Rape of the Sabines*. Underneath the group, trampled underfoot by the rearing horse, one sees a woman and her child; these figures are taken again from David's painting. The woman is, in fact, a transformation of Hersilia. The courageous intercessor has been thrown on the ground; her pleading arms are now spread in a helpless attempt at self-protection, if not in an expression of sheer horror. The group on the extreme left lacks clarity; it seems to involve one, perhaps two women, running away with their children. It should be noted already at this point how radically Picasso changes the purpose of borrowed figures —without changing their attitudes. The noble Romulus becomes a savage barbarian; Hersilia, the pacifier, becomes a victim of war.

Picasso spent the rest of the same day filling the pages of a notebook[3] with an astonishing narrative in fourteen drawings. The first three introduce the subject of a young woman fallen from her bicycle. In spite of its anachronistic nature, this motif was soon to be incorporated in the studies for the *Rape of the Sabines;* it remained part of it until fairly late in the evolution of the theme. Its very inconsistency with the Roman legend suggests an autobiographical root, for we know by now that Picasso's subject matter, if not related to myth or tradition, invariably stems from his own private experience. We have hardly begun to recognize the extent of his reliance upon personal memories, or upon the stuff of his everyday existence. Patrick O'Brian identifies the woman as Marie-Thérèse

*Figure 3. Nicolas Poussin* Rape of the Sabines *oil on canvas, circa 1635–1637. Musée du Louvre, Paris*

*Figure 4. Picasso* Rape of the Sabines *oil on canvas, October 24, 1962*

*Figure 5. Picasso Sketchbook No. 164, p. 1 pencil on paper, October 24, 1962*

*Figure 6. Picasso Sketchbook No. 164, p. 2 pencil on paper, October 24, 1962*

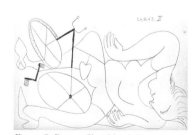

*Figure 7. Picasso Sketchbook No. 164, p. 3 pencil on paper, October 24, 1962*

*Figure 8. Picasso Sketchbook No. 164, p. 4 pencil on paper, October 24, 1962*

*Figure 9. Picasso Sketchbook No. 164, p. 5 pencil on paper, October 24, 1962*

*Figure 10. Picasso Sketchbook No. 164, p. 6 pencil on paper, October 24, 1962*

Walter, Picasso's love of the 1930s, "a passionate cyclist."[4] But this is clearly contradicted by her dark hair in those paintings in which she appears (figures 19, 38), as Marie-Thérèse was blond. It seems much more plausible that the woman is Dora Maar, who supplanted Marie-Thérèse in Picasso's affections. She was no less a passionate cyclist —witness her depiction with her bicycle in Picasso's great painting *Night Fishing in Antibes* (1939).[5] The dark hair, occasional facial distortions, and, not least, the curious hat worn in several drawings and paintings by the woman fallen from her bicycle are all familiar in portraits of Dora Maar.[6] Moreover, there is an incident in her biography that makes the identification all but inevitable. As Picasso told Françoise Gilot, Miss Maar in 1945 went through a period of mental disturbance, for which she was treated by Dr. Lacan. One night, she was

*found by a policeman wandering along the quay near the Pont Neuf (with her hair dishevelled and her clothes torn). She told him she had been attacked by a man who stole her bicycle. The policeman took her home, since she seemed very dazed. Later on . . . her bicycle was found, apparently untouched, right near the spot where she claimed to have been attacked. It looked as though she had just left it there . . . . "I thought she was looking for sympathy," [Picasso] said, "feeling that maybe I wasn't so much interested in her as I had been."[7]*

The personal memory that inspired the first three drawings (figures 5–7) is, therefore, the real or imagined assault suffered by Dora Maar. Picasso works his way toward a balanced composition, adjusting the position of the bicycle wheels between the straddled legs of the figure, and changing the treatment of her face. In the first drawing she cries out in pain, and her features are as grotesquely distorted as in a portrait of Dora Maar of August 29, 1937.[8] In the two following versions, she falls into a swoon; in the latter of these, she is shown with a simple, near-classical profile. The next four drawings (figures 8–11) connect the incident with the *Rape of the Sabines*. They depict a nude woman, subject to the amorous assault of a bearded warrior. She defends herself in wide-eyed horror, pressing her hand against his mouth, or scratching his throat. The drawing in figure 9 proves that she is indeed the woman fallen from her bicycle, for she is wearing Dora Maar's hat, while the raised head of a horse confirms the connection with the *Sabines* (see figure 4). The young warrior in figure 12 is a variation of David's Romulus, brandishing his sword.

Unexpectedly, in the remaining six sketches (figures 13–18) the violence gives way to an idyllic mood. They depict a domesticated "Romulus" dallying with a young girl. With her elbows raised over her head, she strikes an attitude familiar in Picasso's paintings of 1907–1908, from *Les Demoiselles d'Avignon* and its "African" aftermath to the *Three Nudes*.[9] Gradually, the girl loses all her shyness

*Figure 11. Picasso Sketchbook No. 164, p. 7 pencil on paper, October 24, 1962*

*Figure 12. Picasso Sketchbook No. 164, p. 8 pencil on paper, October 24, 1962*

*Figure 13. Picasso Sketchbook No. 164, p. 9 pencil on paper, October 24, 1962*

*Figure 14. Picasso Sketchbook No. 164, p. 10 pencil on paper, October 24, 1962*

*Figure 15. Picasso Sketchbook No. 164, p. 11 pencil on paper, October 24, 1962*

*Figure 16. Picasso Sketchbook No. 164, p. 12 pencil on paper, October 24, 1962*

*Figure 17. Picasso Sketchbook No. 164, p. 13 pencil on paper, October 24, 1962*

*Figure 18. Picasso Sketchbook No. 164, p. 14 pencil on paper, October 24, 1962*

*Figure 19. Picasso* Rape of the Sabines *oil on canvas, October 25, 1962*

and in the last sketch of the day (figure 18), she leans trustingly on her lover's shoulder.

The following day, Picasso continued the story of the unhappy cyclist with an increase of both savagery and tenderness. In a grisaille painting (figure 19) he shows her trodden underfoot by an antique soldier. Only his left foot is visible, which is clearly derived from the soldier in Poussin's *Massacre of the Innocents* (figure 1). This is corroborated by the first of eleven drawings, all done the same day (figure 20). There, the soldier, while stepping over the cyclist, pursues a mother with her child. In the following two sketches (figures 21 and 22) a nude, bald-headed warrior (he, too, trampling upon the woman with the same, oversize foot) threatens to stab her with his sword. Once more, however, the violence is replaced by tender humanity. Six times (figures 23–28), the victim is rescued by paternal or youthful men. Their compassion is conveyed all the more movingly as it is expressed with the utmost economy of line. In one case (figure 25) the woman is helped up by a hero who defiantly looks out for possible contestants. In another (figure 28), the young rescuer calls for help for the lifeless victim.

Yet in the remaining two drawings (figures 29 and 30) the original savagery returns. In the first instance, two giant legs step upon the swooning cyclist, while a rearing horse appears in the background. In the second one, the legs alone stride over the helpless body, in filmlike fragmentation and magnitude. Again, special emphasis is placed on the Poussin-derived left foot.

Even without their anachronisms, these drawings could not be called classical. Picasso made no attempt at creating an illusion of antiquity by way of detailed treatment of armor and weapons, as he had done in his illustrations of Aristophanes' *Lysistrata* (1934). Moreover, if he worked in a classical idiom (as he had done in his paintings and drawings of 1920–1924), he used straight lines and consistent proportions, and suppressed emotion. In the series under discussion, however, the bodies are arbitrarily shaped with all but childlike abbreviations; Picasso drew spontaneously, without preconceived notions of style. Hence, his line transmits pure emotion and instinct.

It is equally obvious that the images themselves emerge, without much conscious control, from the depths of the artist's psyche. The story of the cyclist in its interaction of destruction and compassion appears as a parable of Picasso's relations with women. In those multiple disguises as assailant and lover, Good Samaritan and killer, he is acting out a deeply rooted ambivalence of his own. If, as he said, women were for him either goddesses or doormats, he treated them accordingly. Dora Maar, whose memory was in those days foremost on his mind, was not only a beautiful and exciting lover, but also a splendid companion in all of

*Figure 20. Picasso Sketchbook No. 164, p. 15 pencil on paper, October 25, 1962*

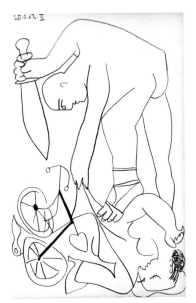

*Figure 21. Picasso Sketchbook No. 164, p. 16 pencil on paper, October 25, 1962*

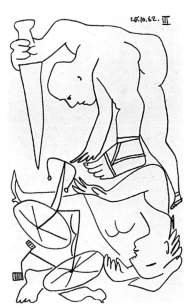

*Figure 22. Picasso Sketchbook No. 164, p. 17 pencil on paper, October 25, 1962*

Picasso's artistic and intellectual pursuits. Yet in his pictorial world she appears more often than not as the *Weeping Woman*,[10] since he loved to make her cry. By the same token, earlier on, he forbade Marie-Thérèse her girlish laughter, and introduced her, in theory and practice, to the doctrines of the Marquis de Sade. Both Marie-Thérèse and Dora Maar ended up as victims on the altar of Picasso's art. As the brutal, destructive lover of both, Picasso depicted himself frequently as a Minotaur.[11] When he was overcome by guilt, however, he showed the Minotaur slain by the innocent young female whom he had made suffer so much.[12] Hence, it is hardly drawing theory too far if we interpret the narrative of the cyclist as a parable of Picasso's compulsion to destroy what he loved most. Linked to the *Sabines* by the common theme of violence done to women, the motif could easily be interwoven with those sources from which he was to distill a statement against violence and war. There is support for this interpretation in the persistence of the soldier's foot, trampling upon the cyclist. Lydia Gasman has collected evidence that Picasso in his surrealist phase used the foot as a symbolic self-image.[13] Suffice it for our purpose to mention that the autobiographical protagonist of Picasso's play *Desire Caught by the Tail* is called Big Foot.[14]

As the *Sabines* series developed, the autobiographical element was gradually superseded by the universal, humanitarian theme. On October 26, Picasso began his working day with a large drawing in fat black crayon, which apparently has been preserved only in a transfer lithograph (figure 31).[15] It is an enlarged version of the painting of October 24 (figure 4) in simple, generalized outlines. As the setting widens, the composition gains in clarity and all the figures and groups receive sufficient space to act out their individual dramas. The backdrop of an antique city overarches the whole composition; it now includes a "Colosseum" and, to the right, a contemporary building with window shutters. The principal figures of the earlier painting—the "Romulus," the horseman, and the "Hersilia" —appear in the same places. However, the "Romulus" is given a much more domineering position. The blade of his sword is aligned with the temple on the horizon. Instead of balancing a struggling female, he carries a shield, like his prototype in the painting by David (figure 2). Most important, he puts his grossly enlarged foot on the cyclist, who is here for the first time integrated in a larger composition. The horseman, who in the first version appeared parallel to the picture plane, now rushes forth from the middle distance. As he reaches down to snatch a woman, he is half hidden behind the head of his horse, a flaw that obscures the fact that "Romulus" aims his sword at him. "Hersilia" laments again underneath the hooves of the rearing horse. To her left, two soldiers try to grab hold of running women. The bodies of two children, one dead, one reaching out for help, indicate that at this point, Picasso has fused the theme of the *Sabines* with that of the *Massacre of the Innocents*.

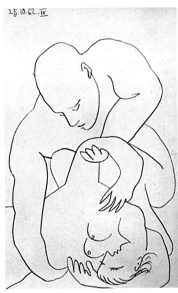

*Figure 23. Picasso Sketchbook No. 164, p. 18 pencil on paper, October 25, 1962*

*Figure 24. Picasso Sketchbook No. 164, p. 19 pencil on paper, October 25, 1962*

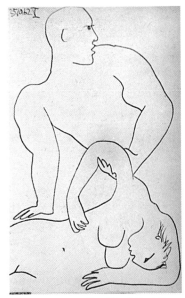

*Figure 25. Picasso Sketchbook No. 164, p. 20 pencil on paper, October 25, 1962*

Figure 26. Picasso Sketchbook No. 164,
p. 21 pencil on paper, October 25, 1962

Figure 27. Picasso Sketchbook No. 164,
p. 22 pencil on paper, October 25, 1962

Figure 28. Picasso Sketchbook No. 164,
p. 23 pencil on paper, October 25, 1962

Upon completing this composition, the indefatigable master took up a new notebook.[16] He filled its first eight pages with paraphrases of motifs from the large composition (figure 31). In the first drawing (page 1) Picasso invents a different formula for the horse, whose baroque fury owes an obvious debt to Poussin's *Rape of the Sabines* (figure 3). Thereafter (page 2) he makes the gesture of "Hersilia" more effective through subtle adjustments in her proportions. The next two sketches elaborate upon the theme of soldiers pursuing women. The helmeted hoplite on page 3 is a new invention, whereas the nude man on page 4 is prefigured in the large composition. He is characterized by oversize buttocks, which are attached to his back like a hump. Note his equally oversize foot! New, likewise, is the attitude of the woman in his grip. The sharp twist between her upper and lower body appears—another instance of Picasso's encyclopedic memory—like an echo of Giovanni Bologna's mannerist sculpture *The Rape of the Sabines*.[17] The simultaneous depiction of a woman's front and rear had become second nature to Picasso, at least since his variations on Delacroix's *Women of Algiers*, 1954–1955.[18] The next drawing (page 5) is a new version of the amorous assault, known from figure 8. There follow two versions of an equestrian abducting a woman, the first one easy and all of a piece, the second one clumsier, with a horse that seems to be weighed down by the struggle going on on its back (pages 6 and 7). A similar group appears in the large composition above the shield of "Romulus." This latter is drawn on the next page (8), once more with disproportionately large legs, yet transformed into an ideal young hero, in accordance with David.

The style in all these quick jottings is a pictorial shorthand, sometimes bordering on caricature. Hence, the following drawing (page 9), a realistic head of an elderly woman in charcoal, can only come as a surprise. This woman, a worn-out proletarian, is portrayed in an extreme state of terror and grief, clutching her head with hands deformed by hard labor. Its high emotional pitch links this drawing to the *Weeping Women* of 1937,[19] but its peculiar brand of realism —one is tempted to call it "social" realism—is out of character for Picasso, except perhaps for a very few works preceding his blue period.[20] It seems hard to determine where this head fits into the evolving, major composition. Yet the artist pursues the motif through four more pencil drawings in a different, linear idiom, with the head facing left and thrown back. In the first version (page 10), realism prevails in the detailed rendition of mouth and nose, seen from below. In the next one (page 11), the head is cast in the same attitude as that of the mother with her dead child in *Guernica* (figure 32). But the attempt to join the averted part of the face to a head seen essentially in profile (albeit with both eyes) only yields a muddled result. In the following drawing (page 12), the head is all but identical to the one in *Guernica*, or its preparatory study (figure 33). But Picasso, unable to repeat himself verbatim, changes the

Figure 29. Picasso Sketchbook No. 164,
p. 24 pencil on paper, October 25, 1962

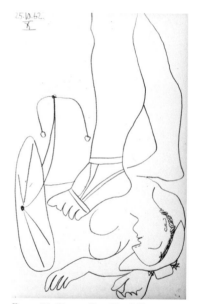

Figure 30. Picasso Sketchbook No. 164,
p. 25 pencil on paper, October 25, 1962

Figure 31. Picasso Rape of the Sabines
crayon on paper, October 26, 1962

concept through the introduction of a divided, or doubled, nose—a formula he further refines on page 13. He concludes this experimental sequence with a drawing of two interpenetrating profiles, further complicated by the inclusion of a hand, reaching across both heads (page 14).

Picasso did not finish work on this fruitful day without returning to the large composition. In a quick charcoal sketch (page 15), he isolates the encounter between "Romulus" and the horseman abducting a woman—without, however, finding an entirely plausible solution regarding the scale and position of the figures.

*Figure 32. Picasso Guernica oil on canvas, 1937. Museo del Prado, Madrid*

It had now become clear to him that the combat between these two would be the main subject of the evolving work. In the only drawing of October 27 (page 16),[21] they fill the entire space with the exception of a small rider chasing a woman, and a reclining draped figure at the feet of "Romulus." She is none other than the cyclist, although deprived of her bicycle. On the following day, Picasso replaced her with the kneeling figure of "Hersilia" (page 17). However, the figure appears here for the first time in a role analogous to that of her prototype in David's *Sabines* (figure 2), as indicated by her oversize arms. One arm reaches the head of the horseman, while the other touches the shield of "Romulus," as she tries to intervene between the combatants, to put an end to their struggle.

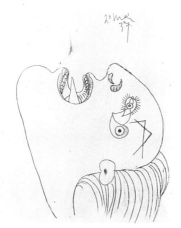

*Figure 33. Picasso Study for "Guernica" crayon and gouache on paper, 1937*

The second drawing of October 28 (page 18) introduces a digression. It is a *Head of a Warrior*, to be followed instantly by three painted versions, and a fourth one dated October 31.[22] In each of these ferocious heads the face is compounded with the antique helmet, a helmet "beginning to resemble a Phrygian cap."[23] One head (figure 34) follows the sketch almost verbatim, with a bearded chin appended like a tassel to a monstrously dilated nose, and two eyes fixed in static horror. All four of these *Warrior*s bespeak the same horror. Is it caused by the evil deeds they are forced to commit in the name of some questionable good?

*Figure 34. Picasso The Warrior oil on canvas, October 28, 1962*

Hélène Parmelin relates at great length how Picasso was

ridden with doubts concerning these *Warriors*; how he asked himself, time and again, whether they really "said something."

They do, heaven knows; most forcibly, perhaps, in a slightly later painting, called innocently by Zervos *Tête de femme* (figure 35).[24] It is, in fact, a portrait of Jacqueline; but Picasso has projected, with their facial distortions, all the horror of the *Warriors* upon her face.

The notebook was then put aside until November 1. On this day Picasso jotted down ideas for one of the most horrifying paintings, not only in this series, but of his entire career. It shows "Hersilia" run over by a ghastly rider (figure 36).

*Figure 36. Picasso* Rape of the Sabines *oil on canvas, November 2, 4, 1962. Private collection*

In the first sketch in colored crayons (page 19), the horse alone is visible. It thrusts its hooves into the woman's armpits, thus forcing her to bend over backward. This rendition suggests, if anything, an amorous assault; the composition recalls indeed Picasso's depictions of the Minotaur raping a woman. Inconsistent both in its scale and position in space, a leg with a giant foot (!) flanks the scene. This leg, complete with greave and sandal, is the subject of the following drawing (page 20)—proof that at this stage it was an integral part of the composition. It does not appear in the final version. The next sketch (page 21) depicts two hands holding daggers; they are used nowhere in the following paintings. Nor did Picasso use the horse's head, page 22. He did, however, make use of the elaborate drawing of a horse turning around from right to left (page 23). Complete with a saddlecloth, the greaved leg of its rider, and part of the body of an abducted woman, this horse gave Picasso an opportunity to try his favorite device, the simultaneous rendition of a figure from front and rear, on an animal's body.

*Figure 35. Picasso* Tête de Femme *oil on canvas, November 14, 1962*

The following day brought only one drawing, yet a magnificent one of a barbarian horseman, brandishing his sword (page 24). He is drawn in undulating lines, which in no way correspond to the real appearance, but convey uncannily the full career of the horse and its rider's savage fury. "Death on a Pale Horse" would be an appropriate title for this eerie improvisation.

So prepared, Picasso could attack, on November 2, a huge canvas of 63¾ by 58⅛ inches (figure 36). If a single picture could contain the sum of all the brutish violence in the world, it would be this one. Painted monochromatically in a brownish earth color interspersed with glaring white, it shows "Hersilia" in the last stage of her transformation from pacifier to victim. Her assuaging arms raised in the panic of impending death, her breasts absurdly (but how plausibly!) thrown back, she cries out underneath the hoof that, split seconds later, will have crushed her. The horse performs its turn like an infernal dance. The rider is "Death on a Pale Horse."

*Figure 37. Picasso* Head of a Horse *oil on canvas, November 3, 4, 1962*

This painting was begun on November 2, left untouched the following day, and finished on November 4. On November 3, Picasso tried out, on a small canvas, a formula for the head of the horse and the rider's fist with the dagger (figure 37). Both fall short of the final version. Thereafter, his thoughts turned to the cyclist. Having "liquidated" the figure of "Hersilia," it was time to put an end to her narrative, also; for from now on the artist wanted to depict collective, not individual, destinies. So he outlined a composition (page 25) with the cyclist reclining in the foreground, a warrior in the center, and a woman lamenting in an open window. The same day it was transferred onto canvas without changes (figure 38). As opposed to the preceding drawings, which showed the woman fallen from her bicycle as a subject of assault or rescue, she is here depicted in a state of rest, an attitude of sleep indistinguishable from death. Most probably she is dead, for the warrior is not aiming his sword at her. He does not even see her (this comes out even more clearly in the sketch). A veritable god of war, he looks out for new cities to destroy, new life to put to death.

This painting marks the point where, within the continuous narration of this cycle, Picasso's personal memories and ambivalences recede and the emphasis shifts to universal concerns. This is indicated also by the woman at the window, obviously a borrowing from *Guernica* (figure 32). Now it becomes clear that she was prefigured in the drawings of pages 10–13. However, the motif continued to occupy Picasso, for the last two drawings of November 3 (pages 26 and 27) develop it further. The figure becomes almost unbearably lifelike in her shrill outcry of pain; and small wonder, since the new conception combines the diagrammatic style of pages 10–13 with the realism of page 9.

Our sketchbook ends here. Yet the whole development traced so far was no more than the preparation for two major works. The painting of November 4, 5, and 8, 1962 (figure 39), repeats, on the whole, the composition of figure 31. But there are essential differences. With the addition of a bullring and modern tenement buildings, the backdrop is now made up in equal parts of antique and contemporary elements. "Romulus" and the horseman abducting a woman face each other, ready for their deadly struggle. The subjects of the *Rape of the Sabines* and the *Massacre of the Innocents* have been completely fused, for both "Hersilia" and the cyclist have been replaced by mothers lamenting their dead children. "Hersilia" has become the woman with torn clothes and raised hands in the left foreground. The cyclist is replaced by the figure to the right, screaming at "Romulus" as her prototype in *Guernica* is screaming at the bull. This is a moving picture, yet one that seems pervaded by a strange ambiguity. Victims and assailants look too much alike; they seem to be treated with equal cruelty by the painter. And, certainly, this painting retains none of the idealism of its sources, the

*Figure 38. Picasso* Rape of the Sabines *oil on canvas, November 3, 1962*

*Figure 39. Picasso* Rape of the Sabines *oil on canvas, November 4, 8, 1962. Musée National d'Art Moderne, Centre Georges Pompidou, Paris*

*Figure 40. Picasso* Rape of the Sabines *oil on canvas, January 9, February 7, 1963. The Museum of Fine Arts, Boston. Juliana Cheney Edwards Collection, Tompkins Collection, and Fanny P. Mason Fund, in memory of Alice Thevin*

works by Poussin and David. Did the art of the past incite in Picasso the same response as his dealings with women, namely, the compulsion to destroy what he loved most?

Such an interpretation fails to realize that Picasso's art is inextricably bound up with the time, his and ours. After Auschwitz and Hiroshima, in the face of the Cuban crisis, even he felt no longer called upon to work in a classical idiom. If Romulus becomes a savage executioner, Hersilia an unredeemed victim, this can only mean that contemporary humanity will soon be divided into merely these two categories. In the painting under discussion, the uniformity of victims and assailants is due to the fact that every face reflects the face of Death. Once this has been seen, one can recognize the compassion behind even the most painful (or ludicrous) distortions.

At this point, Picasso put the subject to rest until January 9, 1963. In an effort that, as he said, almost undid him, he finally created that statement against war and violence toward which all his foregoing attempts were directed. This great painting (figure 40) speaks a much clearer language than the preceding one. The destructive rage of the two combatants contrasts with the stillness of the expiring woman. The bloodshed appears all the more loathsome because it defiles the soil on which a sanctuary stands. The stumbling child, so badly equipped for survival, embodies, in spite of all, a minimal spark of hope.

# Notes

1. Helene Parmelin, *Picasso: The Painter and His Model* (New York: Abrams, n.d.), color plate on p. 115.

2. Helene Parmelin, *Voyage en Picasso* (Paris: Laffont, 1980), p. 75.

3. Sketchbook No. 164 in the catalogue raisonné. Of the original twenty-six drawings the first one is missing. Reproduced entirely in Zervos XXIII, 8–32.

4. Patrick O'Brian, *Pablo Ruiz Picasso*, translated by Henri Morisset (Paris: Gallimard, 1979), p. 574. I accepted this identification in *Picasso: The Last Years* (New York: Solomon R. Guggenheim Museum, 1984), p. 13. I am grateful to Lydia Gasman for providing me with the more plausible interpretation of the figure as propounded below.

5. William Rubin, ed., *Picasso: A Retrospective* (New York: Museum of Modern Art, 1980), color plate on p. 365.

6. See David Douglas Duncan, *Der unbekannte Picasso* (Düsseldorf and Vienna: Econ Verlag GMBH, 1961), color plates on pp. 171, 172, and illustrations on pp. 240–243 passim.

7. Françoise Gilot and Carlton Lake, *Life with Picasso* (New York: McGraw-Hill, 1964), pp. 87–88.

8. Duncan, *Der unbekannte Picasso*, color plate on p. 126.

9. Rubin, *Picasso*, pp. 99, 102, 103, 108, 112–115.

10. *Ibid.*, color plate on p. 344; Zervos IX, 22–25, 32.

11. Rubin, *Picasso*, p. 312; Zervos VIII, 296.

12. Rubin, *Picasso*, p. 334.

13. Lydia Gasman presents this evidence in her dissertation *Mystery, Magic and Love in Picasso, 1925–1938: Picasso and the Surrealist Poets*, to be published by Yale University Press.

14. See Roland Penrose, *Picasso: His Life and Work* (New York: Harper, 1959), pp. 299–303.

15. See Parmelin, *Picasso*, p. 121, and Zervos XXIII, 33.

16. Sketchbook No. 162 in the catalogue raisonné. Front cover inscribed "N.D. de V. / 26.10.62. / 3.11.62." in ink marker. The twenty-seven pages of drawings are reproduced entirely in Zervos XXIII, 34–51, 58–61, 63–65, 67, 68.

17. John Pope-Hennessy, *Italian High Renaissance and Baroque Sculpture* (London and New York: Phaidon Press, 1963), pl. 85.

18. Rubin, *Picasso*, pp. 424–425.

19. See n. 10.

20. E.g., *The Absinth Drinker*, Paris, 1901; Rubin, *Picasso*, p. 33.

21. The principal works of this day are two paintings of Jacqueline, Zervos XXIII, 52, 53.

22. Parmelin, *Picasso*, color plates on pp. 132, 133.

23. *Ibid.*, p. 145.

24. Zervos XXIII, 78; Parmelin, *Picasso*, color plate on p. 141.

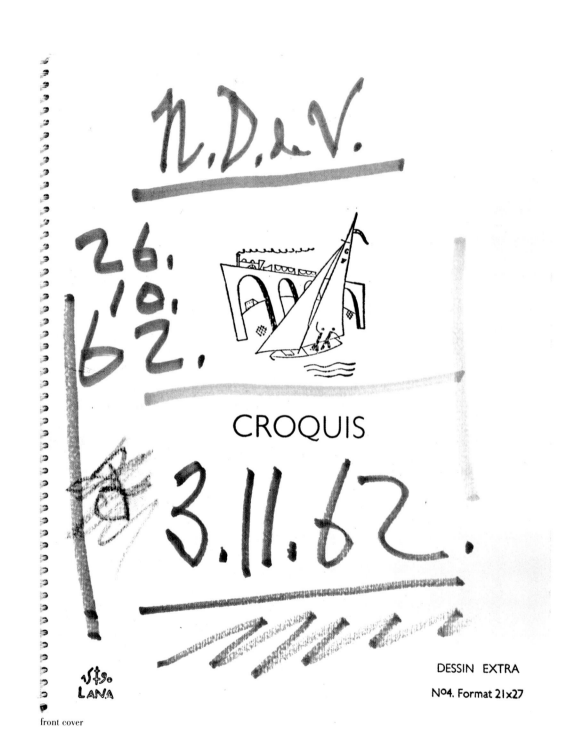

N.D.de V.

26.
10.
62.

CROQUIS

3.11.62.

LANA

DESSIN EXTRA

N°4. Format 21x27

front cover

190

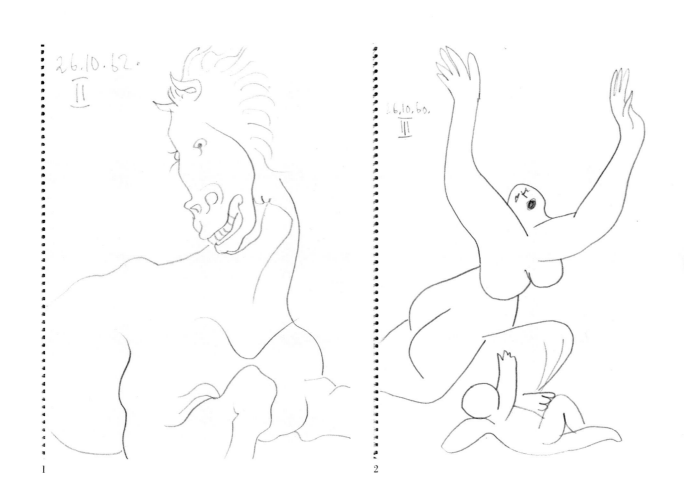

26.10.62.
II

26.10.62.
III

1                    2

3

4

26.10.62.VI

5

26.10.62. VII

6

26.10.62.
VIII

7

26.10.62.
IX

8

9

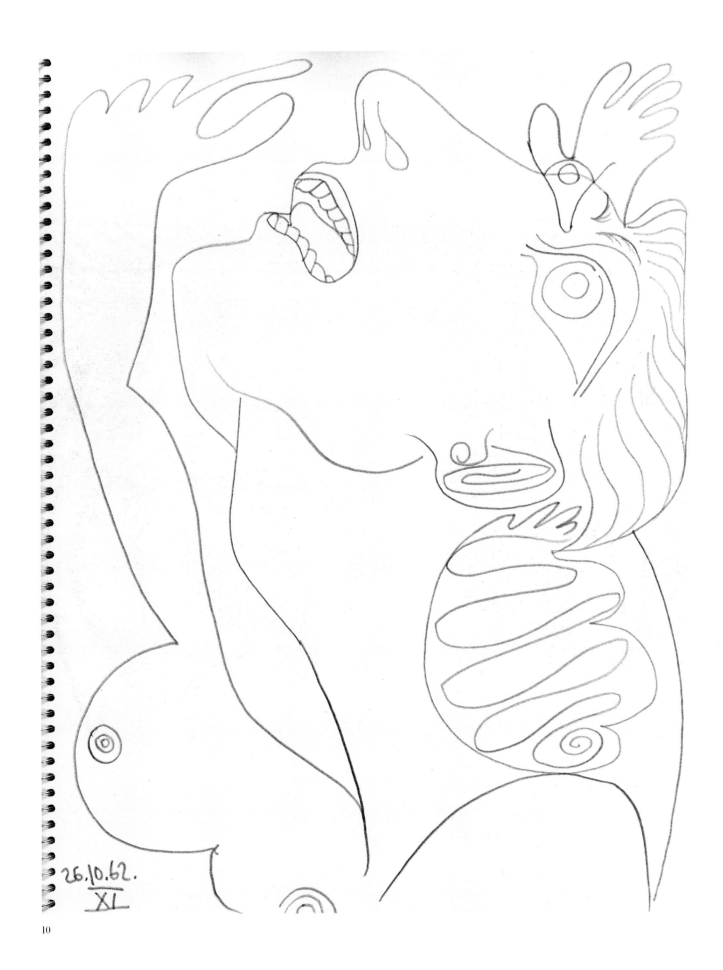

26.10.62.
XI

10

26.10.62. XII

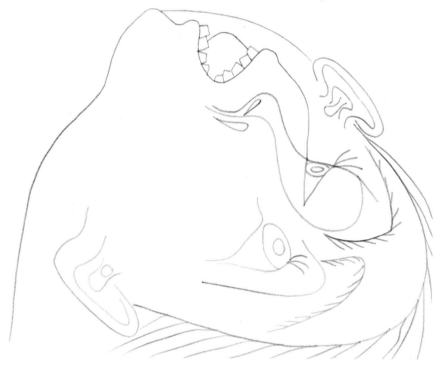

11

26.10.62. XIII

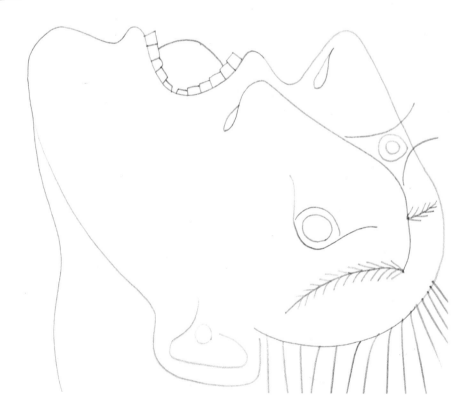

12

198

26.10.62. XIV

13

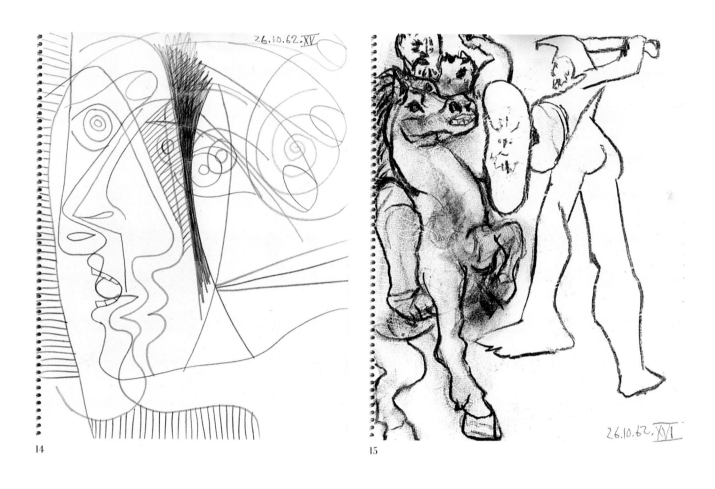

14

15

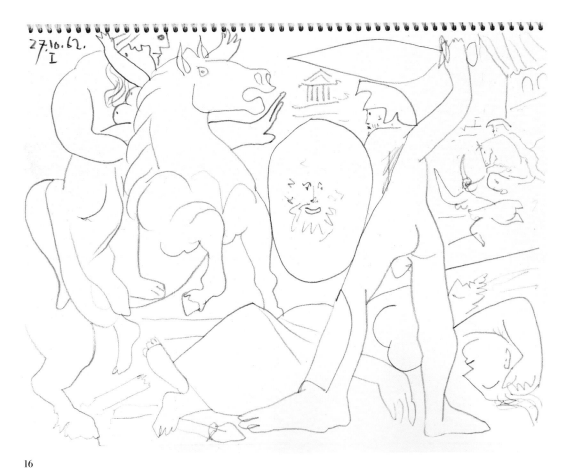

16

17

201

28.10.62.

18

1.11.62.I

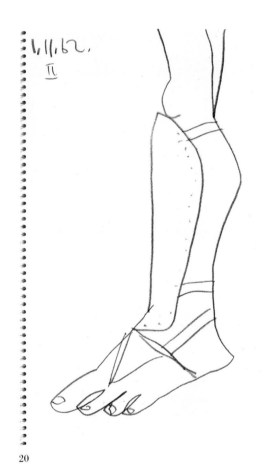

1.11.62.
II

20

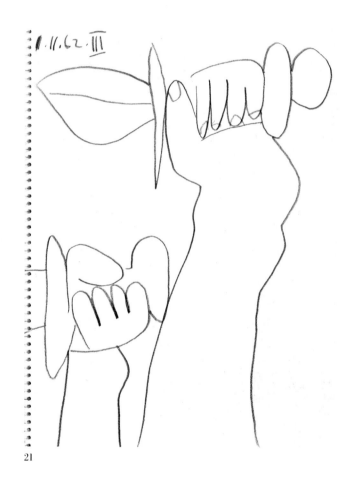

1.11.62. III

21

1.11.62.
IV

22

23

24

25

3.11.62.
II

27

# II. Selections from Other Sketchbooks

# Enigmas for Posterity

by Françoise Gilot

Often painters need to record a fleeting thought, an observation, a new organization of shapes and colors. A sketchbook is a companion, a mirror of dreams, utterly sincere since it is utterly *private* and *personal*. From doodles to scamped or elaborate notations, it bears witness to the early processes of creation. Painters are usually reluctant to show these spontaneous notations, even though they may enjoy discussing a work with pen in hand around a bistro table and demonstrating the matter in question on the very paper that is laid down to protect the linen tablecloth. There is a difference here, since in a sketchbook the artist attempts to capture a new conception as it surges from the limbo of the unconscious, whereas at the bistro he or she publicly displays skill, wit, and well-rehearsed feats of virtuosity.

Pablo Picasso was no exception: if he liked to show friends his recent achievements or to improvise freely in a café-brasserie, nevertheless he remained secretive about his sketchbooks; so I was quite impressed when, by the end of 1945, he started to show me some of the most intimate aspects of his work. At that time, I saw india ink drawings of the blue period within a read and reread copy of Gauguin's *Noa-Noa*, and the pencil studies leading to the composition of *Les Demoiselles d'Avignon*, which were kept in a safe at the bank.

When I came to visit Picasso in the afternoons at 7, rue des Grands Augustins, it was a treat to retrace with him the genesis of famous works. Since he had become so open with me, I had to reciprocate by bringing small oils that I could carry under my arm so that I could play my part in this artistic dialogue. Once his insatiable curiosity was stirred, he started to come to my studio and surprise me at work, wrapped in an old robe full of paint, looking like a witch with my hair all tousled around my face, but against all entreaties I remained evasive about my notations.

Early in 1946 he decided to strike a drastic blow. On the twenty-second of March he greeted me with the most benign smile and said: "I just bought a children's drawing pad with a Gallic rooster on the cover to make some studies of you, but it must become a dialogue. It will be great fun if you collaborate in the elements of your typification."

I did not enjoy the idea, but thought that once he started, he would get so engrossed in his own work that he would forget about the dialogue. Yet I agreed to sketch on my own while he observed me. In the first drawing he made that afternoon, I am seen with a pad in my hands, my eyes bulging out slightly. I remember that I was evoking in my own drawings the likeness of my friend Geneviève (sketchbook No. 116, p. 1). Picasso captured the way I looked beyond rather than at what I was doing while concentrating on an inner vision. He then asked me to braid my hair, "Russian spy fashion," for the second portrait (sketchbook No. 116, p. 2). In this one the position of my upper arms and shoulders suggests that I was still drawing; the eyelids are lowered and the mouth tightly closed in complete self-absorption. When I came the next day, he insisted that I should rise to the challenge of a dialogue apropos of my own image. I laughed: "You start and I'll answer you pencil in hand."

To increase my willingness he made two rather flattering sketches with emphasis on my right eye, lifted brow, and flowing mane of hair (sketchbook No. 116, pp. 3–4). Jokingly I proceeded to depict myself without complacency, one face expanding laterally to give more light to the whole area (No. 116, p. 5), the other puffy and distraught, accentuating the melancholy expressed in Picasso's fourth drawing (No. 116, p. 6). My drawings were not signed but one of them bore, in my own handwriting, "P. Picasso 28 Mars 46," the *P* standing for an abbreviation of *pour* (for) and of course also being understood as the initial of *Pablo*. We giggled: "Let's create enigmas for posterity."

I am sure that a graphologist would have no difficulty distinguishing the altogether different dynamism of Picasso's lines and mine. It is clear that two very different *hands* had been at work quite apart from the disparity of intentions—Picasso bent toward refinement while I was then bent toward raw primitivism.

After this we worked on related themes in a red leather-bound album where Pablo intertwined our last names, given names, and eyes. Later in the spring he made a series of studies of me in a large sketchbook, first with colored crayon and then using collages (No. 115).

Since Picasso wanted me to contribute to the definition of the elements necessary to my depiction, I told him that I thought he had been involved mostly in structure and that my features, though regular, did not reveal a lot about my character. He was interested in form, while I felt that everything about me was a matter of light and shadow, a baroque concatenation of curves; that's when I proceeded to make the collage with sepia pencil superimposed on ragged pieces of tan and buff paper (sketchbook No. 115, p. 2). Pablo was enchanted with my utterly arbitrary approach, my speed, my disregard for elegance. He kissed me.

"I have not had such a good time in a long while. My artist friends shy away from me, but you have guts, you little nihilist!"
"Well, to tell you the truth, it felt sacrilegious to volunteer anything within this gorgeous notebook."
"No, let's go on; for once I am enjoying myself."

I don't remember if Pablo's collage with the turquoise face and sophisticated pencil arabesques in the hair was done before or after (sketchbook No. 115, p. 5). It was a miracle of balance where he kept emphasis on verticality and serenity. Having picked up the bits of paper that had fallen to the ground, I placed them on the next page and added just a few lines in sepia (No. 115, p. 1).

This was an ecstatic moment of perfect comprehension, an experience of nonverbal communication after which we knew that we were bound to explore art and roam the world together, eager to discover more and more in an unusual *mano a mano*.

No. 11, p. 13

No. 11, p. 24

No. 21, p. 11

No. 21, p. 18

No. 26, p. 9

No. 30, p. 2

No. 30, p. 7

No. 33, p. 18

No. 33, p. 35

No. 36, p. 2

No. 36, p. 8

No. 36, p. 58

No. 36, p. 60

No. 38, p. 33

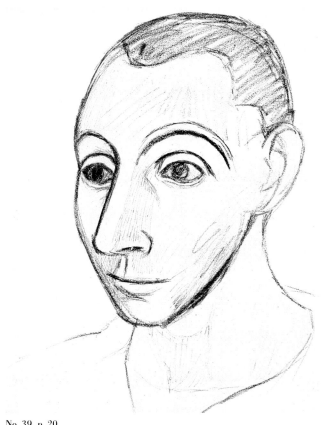

No. 39, p. 20

No. 39, p. 22

No. 41, p. 5

No. 43, p. 10

No. 43, p. 34

No. 43, p. 50

227

No. 44, p. 2

No. 44, p. 10

No. 44, p. 11

No. 44, p. 24

229

No. 45, p. 2

No. 45, p. 14

No. 45, p. 25

No. 45, p. 28

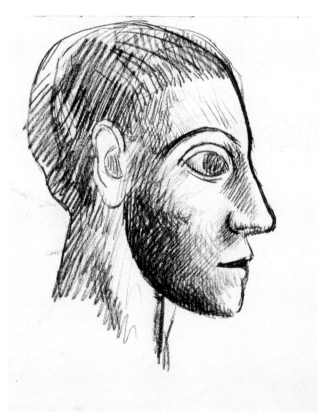

No. 45, p. 49

No. 45, p. 55

No. 45, p. 57

No. 51, p. 4                    No. 51, p. 25

No. 57, p. 5

No. 57, p. 8

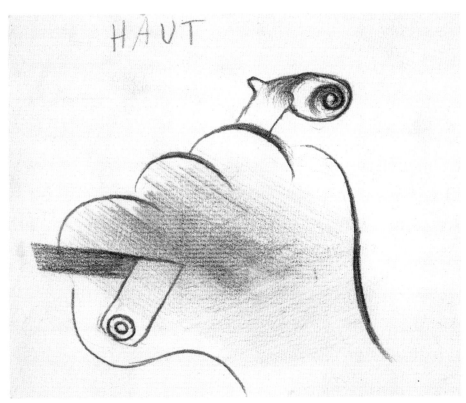

No. 57, p. 9

No. 57, p. 10

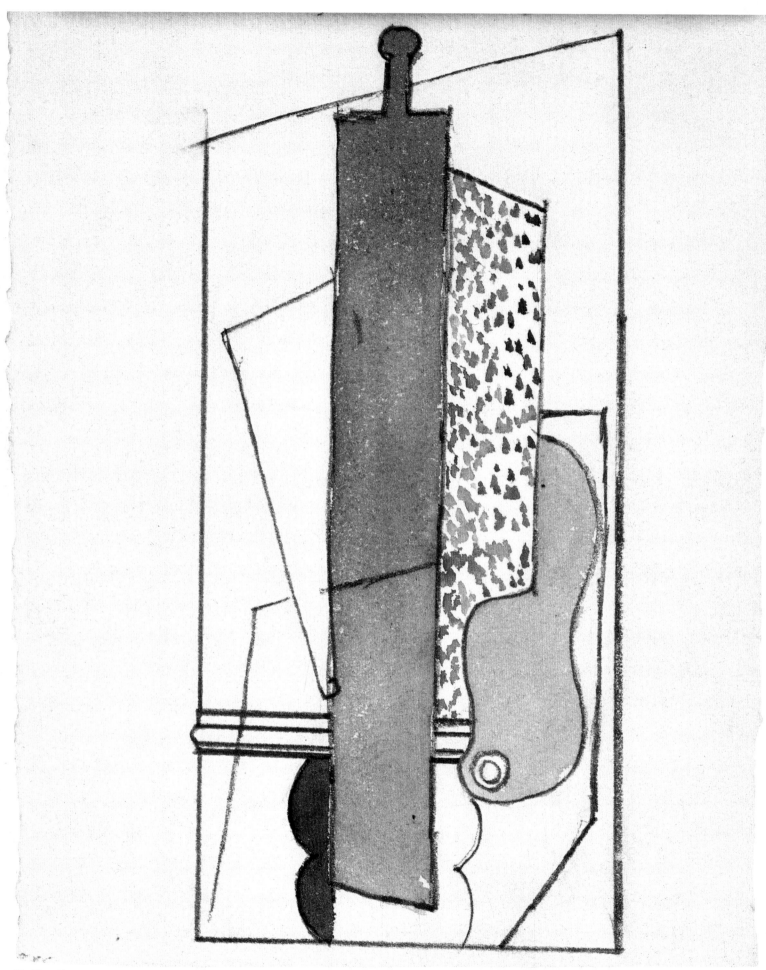

No. 64, p. 31

No. 66, p. 2

No. 66, p. 3

No. 66, p. 16

No. 66, p. 17

No. 66, p. 18

No. 66, p. 20

No. 66, p. 21

No. 66, p. 24

No. 66, p. 27

No. 72, p. 1

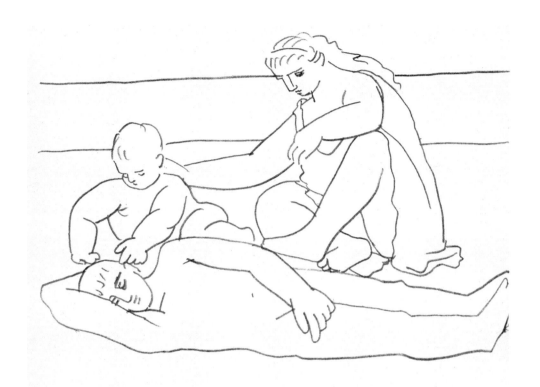

No. 75, p. 30

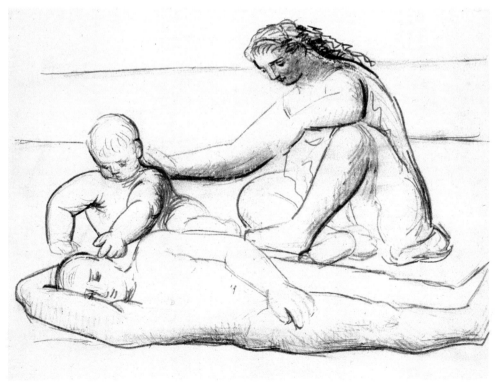

No. 75, p. 31

249

No. 76, p. 2

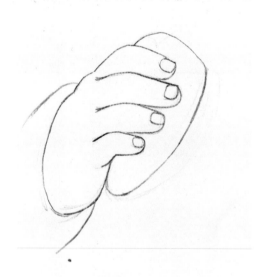

No. 76, p. 40

No. 76, p. 39

No. 77, p. 5

No. 77, p. 8

No. 77. p. 20

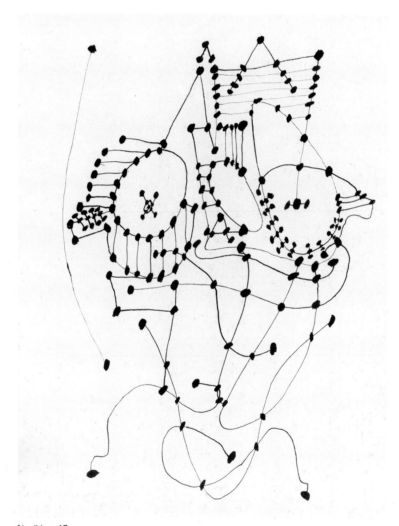

No. 84, p. 17

No. 99, p. 1

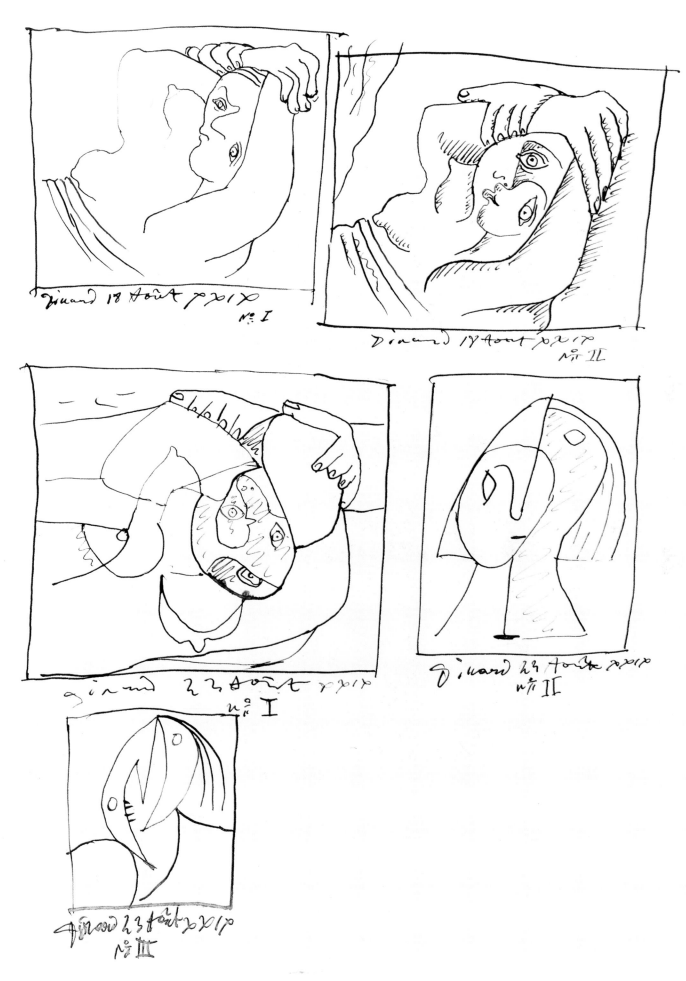

Dinard 18 Août XXIX
Nº I

Dinard 18 Août XXIX
Nº II

Dinard 23 Août XXIX
Nº I

Dinard 23 Août XXIX
Nº II

Dinard 23 Août XXIX
Nº III

No. 99, p. 4

16 septembre

No. 99, p. 5

31 May MCMXXXI.

No. 105, p. 1

No. 105, p. 11

No. 105, p. 22

No. 105, p. 25

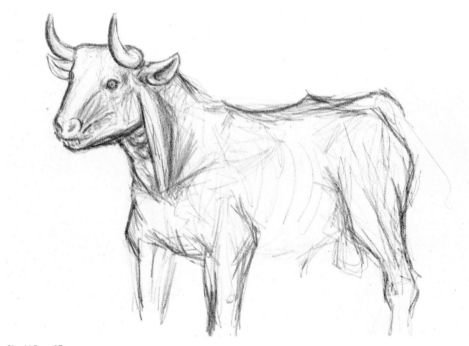

No. 105, p. 27

No. 114, p. 10

21.3.45.

No. 114, p. 21

267

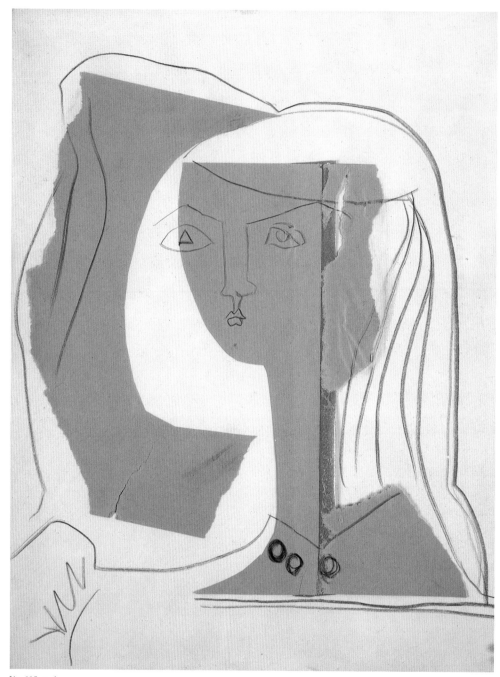

No. 115, p. 1

No. 115, p. 2

No. 115, p. 5

No. 115, p. 6

No. 126, p. 10

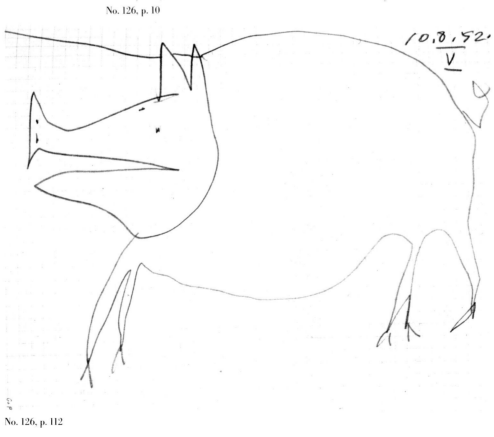

No. 126, p. 112

No. 126, p. 56

No. 126, p. 127

273

No. 131, p. 1

No. 131, p. 2

No. 131, p. 3

No. 131, p. 4

No. 131, p. 5

No. 139, p. 1

No. 139, p. 4

No. 139, p. 7

No. 159, p. 1

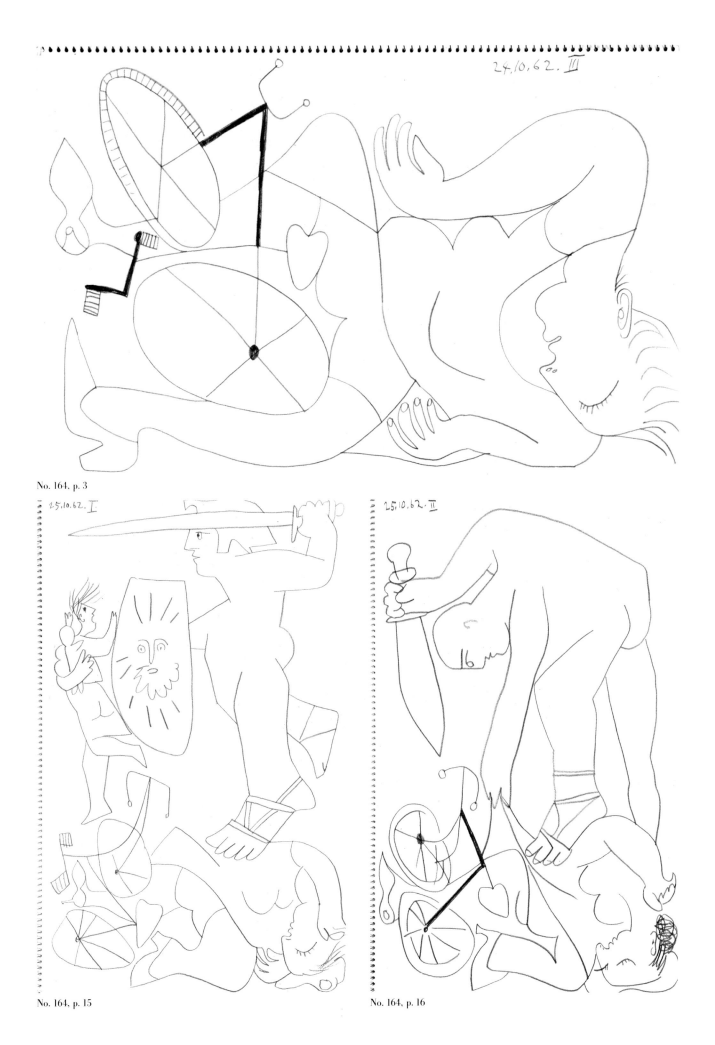

24.10.62. III

No. 164, p. 3

25.10.62. I

No. 164, p. 15

25.10.62. II

No. 164, p. 16

12.7.62.

No. 165, p. 9

No. 165, p. 10

No. 165, p. 23

No. 165, p. 26

2.8.62. I

No. 165, p. 36

No. 165, p. 37

No. 165, p. 43

No. 165, p. 44

No. 171, p. 4

10.2.63. III

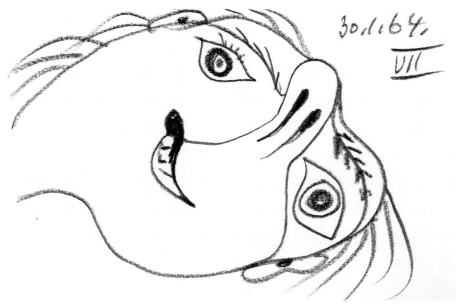

No. 172, p. 5

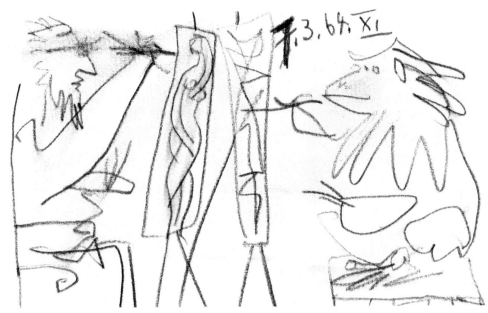

No. 172, p. 25

No. 172, p. 29

17.1.64. IX

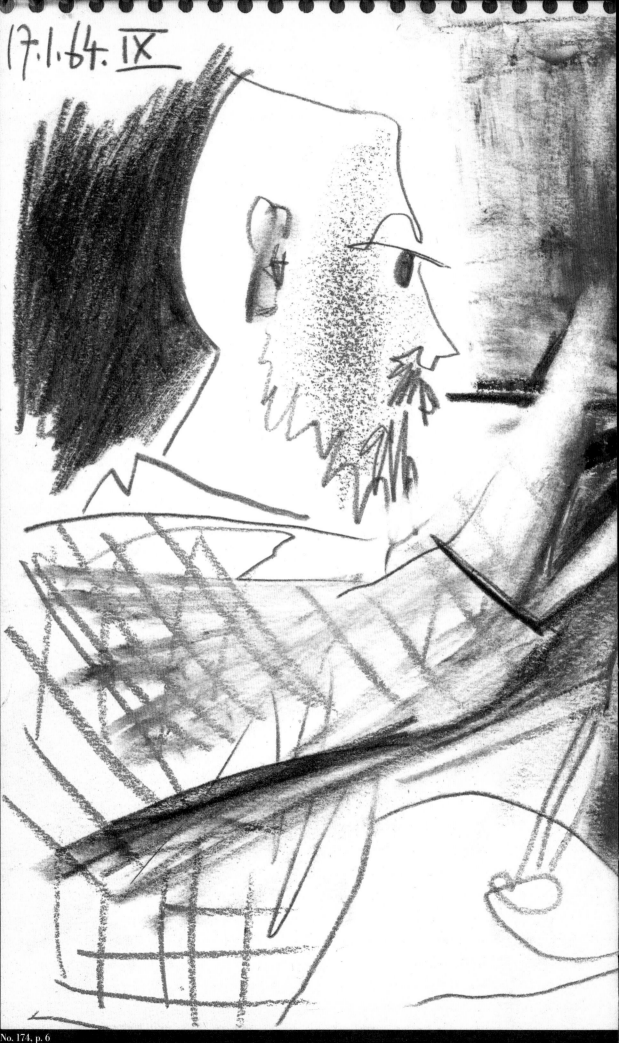

25.1.64.
26.

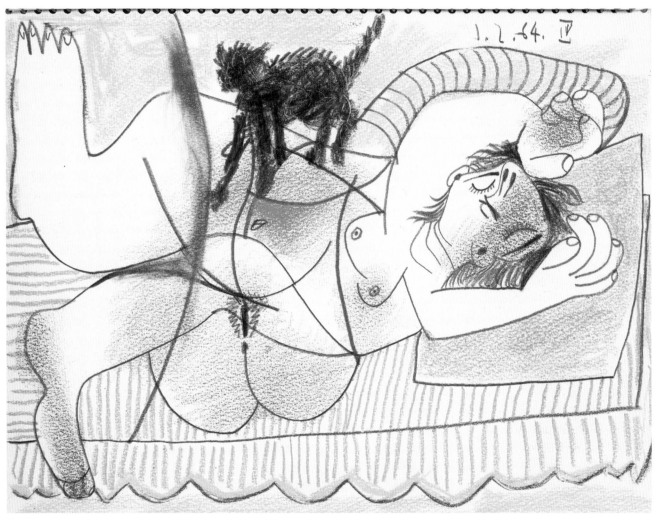

No. 174, p. 13

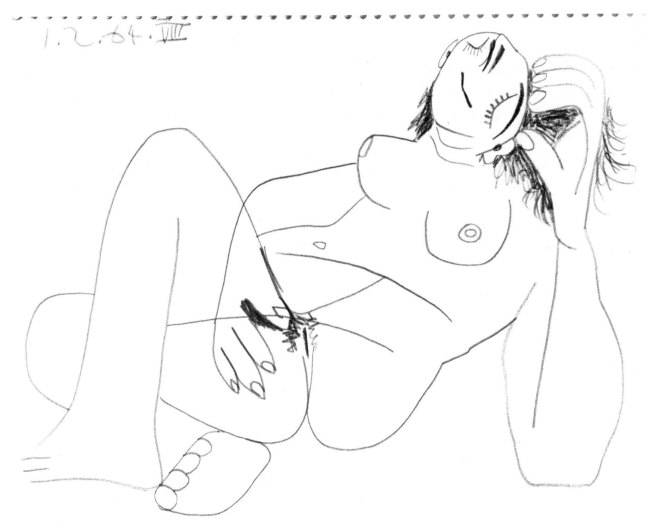

1.2.84.VIII

No. 174, p. 17

# III. Catalogue Raisonné

**No. 1**
Brown cloth-covered notebook
with "Album" printed on front
in gold ink
1894
12.5 x 19 cm

Back Cover: inscribed "Lola Ruiz
Picasso Blasco"
Inside Front Cover: pencil and
ink drawing of a woman, a boy's
head, a standing male figure, and
three spiderwebs
Inside Back Cover: inscribed
"*FIN* / Coruña 20 de septiembre /
del 94 / *P. Ruiz*"
53 Pages: pencil and/or ink drawings, subjects include: male and
female figures, portraits of the
artist's mother and father, landscapes, horses, dogs, and bulls

**No. 2**
Red cloth-covered notebook
with "ALBUM" printed on front
in gold ink
1894–1895
12.5 x 19 cm

Inside Front Cover: pencil
drawing of male nudes and
a foot, inscribed "ALBUM /
*P. Ruiz*"
Inside Back Cover: pencil
drawing of a seated man
8 Pages: ink and/or pencil
drawings of hands
30 Pages: ink, pencil, and/or
watercolor drawings of figures,
including portraits of the
artist's mother and father
1 Page: pencil and watercolor
drawing of a standing male figure
in eighteenth-century costume
6 Pages: ink and/or pencil
drawings of horses and dogs
1 Page: ink and pencil drawing
of a picture frame
1 Page: pencil drawing of a
baroque altar draped with flags
1 Page: pencil drawing of a vase
of flowers
Note: produced as a limited-
edition facsimile, *Carnet de
Picasso: La Coruña, 1894–1895*
(Barcelona: Editorial Gustavo
Gili, 1971)

**No. 3**
Canvas-covered notebook with
pencil loop on side
1895
8 x 12 cm

Inside Front Cover: black crayon
drawing of figures
Inside Back Cover: black crayon
drawing of a male nude and an
animal's head
65 Pages: pencil and/or black
crayon drawings, subjects include:
figures, horses, a boat, portraits
of the artist's mother and father,
a drawing after the sculpture
Venus de Milo, and manuscript
writing

**No. 4**
Canvas-covered notebook with
pencil loop on side
1895
8.2 x 12 cm

Inside Front Cover: black crayon
drawing of swans
Inside Back Cover: black crayon
drawing of the profile of a female
head
83 Pages: pencil, ink, and/or
black crayon drawings, subjects
include: male and female figures,
portraits of the artist's mother,
father, and sister, animals, landscapes, a boat, architectural
studies, and abstract patterns

**No. 5**
Blue canvas-covered notebook
with "Sketches" printed on front
in gold ink
1896
12.5 x 18.5 cm

Inside Front Cover: ink drawing
of seated figures, printed label
"Reeves & Sons, Ld. / London"
Inside Back Cover: black crayon
drawing of an interior with figures
53 Pages: pencil, oil, ink, and/or
black crayon drawings, subjects
include: male and female figures,
animals, portraits of the artist's
father and sister, a bullfight, a
religious scene, and caricatures

**No. 6**
Blue canvas-covered notebook
with "Sketches" printed on front
in gold ink
1896
12.5 x 18 cm

Inside Front Cover: ink drawing
of female heads and nudes,
inscribed "P. Ruiz / 24 Marzo –
96 / Barcelona"
Inside Back Cover: ink and pencil
drawing of figures
1 Page: ink drawing of a female
figure, related to the painting
*First Communion*. Barcelona,
1895–1896. Zervos XXI, 49
56 Pages: ink and/or pencil
drawings, subjects include: male
and female figures, portraits of
the artist's mother and father,
animals, and religious scenes

**No. 7**
Cover missing
1896
7.5 x 10.5 cm

116 Pages: pencil, ink, and/or
black crayon drawings, subjects
include: studies of hands, interior
of an artist's studio, male and
female figures, portraits of the
artist's sister, studies of drapery,
cats, religious scenes, and manuscript writing

**No. 8**
Cover missing
1896–1897
7.5 x 10.5 cm

84 Pages: ink and/or black crayon
drawings, subjects include: male
and female figures, portraits of
the artist's mother and father,
horses, architectural studies, and
manuscript writing

**No. 9**
Cover missing
1897
8 x 12 cm

28 Pages: charcoal drawings,
subjects include: male and female
figures, horses, and a study of an
Egyptian sculpture

**No. 10**
Cover missing
1897–1898
12 x 20 cm

32 Pages: black crayon drawings,
subjects include: male and female
figures, cats, horses, interiors,
and studies of trees, one inscribed
"(Del Retiro)"

**No. 11**
Paper-covered notebook, cover
abraded and worn through
1897–1898
13 x 22 cm

Front Cover: pencil and brown
crayon drawing of abstract
patterns, inscribed "PRP"
Inside Front Cover: pencil
drawing of abstract patterns
1 Page: brown crayon drawing
of a landscape, inscribed
"(Del Retiro)"
12 Pages: brown crayon or charcoal drawings of girls
1 Page: charcoal drawing
of a rooster, inscribed with
mathematical notations
1 Page: pencil drawing of male
and female heads
1 Page: charcoal drawing of two
standing female figures
in long dresses and hats, one
carrying an umbrella,
related to the drawing *The Street
Violinist*. Madrid, 1897–1898.
Not in Zervos
17 Pages: ink or charcoal
drawings of figures in a park
1 Page: charcoal drawing of
a street scene with carriages
2 Pages: brown ink drawings
of a seated guitarist
1 Page: ink drawing of a courtyard
through a window
1 Page: charcoal self-portrait with
brown crayon drawing
of two reclining cats
1 Page: charcoal head of a man
with an art nouveau border
1 Page: pencil drawing of a
reclining huddled woman, related
to the painting *Femme
Accroupie et Enfant*. Paris, 1901.
Zervos I, 115

**No. 12**
Canvas-covered notebook
1898
10.5 x 17.5 cm

Inside Front Cover: inscribed
"R. Picasso / Ruiz / –Picasso– /
Pablilo / Pablo Ruiz Picasso"
Inside Back Cover: manuscript
writing and mathematical
notations, inscribed "Madrid
12 Marzo / de 1898"
44 Pages: ink, watercolor, and/or
crayon drawings, subjects
include: male and female figures,
landscapes, animals, architectural
studies, bullfights, and manuscript
writing
3 Pages: crayon drawings after
drawings by Goya
Note: produced as a limited-
edition facsimile with an introduction by Xavier de Salas,
*Carnet Picasso: Madrid, 1898*
(Barcelona: Editorial Gustavo
Gili, 1976)

**No. 13**
Canvas-covered notebook
1898
12 x 19.5 cm

31 Pages: pencil, charcoal, and/or
black crayon drawings, subjects
include: male and female figures,
landscapes, bullfights, architectural studies, interiors,
caricatures, and manuscript
writing, one inscribed
"23 de Marzo 1898 / Madrid"

**No. 14**
Canvas-covered notebook
1898
9 x 13.5 cm

Inside Front Cover: inscribed
"M/Madrid/M/Madrid/Mayo"
Inside Back Cover: mathematical
notations
20 Pages: ink, watercolor, and/or
crayon drawings, subjects
include: male and female figures,
interiors, rooftops, cats,
and manuscript writing

**No. 15**
Gray canvas-covered notebook
with "The / Public Schools /
Drawing Book / Reeves and Sons,
Ltd. / London" printed on
front and "Reeves & Sons, Ltd. /
1777 / Artists Colours /
London" printed on back
1898
13 x 18.5 cm.

16 Pages: charcoal drawings, subjects include: male and female
figures, horses, and a still life

**No. 16**
Cover missing
1898–1899
16 x 24 cm

31 Pages: charcoal drawings, subjects include: male and female
figures, landscapes, an interior
of an artist's studio, and a portrait
of the artist's father

**No. 17**
Cover missing
circa 1899
12 x 19.5 cm

39 Pages: charcoal and/or ink
drawings of male and
female figures

**No. 18**
Linen-covered notebook
circa 1899
10 x 16 cm

Front Cover: inscribed "2238/PP"
Inside Front Cover: inscribed
"PRP/Málaga"
5 Pages: manuscript writing
9 Pages: charcoal drawings of
male heads, one inscribed
"Calle Grava−2−Casa d'amor [?]"
14 Pages: charcoal or crayon
drawings of male and female
figures

**No. 19**
Canvas-covered notebook
1900
6 x 10.5 cm

Front Cover: mathematical
notations
Inside Front Cover: mathematical
notations
47 Pages: watercolor, ink, and/or
crayon drawings of male and
female figures

**No. 20**
Linen-covered notebook with
"ALBUM" printed on front
circa 1900
16 x 24 cm

Back Cover: inscribed '2239/PP'
16 Pages: crayon and/or pencil
drawings of male and
female figures
1 Page: blue crayon drawing of
a female head, related to the
painting *French Cancan*.
Paris, 1901. Zervos XXI, 209
1 Page: blue crayon drawing
of a female head and embracing
lovers
1 Page: charcoal drawing of an
old woman and a hand
holding a stick of charcoal
1 Page: blue crayon drawing
of a café scene with a standing
female figure in the foreground
and a group of figures seated in
the rear, a sign on the wall
inscribed "Anis"

**No. 21**
Linen-covered notebook with
"ALBUM" printed on front, pencil
loop on side, and ribbon closure
circa 1900
12 x 18 cm

Back Cover: ink drawing
of a bearded old man smoking
a pipe
Inside Front Cover: black crayon
drawing of a woman in bed
1 Page: black crayon drawing
of a seated man
1 Page: blue crayon drawing
of a seated woman with a hat
3 Pages: black crayon line
drawings of two pairs of standing
lovers, related to the
painting *The Embrace*. Barcelona,
1903. Zervos I, 161
9 Pages: black crayon drawings
of male and female figures
1 Page: black crayon drawing
of a female profile, related to the
painting *The Absinth Drinker*.
Paris, 1901. Zervos I, 62

**No. 22**
Linen-covered notebook with
"ALBUM" printed on front, pencil
loop on side, and ribbon closure
1900–1901
12 x 19 cm

8 Pages: black crayon drawings of
a female figure kneeling before
a large figure
3 Pages: black crayon portraits of
an old woman
3 Pages: black crayon drawings of
kneeling or seated female nudes
6 Pages: black crayon drawings
of a woman with a large hat
2 Pages: black crayon drawings of
male and female heads

**No. 23**
Linen-covered notebook
circa 1900–1901
11.5 x 18 cm

Back Cover: ink drawing
of a head
1 Page: black crayon drawing of
a male head, inscribed "Paris"
27 Pages: black crayon drawings
of standing or seated women
with large hats, one inscribed
with color notations
1 Page: pencil drawing of a female
head
8 Pages: black crayon drawings of
standing male figures

**No. 24**
Linen-covered notebook with
pencil loop on side
circa 1900–1901
13 x 22 cm

1 Page: black crayon and red
pastel drawing of a seated
woman wearing a large flowered
hat
1 Page: black crayon drawing
of a toreador
1 Page: charcoal drawing of
a female profile, related to the
painting *Le Moulin de la Galette*.
Paris, 1900. Zervos I, 41
1 Page: charcoal drawing of
a seated woman, related to the
painting *Woman in Blue*. Madrid,
1901. Zervos XXI, 211
1 Page: charcoal drawing
of a woman in bed
1 Page: charcoal drawing of
figures in a park
10 Pages: brown ink drawings of
dancing women in long skirts
9 Pages: charcoal, black crayon,
or brown ink drawings of male
and female heads, two pages
colored with red pastel, one
inscribed "Madrid" and another
"Plaza de St Domingo"
Note: this notebook has been
recently dismantled; individual
pages exhibited and sold during
the exhibition "Les Noces
Catalanes: Barcelone–Paris,
1870–1970" at Artcurial: Centre
d'Art Plastique Contemporain,
Paris, May–July 1985

**No. 25**
Linen-covered notebook with
perforated pages, pencil loop on
side, and ribbon closure, bound
with two metal rivets
1901
15.5 x 23.5 cm

Front Cover: blue pencil drawing
of a male profile with a pipe
Back Cover: inscribed "2217/PP"
4 Pages: black and red crayon
drawings of an old woman
1 Page: blue pencil drawing
of a landscape
1 Page: black crayon drawing
of a female head, a boy's head,
and a back view of a standing
female figure
1 Page: blue crayon drawing of
an old man with a pipe, inscribed
"Donner / 1901 / Lobo de mar"
(does not appear to be by
Picasso)
1 Page: black crayon drawing
of a seated female figure
1 Page: three black crayon portraits of a man with a mustache,
inscribed "Georgius [?] du poete /
Alberto Lozano / Madrid 1901"

**No. 26**
Gray canvas-covered notebook
with "The / Public Schools /
Drawing Book / Reeves and Sons,
Ltd. / London" printed on front
and "Reeves & Sons, Ltd. /
1777 / Artists Colours / London"
printed on back
circa 1901
13 x 18.5 cm

Front Cover: blue and black
crayon drawing of a small
geometric design and a male
forehead
Back Cover: black crayon drawing
of profiles of four male heads
11 Pages: black crayon and/or
pencil drawings of male and
female figures, one inscribed
"Madrid"
1 Page: black crayon drawing
of a street scene with trees
2 Pages: black crayon drawings
of a woman wearing a flowered
dress with a ribbon in her hair,
one inscribed "PRP / Salon
Japones"
1 Page: blue crayon drawing of an
interior
1 Page: black crayon drawing of
a large building with a horse and
carriage in front, inscribed
"Teatro/PRP"
1 Page: manuscript writing

**No. 27**
Linen-covered notebook
1900–1901
11 x 17.5 cm

Front Cover: pencil drawing
of a female profile
1 Page: inscribed "Madame
Leonida Blond [?] / Rue
Dunkerque 93 / Dunkerque"
5 Pages: black crayon drawings
of dancing or singing female
figures
31 Pages: black crayon drawings
of male and female figures in
a park
1 Page: black crayon drawing
of a woman at a table resting her
head on her hand
1 Page: black crayon drawing
of a dancing soldier and woman

**No. 28**
Linen-covered notebook with
pencil loop on side and ribbon
closure
1901
12 x 20 cm

Back Cover: black crayon self-
portrait
Inside Back Cover: two separate
sheets of letters from Guillaume
Apollinaire
56 Pages: black crayon or ink
drawings of male and female
figures, many caricature-like,
one inscribed "Poutain"

**No. 29**
Linen-covered notebook
1901–1902
13 x 21 cm

Front Cover: ink drawing of
a reclining female nude in
a landscape
Back Cover: ink drawing of
a female profile
7 Pages: black crayon or pencil
drawings of landscapes and
stick figures, several inscribed
"Sarah," "Marie-Thérèse,"
or "Lucie" (these do not appear
to be by Picasso)
45 Pages: ink or pencil drawings
of male and female figures

**No. 30**
Paper-covered notebook
1903
12 x 23 cm

Front Cover: pencil and blue
crayon drawing of abstract
patterns
1 Page: inscribed "Oct. 1903 /
Barcelona / 2234 / PP"
1 Page: brown ink drawing of
a standing male figure with
a detail of long, thin fingers
at lower right
1 Page: brown ink drawing
of a female head
4 Pages: brown ink drawings
of dancing or bending female
nudes, one with a male head
at bottom
1 Page: brown ink drawing of a
male profile with an open mouth
1 Page: brown ink drawing of
a still life
1 Page: brown ink drawing
of a female profile
1 Page: pencil drawing of two
reclining female nudes
2 Pages: pencil drawings of two
seated female figures, related
to the painting *Two Women at
a Bar*. Barcelona, 1902.
Zervos I, 132
1 Page: pencil drawing of a still
life
1 Page: pencil drawing of a cup
and saucer
1 Page: pencil drawing of a hand
3 Pages: pencil drawings of a
standing harlequin, one with
a female figure at left
1 Page: pencil drawing of a
cloaked female figure with a
child, inscribed with color
notations
1 Page: pencil drawing of a
standing female figure with
an outstretched arm
1 Page: pencil drawing of an
interior with three figures at
a hearth and a goblet at lower
right

1 Page: brown ink drawing of a
pointing hand
1 Page: pencil drawing of a female
profile
1 Page: pencil portrait of a
woman, related to the painting
*Corina Pere Romeu*. Barcelona,
1902. Zervos I, 130
1 Page: brown ink drawing of a
woman and child
1 Page: pencil drawing of a
standing female nude

**No. 31**
Blue paper-covered notebook
with lined paper
circa 1904
9.5 x 14.5 cm

Front Cover: inscribed
"JACOB/JACOB/Jacob"
Back Cover: inscribed
"max/max/max/MAX"
Inside Front Cover: brown ink
drawing of a female nude
Inside Back Cover: brown ink
self-portrait; four separate
sheets of brown ink drawings
of standing female figures and
two calling cards
1 Page: printed and manuscript
inscription "CARNET / de
*Odéon* / Appartenant / à M^r *Max
Jacob / 33 Bd. Barbes / PARIS*"
48 Pages: manuscript writing in
pencil and ink (does not all
appear to be by Picasso)
14 Pages: pencil or ink drawings
of female figures, one related
to the drawing *Mother and Child*.
Paris, 1904. Zervos I, 220
1 Page: blue crayon drawing
of a standing figure, inscribed
with color notations
1 Page: brown ink drawing of
seated babies
1 Page: pencil drawing of
a reclining male figure
1 Page: brown ink drawing of a
seated harlequin holding a baby
1 Page: brown ink drawing of a
male head with a pipe
1 Page: brown ink drawing
of a cat

**No. 32**
Notebook with blue endpapers,
cover missing
1905
10 x 16 cm

Front Endpaper: ink caricature
of a standing figure
Inside Back Endpaper: ink drawing of a reclining figure
1 Page: ink drawing of a seated
female saltimbanque with a
crown holding a bowl
1 Page: ink drawing of two female
figures looking in a mirror
and a seated female saltimbanque
with a crown
1 Page: ink drawing of a female
nude
1 Page: ink drawing of a
landscape

**No. 33**
Paper-covered notebook with
"Schetsboek" printed on front
1905
12 x 16 cm

Front Cover: inscribed "Schoorl"
2 Pages: ink and/or pencil drawings of the head of a Dutch girl,
one inscribed "Alkmarr/1905"
3 Pages: ink, pencil, and watercolor drawings of Dutch city-
scapes and landscapes, each
inscribed "1905"
17 Pages: ink or pencil drawings
of standing male figures wearing
costumes
3 Pages: pencil or ink drawings
of hands
1 Page: ink line drawing of a
reclining male nude
2 Pages: ink drawings of a large
seated harlequin with a thin
harlequin standing at left, one
inscribed with color notations,
related to the painting
*Family of Saltimbanques.*
Paris, 1905. Zervos I, 285; and the
drypoint *Salomé*. Paris, 1905.
Geiser 17
8 Pages: ink drawings of male and
female figures
1 Page: ink drawing of harlequins,
related to the drypoint *Les
Saltimbanques.* 1905. Geiser 9
1 Page: ink drawing of a child and
a standing harlequin carrying
a box
3 Pages: manuscript writing, one
inscribed "Schoorl Hollande /
Schoorl/Schoorl/Schoorl/
Alkmarr"

**No. 34**
Linen-covered notebook with
ribbon closure
1905
12.5 x 18.5 cm

Inside Front Cover: inscribed
"Junio y Julio"
Inside Back Cover: inscribed
"Junio y Julio," printed label
"Geo. Rowney & Co.'s / School of
Art / canvas-covered / Sketch
Book. / 30 Leaves / made in
England"
1 Page: ink portrait of André
Salmon
1 Page: pencil and gray watercolor drawing of a harlequin and
a woman holding a jug on her
head
3 Pages: ink caricatures of lovers
4 Pages: ink drawings of a
bearded harlequin, one colored
with gouache
1 Page: ink drawing of the head
of an old harlequin, related to
the sculpture *The Jester*. Paris,
1905. Spies 4
2 Pages: ink drawings of standing
costumed figures
15 Pages: ink, pencil, and/or
watercolor drawings of Dutch
scenes, subjects include: women
carrying buckets, landscapes
with windmills, houses, Dutch
girls, and a man smoking a pipe

**No. 35**
Blue paper-covered notebook
with perforated pages
1905
9 x 14.5 cm

6 Pages: ink drawings of a thin
seated male figure
3 Pages: pencil drawings of a
profile of a girl's head
colored with gouache, watercolor,
or crayon
1 Page: charcoal and brown ink
drawing of a long-haired
standing girl holding a hoop
1 Page: ink and blue watercolor
drawing of a standing harlequin
15 Pages: ink and/or watercolor
drawings of male and female
figures
1 Page: ink drawing of a caricature of a man as a pitcher
1 Page: ink and pink watercolor
drawing of a large harlequin
seated on a cube, related to the
drypoint *Le Saltimbanque
au Repos*. Paris, 1905. Geiser 12
9 Pages: manuscript writing with
various addresses and a list of
art supplies (?), one inscribed
"3 de Mayo / 1905"

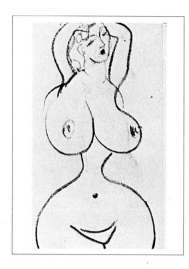

**No. 36**
Leather-covered notebook with
snap closure
1905–1906
13 x 18.5 cm

Inside Front Cover: postcard
from Guillaume Apollinaire
dated 1905, inscribed with
the poems "Spectacle" and
"Les Saltimbanques"
1 Page: pencil drawing of a seated
woman, related to the painting
*La Coiffure*. Paris, 1905.
Zervos I, 309
1 Page: pencil drawing of a table
2 Pages: pencil caricatures of
a bearded man
1 Page: pencil drawing of
a standing female nude
1 Page: pencil and watercolor
drawing of a female nude
with long hair, related to the
painting *The Harem*. Gosol,
1906. Zervos I, 321
2 Pages: pencil drawings of a goat
2 Pages: pencil and watercolor
drawings of women combing
their hair, one related to the
painting *The Harem*.
7 Pages: watercolor drawings
of women carrying buckets or
a bunch of twigs
1 Page: pencil and watercolor
drawing of a dancing couple
1 Page: ink drawing of studies
of a standing nude child
15 Pages: ink or pencil drawings
of heads of men or women
33 Pages: ink and/or pencil
drawings of studies of
saltimbanque figures

**No. 37**
Leather-covered notebook
1906
7.5 x 12 cm

Inside Front Cover: brown ink
drawing of a bird and a caricature
of a standing male figure
Inside Back Cover: manuscript
writing
42 Pages: ink and/or crayon
drawings of male and female
figures, several related to the
painting *The Harem*. 1906.
Zervos I, 321; and to the drypoint
*L'Abreuvoir*. 1905. Geiser 10
1 Page: black crayon caricature of
Guillaume Apollinaire, inscribed
"Don/Guillermo/Appoline"
12 Pages: manuscript writing
Note: produced as a limited-
edition facsimile with an introduction by Douglas Cooper,
*Picasso: Carnet Catalan* (Paris,
Berggruen & Cie., 1958)

**No. 38**
Patterned silk-covered notebook
1906–1907
11 x 15 cm

Inside Front Cover: pencil drawing of a female nude with raised
arms, inscribed "2246/PP"
54 Pages: pencil drawings of
standing or seated monumental
female nudes, many related to
the paintings *Two Nudes*. Paris,
1906. Zervos I, 366; and *Seated
Nude (Study for "Les Demoiselles
d'Avignon")*. Paris, 1906–1907.
Zervos II**, 651
11 Pages: pencil and ink drawings
of abstracted heads
3 Pages: ink drawings, related to
the painting *Les Demoiselles
d'Avignon*. Paris, 1907.
Zervos II*, 18

**No. 39**
Linen-covered notebook
1906
20 x 26 cm

Front Cover: inscribed "2240/PP"
Inside Back Cover: separate sheet
with an ink drawing of a standing
female nude pasted in
2 Pages: pencil self-portraits,
related to the painting *Self-
Portrait with a Palette*. Paris,
1906. Zervos I, 375
1 Page: pencil drawing of a female
head
1 Page: pencil drawing of a
standing female nude, related to
the painting *Two Nudes*. Paris,
1906. Zervos I, 366
54 Pages: pencil and/or ink drawings of monumental female nudes
and monumental heads and feet

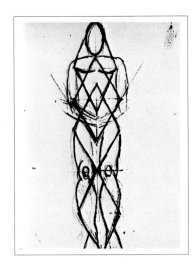

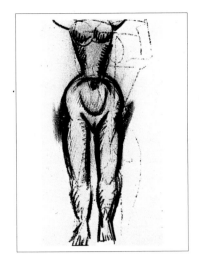

**No. 40**
Paper-covered graph-paper note-book, "Cahier" printed on front and "Table de Multiplication" printed on back, cover abraded and worn through
circa 1906–1907
17 x 22.5 cm

Front Cover: printed and manu-script inscription "*Je suis / le / CAHIER / APPARTENANT à Monsieur Picasso peintre / 13 Rue Ravignan / Paris XVIII*ᵉ"
Back Cover: inscribed "2221/PP"
Inside Back Cover: inscribed "Fernande/Raymonde/Pablo"
71 Pages: pencil and/or ink drawings of abstracted female figures, heads, and still lifes, several related to the painting *Nude with Drapery*. Paris, 1907. Zervos II*, 47
2 Pages: manuscript writing

**No. 41**
Drawn on blank pages of cata-logue for "Exposition Daumier" at Galerie L. & P. Rosenberg Fils, 38, avenue de l'Opéra, Paris, April 1907
1907
Size undetermined

4 Pages: pencil drawings of abstracted female figures
1 Page: pencil and ink drawing of an abstracted head, related to the painting *Woman with Joined Hands (study for "Les Demoiselles d'Avignon")*. Paris, 1907. Zervos II**, 662

**No. 42**
Leather-covered notebook
1907
11 x 16.5 cm

Inside Back Cover: twenty-three photographs of cubist paintings and constructions, one drawn on in ink and one showing Picasso standing next to a painting; six sheets of pencil or ink drawings of standing female nudes, one drawn on recto/verso; one sheet with a pencil drawing of a tree, related to the painting *Landscape*. Paris, 1907. Zervos II**, 681; and two sheets of ink drawings of a composition with figures, related to the painting *Les Demoiselles d'Avignon*. Paris, 1907. Zervos II*, 18
39 Pages: black crayon drawings of male and female figures
3 Pages: manuscript writing mentioning Gertrude Stein and Georges Braque

**No. 43**
Paper-covered notebook
1907
13.5 x 21 cm

Back Cover: inscribed "2229/PP"
11 Pages: charcoal and pencil drawings of figures, one related to the painting *Bather*. 1908–1909. Zervos II*, III; and another to the painting *The Dryad*. Paris, 1908. Zervos II*, 113.
2 Pages: charcoal drawings of still lifes, related to the painting *Vase of Flowers*. Paris, 1907. Zervos II*, 30
1 Page: pencil and ink drawing, related to the drawing *Sailors in a Bordello*. Paris, 1906–1907. Zervos XXVI, 188
7 Pages: pencil drawings of a seated male figure, related to the painting *Seated Male Nude*. Paris, 1908–1909. Zervos II*, 117.
2 Pages: pencil drawings of still lifes, one a complete composi-tional sketch with color notations of the painting *Bowls and Jug*. Paris, 1908. Zervos II*, 63
2 Pages: pencil drawings of a composition with a winged figure
1 Page: ink and pencil drawing of figures beside a table, related to the drawing *Study for Carnival at the Bistro*. Paris, 1908–1909. Zervos VI, 1074; and to the painting *Bread and Fruit Dish on a Table*. Paris, 1909. Zervos II*, 134
1 Page: pencil drawing of an abstracted landscape

**No. 44**
Patterned cloth-covered notebook
1907
10.5 x 13.5 cm

12 Pages: ink drawings, related to
the painting *Les Demoiselles
d'Avignon*. Paris, 1907.
Zervos II*, 18
1 Page: charcoal drawing of
a landscape, related to the
painting *Landscape*. Paris, 1907.
Zervos II**, 681
25 Pages: charcoal or ink
drawings of figures
18 Pages: pencil drawings of a dog
with suckling puppies

**No. 45**
Linen-covered notebook with
ribbon closure
1907
19.5 x 24.5 cm

3 Pages: pencil drawings of a dog
with suckling puppies
96 Pages: pencil, pastel, and/or
ink drawings, related to the
painting *Les Demoiselles
d'Avignon*. Paris, 1907. Zervos II*,
18; subjects include: compositional studies, individual figures,
and still lifes

**No. 46**
Paper-covered notebook with
"Cahier de Dessins" printed
on front
1907
17.5 x 22.5 cm

Front Cover: pink, blue, and
brown ink drawing of abstract
patterns
Back Cover: brown watercolor
line drawing of a stylized bird
Inside Front Cover: ink drawing
of a standing female nude,
inscribed "Málaga," related to
the painting *Bather*. Paris,
1908–1909. Zervos II*, 111
Inside Back Cover: pencil drawing
of a standing female nude
6 Pages: ink and watercolor
drawings of heads, several
related to the watercolor *Head
of a Man (Study for
"Les Demoiselles d'Avignon")*.
Paris, 1907. Zervos VI, 977
4 Pages: watercolor drawings
of still lifes
3 Pages: watercolor drawings of a
standing female nude, related to
the painting *Nude with Drapery*.
Paris, 1907. Zervos II*, 47
4 Pages: ink drawings of
abstracted figures
2 Pages: printed with tattoo
transfers (?)

**No. 47**
Paper-covered notebook with
lined paper
1907
17 x 22 cm

Front Cover: printed and manuscript inscription "120 pages
Réglées / Prix 10 Centimes /
Cahier / de *Dessins* /
Appartenant / à *Monsieur
Picasso*" with a small ink drawing of a bird at top, inscribed
"1770/PP"
1 Page: red watercolor line
drawing of a stylized bird drawn
over a light pencil drawing of a
landscape
24 Pages: ink drawings of a
standing female nude, related
to the painting *Nude with
Drapery*. Paris, 1907. Zervos
II*, 47
6 Pages: ink or pencil line
drawings of stylized birds
43 Pages: pencil drawings of male
and female figures, several
related to the painting *Nude with
Raised Arms Seen from Behind*.
Paris, 1907. Zervos XXVI, 189
8 Pages: ink drawings of still lifes

**No. 48**
Paper-covered notebook with
"Cahier de Dessin" printed
on front
1907
18 x 22 cm

Front Cover: watercolor and ink
drawing of a bird
Back Cover: watercolor line
drawing of a bird, inscribed
"1907/Paris"
Inside Front Cover: pencil and
brown watercolor drawing of
stylized birds
Inside Back Cover: brown watercolor drawing of stylized birds
13 Pages: pencil drawings of an
abstract landscape-like design,
one with a figure and an
abstracted head in the center
of the image, possibly related to
the painting *Les Demoiselles
d'Avignon*. Paris, 1907. Zervos II*,
18; one inscribed "Ravignan/
Ravignan/Ravignan"
2 Pages: pencil drawings of
abstract patterns
1 Page: pencil drawing
of a woman at a table
6 Pages: pencil drawings of
female nudes, related to the
painting *Les Demoiselles
d'Avignon*.
1 Page: inscribed "Ravignan/
Barcelona/Monsieur/France/
Madrid/Málaga" over a slight
pencil drawing of a figure

**No. 49**
Blue paper-covered notebook
with "Cahier de Dessin"
printed on front
1907
17.5 x 22.5 cm

Front Cover: ink and pencil
drawing of abstract patterns
Back Cover: ink line drawing
of a jug
Inside Front Cover: pencil
drawing of a standing female
nude, related to the painting
*Bather*. Paris, 1908–1909.
Zervos II*, 111
11 Pages: ink and/or pencil
drawings of standing female
nudes, several related to
the paintings *Bather* or
*The Dryad*. Paris, 1908.
Zervos II*, 113

**No. 50**
Paper-covered notebook with
"Cahier de Dessin" printed on
front
1907
17.5 x 22.5 cm

Front Cover: pencil and brown
watercolor drawing of abstract
patterns
Back Cover: inscribed "1763/PP"
5 Pages: pencil or watercolor
drawings of heads or standing
female figures, related to the
watercolor *Study for "Nude
with Drapery."* Paris, 1907.
Zervos II*, 45
1 Page: pencil drawing of plants
1 Page: pencil drawing of a vase
of flowers
3 Pages: pencil or ink drawings
of abstracted female figures, two
related to the painting
*The Dryad*. Paris, 1908.
Zervos II*, 113
1 Page: ink line drawing of an
abstracted landscape, related
to the painting *Landscape*. Paris,
1907. Zervos II**, 681
1 Page: imprint of a pastel
drawing of a still life from the
facing page, which is now missing

**No. 51**
Paper-covered notebook with
"Cahier de Dessin" printed
on front
1908
17.5 x 22.5 cm

Back Cover: ink line drawing of
a stylized bird and a small blue
pencil drawing of a snail
Inside Front Cover: brown
watercolor line drawing of a
stylized bird and a pencil line
drawing of a stylized elephant
Inside Back Cover: pencil line
drawing of a stylized bird
12 Pages: pencil drawings of
an abstracted landscape
18 Pages: pencil drawings
of male and female figures
1 Page: pencil drawing of a vase
of flowers

**No. 52**
Paper-covered graph-paper notebook with "Livres de Compte /
Offert par / L'Abeille / Sociétés
d'Assurances / Paris" printed
on front
1908
9.5 x 14.5 cm

1 Page: inscribed "11 h. Pour
Bougival / La Celle St. Cloud /
Samedi à midi"
1 Page: ink drawing of a standing
female nude, related to the
painting *Three Women*. Paris,
1908–1909. Zervos II*, 108
1 Page: ink drawing of a detail of
the head from the previous sheet
6 Pages: ink drawings of an
abstract composition, related
to the painting *Three Women
(version rhythmée)*. Paris,
1908. Zervos II*, 107

**No. 53**
Cloth-covered graph-paper
notebook with ribbon closure
1912
9 x 13.5 cm

37 Pages: pencil and/or ink
drawings of transitional analytic/
synthetic cubist compositions,
subjects include: still lifes with
guitars and violins; standing
figures; and male heads with
mustaches, several related to the
paintings *The Aficionado*.
Sorgues, 1912. Zervos II*, 362;
and *Man with Guitar*. Paris,
1911–1913. Zervos XXVIII, 57
1 Page: ink drawing of a city
scene with a café, inscribed
"Apéritif" on the awning and
"Souvenir de Marseille 9 Août
1912" at bottom
1 Page: collage of a dried
carnation, inscribed "SORGUE"
1 Page: inscribed "trouver
l'équilibre / entre la nature
et / votre imagination"
1 Page: inscribed "2232 / PP /
2 homme à la mandoline /
3 maisons Estaque / 4 nature
morte Kramar"
1 Page: inscribed "Carnet
Appartenant à PP"

**No. 54**
Linen-covered notebook edged
in leather with ribbon closure
1912–1914
9 x 14 cm

Inside Back Cover: two separate
sheets, one inscribed "Vive La /
France / Avignon / 1914" and
the other inscribed with the
addresses of Max Jacob, Georges
Braque, and Gertrude Stein
103 Pages: pencil and/or ink
drawings of synthetic cubist
compositions, several drawn
on pieces of newspaper and
pasted in, several with wallpaper
collage, and several inscribed
with color notations, subjects
include: still lifes, figures
with guitars, and portraits of men
with mustaches, many related
to the paintings *Geometric
Composition: The Guitar*. 1913.
Not in Zervos; and *Student with
a Pipe*. Paris, 1913. Zervos II**,
444; and the sculpture *Bouteille
et Guitare*. Paris, 1913. Spies 56

**No. 55**
Paper-covered notebook with
perforated pages
1913
8.5 x 11.5 cm

2 Pages: manuscript writing
concerning sales of paintings
and drawings to Gertrude Stein,
Kahnweiler, and Rosenberg
among others, prices indicated
with dates from October 1913 to
January 1915, and an additional
inscription dated 1916
26 Pages: pencil and/or ink
drawings of synthetic cubist compositions, line drawings of stars,
and mathematical notations

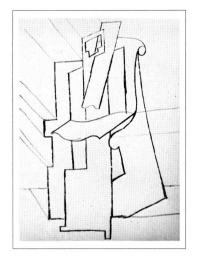

**No. 56**
Cloth-covered notebook
1915
14.5 x 17 cm

8 Pages: synthetic cubist watercolor and pencil drawings of
seated figures
1 Page: synthetic cubist pencil
drawing of a seated female
figure, related to the painting
*Man before a Fireplace*.
Paris, 1916. Not in Zervos

**No. 57**
Handmade cardboard-covered
notebook bound with twine
1915
14 x 16 cm

Inside Front Cover: inscribed with
the company numbers of friends
fighting in World War I, including
André Salmon and Guillaume
Apollinaire
22 Pages: pencil, ink, pastel, and/
or watercolor drawings of synthetic cubist subjects, including:
seated figures, rooftops, an armchair, and a cylindrical abstract
design, three related to the
painting *Man with a Pipe*.
Paris, 1915. Zervos II**, 564

**No. 58**
Linen-covered notebook with
pencil loop on side and
ribbon closure
1914–1915
13.5 x 20.5 cm

Inside Front Cover: inscribed with
Braque's regiment and ambulance
number and "2225/PP," printed
label "Couleurs & Vernis /
R. Charbo / 96, Boulevard
Montparnasse, 96"
Inside Back Cover: pencil drawing
of an abstract cubist design
9 Pages: pencil or crayon drawings of a goblet
2 Pages: pencil drawings of a side
chair seen from different angles
superimposed on one another
1 Page: pencil drawing of a still
life with a book on a table
4 Pages: pencil drawings of a
seated male figure
2 Pages: pencil drawings of nuns,
one inscribed "Soeur"

**No. 59**
Cardboard-covered notebook
with perforated pages
1916
24 x 31 cm

3 Pages: pencil drawings of a bowl
of fruit
12 Pages: synthetic cubist pencil
drawings of seated figures
1 Page: pencil drawing of a
covered bowl
1 Page: pencil drawing of the
upper torso of a mustachioed
harlequin holding a Pulcinella
mask and a club
1 Page: synthetic cubist pencil
drawing of a still life on a table
2 Pages: pencil drawings of a
seated harlequin playing a guitar,
related to the painting *Pierrot*.
Paris, 1918. Zervos III, 137
1 Page: synthetic cubist pencil
drawing of standing figure with
a guitar
13 Pages: pencil drawings of
a harlequin holding a club and
a Pulcinella mask, one depicting
the harlequin in an interior with
a seated man wearing a top hat
at left
3 Pages: pencil drawings of
standing female nudes
1 Page: pencil drawing of a hand

**No. 60**
Cardboard-covered notebook with
blue and black design printed
on front
1917
10.5 x 15 cm

Inside Back Cover: inscribed
"Barcelona 1917 / 2213 / PP";
a calling card, a piece of
stationery from the Madrid
Palace Hotel with notes about
characters from *Pulcinella*
and a sketch for a stage design,
five postcards related to
*Pulcinella*, and two clippings
from a Spanish newspaper:
an advertisement for a new
edition of *Don Quijote de la
Mancha* and a notice from the
*Burlington Magazine* mentioning
"nuestro Pablo Picasso"
64 Pages: pencil drawings,
subjects include: synthetic cubist
compositions of a man leaning on
a table, bullfights, horses, still
lifes with guitars, standing harlequins, dancing figures, hands,
toreadors, one inscribed "Plaza
de Toros"

**No. 61**
Linen-covered notebook with
ribbon closure
1917
Size undetermined

Inside Front Cover: inscribed
"Ce dans la nature que les
peintres / ont toujours cherché
la réalité – / mais la recherche
est dans la / peinture ce n'est que
par elle / qu'elle nous apparaît
alors / en d'autre dans la nature"
1 Page: pencil portrait of a woman
1 Page: pencil drawing of a female
nude

**No. 62**
Green leather-covered notebook
with "Album" printed on front
in gold ink
circa 1917–1920
16 x 24 cm

1 Page: pencil drawing of a cubist
seated figure
14 Pages: pencil drawings of a
bull attacking a horse, related
to the painting *Bullfight*. 1922.
Not in Zervos
1 Page: pencil drawing of a seated
girl in a flowered hat
4 Pages: pencil drawings of bullfights, one related to the painting
*Mlle. V. . . . in the Costume of
an Espada* by Edouard Manet,
1862 (The Metropolitan Museum
of Art, New York)

**No. 63**
Red leather-covered notebook
with "Album" printed on
front in gold ink
1917–1918, 1923–1924
16 x 24 cm

16 Pages: pencil portraits of Olga
Koklova, some representational
and others abstract, one depicting
a woman seated on a balcony with
rooftops behind, another depicting a woman wearing a mantilla,
related to the paintings *Woman
in a Spanish Costume (La
Salchichona)*. Barcelona, 1917.
Zervos III, 45; and *Olga Picasso
in a Mantilla*. Barcelona, 1917.
Zervos III, 40
1 Page: pencil drawing of a
masked harlequin
1 Page: pencil drawing of a group
of women and girls
12 Pages: synthetic cubist pencil
drawings of still lifes with a
guitar on a table, related to the
painting *Table, Guitar, and
Bottle*. Paris, 1919. Zervos III, 437

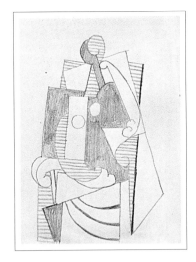

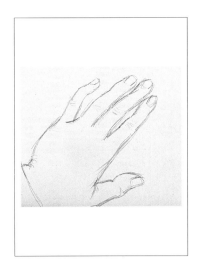

**No. 64**
Linen-covered notebook with
pencil loop on side and ribbon
closure
circa 1918
9.5 x 14 cm

1 Page: pencil drawing of a synthetic cubist composition with
a figure at a table holding a guitar
18 Pages: pencil drawings of landscape and figure studies
24 Pages: pencil or ink line
drawings of stylized birds
1 Page: pencil self-portrait
1 Page: draft of a letter to a doc-
tor, mentioning Olga Koklova
2 Pages: pencil drawings of
abstract patterns
1 Page: pencil drawing of a
reclining female nude, related
to the painting *La Grande
Odalisque* by J.-A.-D. Ingres,
1814 (Musée du Louvre, Paris)
1 Page: pencil drawing of
a mustachioed man holding
a barbell
1 Page: pencil portrait of a woman
1 Page: pencil portrait of a
bearded man
1 Page: inscribed "train pour /
Biarritz / 8 heures 25 m." and
with Guillaume Apollinaire's
address

**No. 65**
Linen-covered notebook with
ribbon closure
1918
24 x 31.5 cm

Inside Front Cover: inscribed
"Tous les dessins de cet album
ont été faits chez Madame
Eugenia Errazuriz à Biarritz"
6 Pages: pencil drawings of
cubist still lifes
1 Page: pencil drawing of an
interior scene
1 Page: pencil drawing of a standing female nude with a guitar
7 Pages: pencil drawings of a
seated cubist figure, related
to the painting *Harlequin Playing
a Guitar*. Paris, 1918. Not in
Zervos
1 Page: pencil drawing of a family
group seated in an interior,
inscribed "Dessin fait à Biarritz
en 1918 chez Madame Eugenia
Errazuriz / pour un portrait à
faire de la famille Paul
Rosenberg"
3 Pages: pencil drawings of
a female figure, one inscribed
"Portrait de Madame
Deidamia Patri"

**No. 66**
Red silk-covered notebook
1918
13 x 16 cm

Inside Front Cover: inscribed
"32 dessins / Biarritz /
«La Mimoseraie» / 1918"
17 Pages: pencil drawings of a
seated female figure, some
representational and others
abstract, five colored with
watercolor
8 Pages: pencil or ink landscape
drawings, five depicting the
landscape seen through a window,
three colored with watercolor
5 Pages: pencil, ink, or watercolor
drawings of three female
nudes holding a garland and
dancing around a reclining
female nude
1 Page: ink line drawing of
a standing Pierrot
1 Page: pencil drawing of a still
life with a basket of fruit

**No. 67**
Purple paper-covered notebook
with "Dessin" printed on front
1919
17.5 x 22.5 cm

Front Cover: pencil and watercolor drawing of abstract patterns
Back Cover: inscribed "Charles—
Maurice Denis—Cocteau /
Carolus—Durand-Ruel / Claude—
Manet—Sully—Proudhomme"
3 Pages: pencil drawings of
a cubist still life, one inscribed
with color notations
9 Pages: pencil drawings of a
hand
1 Page: pencil drawing of a
composition with figures

**No. 68**
Purple paper-covered notebook
with "Dessin" printed on front
1919–1920
17.5 x 22.5 cm

Inside Cover: inscribed "Ragtime"
1 Page: inscribed "Entre Bonnard
et / moi—couvrez vous / Madame
vous / êtes dans un courrant /
d'air [sic]"
1 Page: inscribed "Igor
Stravinsky"
12 Pages: pencil drawings,
subjects include: rooftops seen
through an open window, studies
of hands, a reclining nude, a
horse, a cubist composition with
a guitar, a dog, a dove, two dancing female nudes, and a head of
a woman

**No. 69**
Leather-covered notebook
1919–1920
14.5 x 20.5 cm

1 Page: pencil drawing of a head
of a woman
2 Pages: watercolor drawings
of still lifes in front of an open
window, one inscribed
"24 Décembre 1919"
3 Pages: pencil line drawings
of rooftops
4 Pages: pencil drawings of
female nudes
2 Pages: pencil drawings of
female figures
1 Page: pencil drawing of
a studio interior
3 Pages: pencil drawings of hands
2 Pages: pencil drawings of a
seated cubist figure
4 Pages: pencil and/or crayon
drawings of a cubist still life on
a table, related to the painting
*Table, Guitar, and Bottle.*
Paris, 1919. Zervos III, 437
1 Page: pencil drawing of a
masked Pierrot

**No. 70**
Cloth-covered notebook edged in
leather with ribbon closure
circa 1920
12 x 17.5 cm

6 Pages: pencil line drawings
of phalluses
1 Page: pencil drawing of
a female profile
1 Page: pencil drawing of a synthetic cubist composition with
a guitar, inscribed "Strawinsky"
7 Pages: pencil drawings of a
dancing woman, one inscribed
with color notations, related to
Picasso's costume design for
the Petite Fille in the ballet
*Parade*
3 Pages: pencil drawings of an
abstracted horse, related to
Picasso's costume design for
the Third Manager in the
ballet *Parade*
4 Pages: pencil drawings, related
to costume designs for the
ballet *Pulcinella*
1 Page: pencil drawing
of a Pulcinella mask
1 Page: pencil drawing
of a landscape
1 Page: manuscript writing
concerning a meeting with
Stravinsky, a premier with Bakst,
and a luncheon appointment
with the Princesse de Broglie
1 Page: manuscript writing
of a list of characters for a theatrical production
1 Page: inscribed "moi / Hôtel
Vesuvio / Naples / Chambre / 114"
1 Page: inscribed "Diaghilev / Via
Del Parlamento" and "Olga /
Hôtel Vittoria / Napoli"

**No. 71**
Linen-covered notebook
1920
9.5 x 11 cm

Front Cover: inscribed "Juan les
Pins 1920"
Back Cover: inscribed "2215/PP"
14 Pages: pencil landscape
drawings
1 Page: pencil drawing of an
armchair
1 Page: pencil drawing of
a reclining woman
1 Page: pencil drawing of a
woman looking in a mirror
3 Pages: pencil drawings of hands
3 Pages: pencil drawings of a
woman seated in a chair
2 Pages: pencil drawings
of curtains in an interior

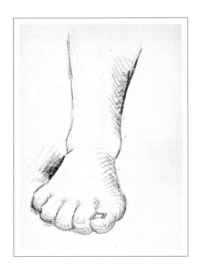

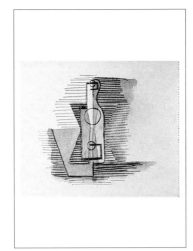

**No. 72**
Cloth-covered notebook
1920
20.5 x 25 cm

1 Page: pastel portrait of a woman

**No. 73**
Linen-covered notebook
circa 1920
8.5 x 13.5 cm

1 Page: inscribed with a list of
paintings, possibly in preparation
for an exhibition, and three small
pencil drawings of paintings,
including one of the painting
*Mother and Child*. Paris, 1907.
Zervos II*, 38
2 Pages: pencil drawings of
synthetic cubist compositions
18 Pages: pencil drawings of
cubist still lifes, four colored
with pastel
22 Pages: pencil drawings of
monumental figures, including
male and female nudes and
a dancing couple
22 Pages: pencil drawings of
monumental hands and feet

**No. 74**
Cardboard-covered notebook
with perforated pages
circa 1921
11.5 x 15 cm

49 Pages: pencil drawings of
cubist still lifes, sixteen colored
with watercolor

**No. 75**
Cardboard-covered notebook with
colored pattern printed on the
front
circa 1922
10.5 x 13.5 cm

Inside Back Cover: inscribed
"50 francs à L. A. Rosenberg"
18 Pages: pencil drawings of
landscapes
8 Pages: pencil drawings of a
child's hands and legs
1 Page: pencil drawing of a stool
7 Pages: pencil drawings of plants
2 Pages: pencil drawings
of an interior
2 Pages: pencil drawings of a
man, woman, and child on a
beach, related to the painting
*Famille au bord de la Mer*.
Dinard, 1922. Not in Zervos
7 Pages: pencil drawings of a little
boy playing
1 Page: pencil drawing of a
monumental seated female nude
1 Page: inscribed "Dinard / Villa
Beauregard / Grand rue"

**No. 76**
Cardboard-covered notebook with
perforated pages and "Sennelier
Album de Dessin" printed on
front
1922
11.5 x 15.5 cm

25 Pages: pencil, watercolor, and/
or pastel drawings of a seated
monumental woman and child
and studies of hands, knees,
and legs, related to the painting
*Mother and Child*. Dinard, 1922.
Zervos IV, 371
3 Pages: pencil drawings of a
seated woman with a child at
her feet and a standing woman
behind, related to the lithographs
*La Coiffure*. 1923. Geiser 234;
and *La Toilette*. 1923. Geiser 235
10 Pages: pencil drawings of landscape, trees, and plants
1 Page: pencil drawing of a table

**No. 77**
Cardboard-covered notebook
with perforated pages
circa 1922
30.5 x 42 cm

Inside Back Cover: inscribed
"Dinard/Olga"
1 Page: pencil drawing of leaves
2 Pages: pencil drawings of a bowl
of fruit
6 Pages: pencil drawings of
landscapes
4 Pages: pencil drawings of
interiors
1 Page: pencil drawing of a
woman and child in a garden
1 Page: pencil drawing of child's
hands holding an object
3 Pages: pencil drawings of
monumental female nudes
5 Pages: pencil drawings of a
seated woman with a child at
her feet and a woman standing
behind, related to the lithographs
*La Coiffure*. 1923. Geiser 234;
and *La Toilette*. 1923. Geiser 235
3 Pages: pencil drawings of a
monumental seated woman
with a child, two related to the
painting *Mother and Child*.
Dinard, 1922. Zervos IV, 371
1 Page: pencil drawing of the
outline of a hand
1 Page: pencil drawing of abstract
patterns

**No. 78**
Canvas-covered notebook
1922
24 x 30.5 cm

27 Pages: charcoal drawings of
a composition with three monumental female nudes and studies
of hands and feet, related to
the painting *Three Women at
the Spring*. Fontainebleau, 1921.
Zervos IV, 322
2 Pages: charcoal drawings of a
monumental woman and child
4 Pages: charcoal drawings of a
male nude
4 Pages: charcoal drawings of a
boy playing pipes

**No. 79**
Cardboard-covered notebook with
"Carnet/Croquis" printed on front
1923
14 x 21 cm

31 Pages: pencil drawings of
cubist still lifes, seven colored
with pastel or watercolor
20 Pages: pencil drawings
of rooftops
2 Pages: brown ink drawings
of classical heads
1 Page: pencil drawing of
a monumental female figure
1 Page: pencil drawing of a figure
wearing a mask, possibly a
costume study for the ballet
*Pulcinella*
1 Page: inscribed with Man Ray's
address and telephone number

**No. 80**
Folded paper maquette for
a program
1923
25 x 32.5 cm

10 Pages: pencil line drawings of
a dancer in a dressing room,
related to a program design for a
Monte Carlo performance of
Diaghilev's Ballets Russes

**No. 81**
Linen-covered notebook
1923
26.5 x 36.5 cm

11 Pages: ink drawings of female
nudes on a beach
7 Pages: ink line drawings of
female heads
1 Page: inscribed "Cap d'Antibes /
1923"

**No. 82**
Linen-covered notebook with
ribbon closure
1923
27 x 36 cm

32 Pages: ink drawings of female
figures

**No. 83**
Linen-covered notebook with
pencil loop on side and ribbon
closure
1924
10 x 11.5 cm

Front Cover: inscribed "2236/PP"
Inside Front Cover: inscribed
"30 mars 1924"
4 Pages: pencil drawings of cubist
still lifes with goblets, three
colored with pastel
1 Page: pencil drawing of a standing male figure
6 Pages: pencil line drawings
of horses
3 Pages: pencil drawings of
seated baboons, one inscribed
"12 Octobre 1924"
13 Pages: pencil line drawings,
possibly preliminary endpaper
designs for *Le Chef-d'oeuvre
inconnu* by Honoré de Balzac
(Paris: Ambroise Vollard, 1931)

**No. 84**
Cloth-covered notebook
1924
23.5 x 31 cm

1 Page: inscribed "Juan les Pins /
1924"
18 Pages: ink drawings, related
to the endpaper designs for *Le
Chef-d'oeuvre inconnu* by Honoré
de Balzac (Paris: Ambroise
Vollard, 1931)
3 Pages: ink drawings of landscapes and buildings
4 Pages: ink drawings of female
heads
1 Page: ink drawing of a hand
covered with multiple ink lines

**No. 85**
Canvas-covered loose-leaf ring
binder with "Cartridge Paper /
C. Rowney & Co. / Sketchbooks"
printed on front
1924
11.5 x 14.5 cm

1 Page: pencil drawing of a foot
1 Page: pencil drawing of a female
head at a windowsill surrounded
by pots of flowers
1 Page: ink drawing of a dancer
at a bar
1 Page: pencil drawing of flowers
in a vase
4 Pages: pencil drawings of stick
figures
1 Page: pencil drawing of women's
shoes
4 Pages: shopping lists and
addresses in London
1 Page: inscribed with Blaise
Cendrars's address in Nice

**No. 86**
Cardboard-covered notebook with
printed "Sennelier" label
1924
23.5 x 31 cm

4 Pages: ink drawings of figures
6 Pages: ink drawings of cubist
still lifes, one colored with
brown and black pastel
1 Page: brown and black pastel
drawing of a landscape with a
large tree in the foreground
24 Pages: ink drawings, including
those that were eventually
reproduced as the endpapers for
*Le Chef-d'oeuvre inconnu* by
Honoré de Balzac (Paris:
Ambroise Vollard, 1931)
1 Page: inscribed "Juan les Pins"

**No. 87**
Cardboard-covered notebook with
printed "Sennelier" label
1925
23 x 30 cm

21 Pages: ink drawings of still
lifes, several related to the
paintings *Studio with Plaster
Head.* Juan-les-Pins, 1925.
Zervos V, 445; and *Tête de
Bélier.* Juan-les-Pins, 1925.
Zervos V, 443
19 Pages: ink drawings of figures
2 Pages: ink drawings of cubist
abstractions
1 Page: inscribed "Juan les Pins
1ère Août 1925"

**No. 88**
Linen-covered notebook with
ribbon closure
1925
23 x 31 cm

Front Cover: inscribed "Juan les
Pins / 1925"
Inside Front Cover: inscribed
"Juan les Pins / Villa Belle Rose /
20 Août 1925"
32 Pages: ink drawings of figures
and heads, two colored with
watercolor, several related to the
painting *The Milliner's Workshop*. 1926. Zervos VII, 2
1 Page: pencil drawing of a still
life
6 Pages: ink drawings of still lifes,
two colored with watercolor
1 Page: ink drawing of an abstract
pattern based on the letters of
the word *serenade*
6 Pages: ink drawings of abstract
designs
1 Page: inscribed "Juan les Pins
13 Septembre 1925"

**No. 89**
Linen-covered notebook with
pencil loop on side and ribbon
closure
1925
27 x 36 cm

2 Pages: pencil drawings of heads,
one signed and inscribed
"Nov. 1925"
1 Page: pencil and watercolor
drawing of a still life with two
small separate sheets of ink
drawings of heads pasted in
15 Pages: pencil drawings of still
lifes
1 Page: pencil drawing of a female
head
5 Pages: ink drawings of clasped
hands
4 Pages: ink drawings of male and
female figures

**No. 90**
Cardboard-covered notebook with
perforated pages and printed
"Sennelier" label
1926
11 x 15 cm

Inside Front Cover: inscribed
"PARIS — Décembre / 1925"
Inside Back Cover: inscribed
"20 Mars / 1926"
26 Pages: ink drawings of cubist
still lifes
4 Pages: ink drawings of a female
figure, related to the paintings
*The Milliner's Workshop*. 1926.
Zervos VII, 2; and *Painter and
Model*. 1926. Zervos VII, 30
6 Pages: ink drawings of heads,
related to the painting *The
Milliner's Workshop*.

**No. 91**
Cardboard-covered notebook with
printed "Sennelier" label
1926
16 x 21 cm

Inside Front Cover: inscribed
"Juan les Pins — Août 1926"
26 Pages: ink drawings of heads
3 Pages: ink drawings of reclining
female nudes
7 Pages: ink drawings of a
landscape, one colored with
watercolor
5 Pages: ink drawings of abstract
patterns
6 Pages: ink drawings of horses
1 Page: inscribed "22 Septembre
1926 / Antibes"

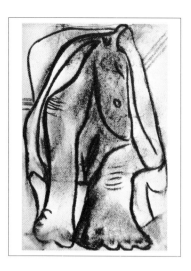

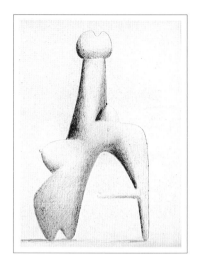

**No. 92**
Cardboard-covered notebook
1926
32.5 x 49 cm

Inside Front Cover: inscribed
"Paris / 21 mars / 1926"
Inside Back Cover: inscribed
"20 juin / 1926 / PARIS"
4 Pages: ink drawings of a female
figure
5 Pages: ink drawings of the
female head, related to the painting *The Milliner's Workshop*.
1926. Zervos VII, 2
1 Page: three ink drawings of
abstracted guitars, related to
the assemblages *Guitar*. Paris,
1926. Zervos VII, 9; and *Guitar*.
Paris, 1926. Not in Zervos
6 Pages: ink and/or blue pencil
drawings of abstract patterns
1 Page: collage of a leaf

**No. 93**
Linen-covered notebook with
pencil loop on side
1926–1927
17.5 x 26 cm

Inside Front Cover: inscribed
"PARIS / Décembre 1926"
Inside Back Cover: inscribed
"8 Mai 927"
5 Pages: pencil and/or ink
drawings of heads, related to the
painting *The Embrace*. Juan-les-
Pins, 1925. Zervos V, 460
41 Pages: pencil, ink, or charcoal drawings of seated female
nudes, many related to the painting *Woman in an Armchair*.
Paris, 1927. Zervos III, 79;
and the sculpture *Bather
(Metamorphosis I)*. Paris, 1928.
Spies 67

**No. 94**
Cardboard-covered notebook with
printed "Sennelier" label
1927
23 x 30.4 cm

Inside Front Cover: inscribed
"Chalet Madrid / Bd
Alexandre III / Cannes /
17 Juillet 1927"
Inside Back Cover: inscribed
"Dimanche 11 Septembre /
1927 / Cannes / Chalet Madrid"
1 Page: ink drawing of two still
lifes and a female nude,
related to the painting *Bust
of a Woman with Self-Portrait*.
Paris, 1929. Zervos VII, 248
1 Page: ink drawing of a female
nude, related to the painting
*Nude in an Armchair*. Paris,
1929. Zervos VII, 263
38 Pages: pencil drawings of
female bone figures on a beach
9 Pages: pencil drawings of
an abstracted bull attacking
a horse
1 Page: pencil drawings of
abstracted open mouths

**No. 95**
Cardboard-covered notebook with
printed "Sennelier" label
1927
23 x 30.5 cm

Inside Front Cover: inscribed
"Chalet Madrid /
Bd Alexandre III / Cannes /
11 Septembre 1927"
6 Pages: pencil drawings of
female bone figures
8 Pages: pencil drawings, related
to the sculpture *Wire Construction*. Paris, 1928. Spies 68
1 Page: inscribed "24 Septembre
1927 – Chalet Madrid Bd
Alexandre III Cannes"

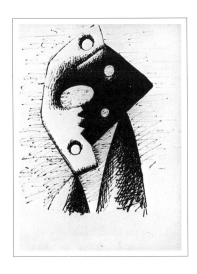

**No. 96**
Cardboard-covered notebook with perforated pages and printed "Sennelier" label
1928
31 x 38 cm

Inside Front Cover: inscribed "Dinard / Vendredi 27 Juillet 1928"
Inside Back Cover: inscribed "PARIS / 23 R. La Boétie / 17 Decembre 1928"
10 Pages: ink drawings of female bone figures
13 Pages: ink line drawings, related to the sculpture *Wire Construction*. Paris, 1928. Spies 68
8 Pages: ink drawings of compositions with figures on a beach, possibly an inventory of paintings, several related to the paintings *Bather and Cabin*. Dinard, 1928. Zervos VII, 211; and *Bathers with Beach Ball*. Dinard, 1928. Zervos VII, 226
22 Pages: ink drawings of figures on a beach, related to the painting *Bathers with Beach Ball*.
1 Page: ink drawing of a woman
3 Pages: ink drawings, related to the series of drawings *An Anatomy*. Paris, 1933. Not in Zervos
1 Page: inscribed "23 R. La Boétie / PARIS / 11 Novembre / 1928"

**No. 97**
Cardboard-covered notebook with string binding
1928
23.5 x 31 cm

Inside Front Cover: inscribed "Paris / 18 Juin 1928"
Inside Back Cover: inscribed "PARIS 23 R. La Boétie / Dimanche Le 8 Juillet 1928"
6 Pages: ink drawings of abstracted heads, related to the painting *Seated Bather*. Paris, 1930. Zervos VII, 306
9 Pages: ink drawings of animals, including horses' heads, eagles, and doves
17 Pages: ink drawings of figures, related to the series of drawings *An Anatomy*. Paris, 1933. Not in Zervos
4 Pages: ink drawings of entangled men and horses

**No. 98**
Mottled black and brown cardboard-covered notebook
1929
24.5 x 31 cm

Inside Front Cover: inscribed "Paris Lundi 25 Février 1929 / 23 Rue La Boétie"
Inside Back Cover: inscribed "PARIS / Dimanche / 12 Janvier / XXX"
40 Pages: pencil drawings of figures, related to the paintings *Painter and Model*. Paris, 1928. Zervos VII, 143; and *Figures by the Sea*. Paris, 1931. Zervos VII, 328; and to the sculpture *Woman in a Garden*. Paris, 1929–1930. Spies 72
2 Pages: pencil drawings of a man bending over a reclining female nude, related to the etching *Homme dévoilant une femme*. June 20, 1931. Geiser 203
4 Pages: pencil drawings of a composition with figures, a horse, a warrior, and a ladder, related to the painting *Crucifixion*. Paris, 1930. Zervos VII, 287
15 Pages: pencil drawings, related to the paintings *The Swimmer*. Paris, 1929. Zervos VII, 419; and *Acrobat*. Paris, 1930. Zervos VII, 310

**No. 99**
Cardboard-covered notebook with perforated pages and printed "Sennelier" label
1929
30 x 37.5 cm

Inside Front Cover: inscribed "Dinard / Villa Bel-Event / Le 16 Août 1929"
1 Page: ink drawing of a sculptural bone figure on a beach
1 Page: ink drawing of a head with a double profile
1 Page: three ink drawings of a reclining female nude and two ink drawings of sculptural heads, possibly an inventory of paintings
1 Page: three ink drawings of sculptural heads
2 Pages: ink drawings of standing sculptural figures
1 Page: pencil and brown pastel drawing of a still life of fruit in a bowl, inscribed "20 Septembre XXIX"

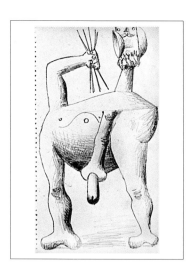

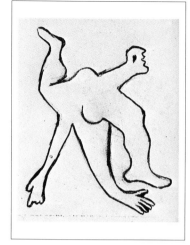

**No. 100**
Blue paper-covered notebook
with perforated pages
1930
11 x 17 cm

Inside Front Cover: inscribed with
Vollard's and Gonzalez's addresses
31 Pages: pencil drawings of
sculptural heads and figures,
several related to the sculpture
*Head*. Paris, 1930. Spies 80
1 Page: inscribed "Boisgeloup 30
Juillet 1930"

**No. 101**
Linen-covered notebook with
ribbon closure
1930–1931
28 x 42 cm

Inside Front Cover: inscribed
"Boisgeloup / 8 Novembre
M.C.M.XXX."
Inside Back Cover: inscribed
"Boisgeloup / 10 Septembre /
XXXI"; a separate sheet with
an ink drawing of an abstract
pattern; and a photograph of
Picasso standing next to a plaster
version of the sculpture *Head
of a Woman*. Boisgeloup, 1932.
Spies 110
8 Pages: ink drawings of standing
female nudes related to the
sculpture *Bather*. Boisgeloup,
1932. Spies 108
3 Pages: ink drawings of abstract
patterns
42 Pages: ink drawings of male
and female heads, including a
self-portrait and a portrait of
Marie-Thérèse Walter, inscribed
"16 Mai XXXI"
20 Pages: ink drawings of reclining sculptural female nudes,
seated female nudes, and heads of
women, related to the sculptures
*Head of a Woman*. Boisgeloup,
1931. Spies 128; and *Head of
a Woman*. Boisgeloup, 1931–
1932. Spies 132

**No. 102**
Cardboard-covered notebook with
printed "Sennelier" label
1930–1932
20.5 x 24.5 cm

Inside Front Cover: inscribed
"Paris—23 R. La Boétie /
2–II–XXX"
4 Pages: ink or pencil drawings of
sculptural seated bone women,
related to the painting
*Seated Bather*. Paris, 1930.
Zervos VII, 306
3 Pages: pencil and ink drawings
related to the painting *Acrobat*.
Paris, 1930. Zervos VII, 310
8 Pages: pencil drawings of interiors with plants, related to the
painting *The Lamp*. 1931.
Zervos VII, 347
1 Page: ink drawing of a figure,
related to the painting
*Crucifixion*. Paris, 1930.
Zervos VII, 287
25 Pages: blue ink line drawings,
related to the series of drawings
*Figures Making Love*. Boisgeloup,
1933. Zervos VIII,
104–111

**No. 103**
Cardboard-covered notebook with
printed "Sennelier" label
1931
30 x 36.5 cm

Inside Front Cover: inscribed
"Boisgeloup / 8 Octobre /
M.C.M.XXXI."
Inside Back Cover: inscribed
"Boisgeloup / 12 Decembre /
M.C.M.XXI [sic]"
25 Pages: pencil drawings of
cubist heads with double profiles
3 Pages: pencil portraits of Marie-
Thérèse Walter
1 Page: pencil drawing of an
abstract pattern of eyes
1 Page: ink drawing of a standing
bearded man facing a sculpture
bust on a pedestal
20 Pages: ink line drawings of
abstracted female nudes as plants,
inscribed "12 Décembre XXXI"

**No. 104**
Cardboard-covered notebook
1933
34 x 45 cm

Inside Front Cover: newspaper
clipping of a photograph of a
bearded man
1 Page: ink drawing of a bearded
man, a copy of the newspaper
photograph, inscribed "Cannes 15
Août XXXIII"

**No. 105**
Linen-covered notebook
1939
11 x 17 cm

Front Cover: inscribed "Royan/
3.11.39"
Back Cover: inscribed "Royan/
9.11.39"
Inside Front Cover: inscribed
"Royan/3.11.39"
3 Pages: ink or pencil drawings
of the head of a woman after the
late-fifteenth-century painting
*Portrait of a Young Princess* by
the Master of Moulins (The
Metropolitan Museum of Art,
New York)
23 Pages: ink or pencil drawings
of women, several related to
the paintings *Woman Seated in a
Garden*. Paris, 1938. Zervos IX,
232; and *Dora Maar Sitting*.
1939. Not in Zervos
3 Pages: ink drawings of a young
girl with a ribbon in her hair
seated at a table
5 Pages: pencil drawings of a
horse wearing a plumed costume
1 Page: pencil drawing of a bull

**No. 106**
Linen-covered graph-paper
notebook with "Croquis" printed
on front
1939
17.5 x 23.5 cm

Front Cover: inscribed
"Royan/29.11.39"
Inside Front Cover: pencil
drawing of a head of a woman
30 Pages: ink or pencil drawings
of a seated female figure
56 Pages: poems, one inscribed
"Janvier 1940"
17 Pages: pencil or ink drawings,
related to the painting *Woman
Dressing Her Hair*. Royan, 1940.
Zervos X, 302

**No. 107**
Linen-covered graph-paper
notebook
1940
17.5 x 23.5 cm

Front Cover: inscribed "Royan/
29.1.40"
Back Cover: inscribed "Royan/
30.1.40"
Inside Front Cover: inscribed
"Royan/29.1.40/Les Voiliers"
Inside Back Cover: inscribed
"Les Voiliers / Royan / 30.1.40"
20 Pages: pencil drawings of
seated woman
38 Pages: pencil drawings of
female nudes
11 Pages: pencil drawings of
heads of Dora Maar, one
inscribed "30.1.40 / Esquisse
du tableau du 20.10.39" and
another "tableau 16.10.39 *20F.* /
ETAT 30.1.40," related to the
painting *Dora Maar Sitting*.
1939. Not in Zervos
2 Pages: pencil drawings of
clasped hands

**No. 108**
Notebook with lined paper
1940
12 x 19 cm

Inside Front Cover: inscribed
"Les Voiliers"
Inside Back Cover: inscribed
in large abstract letters "Les
Voiliers"
Front Endpaper: inscribed "Les /
Voiliers / Bᵈ Thiers / Royan"
64 Pages: ink drawings of standing or seated female nudes, one
inscribed "4.3.40/Royan"
60 Pages: ink drawings of abstract
heads, related to the paintings
*Head of a Woman with Two
Profiles*. Paris, 1939. Zervos IX,
282; and *Woman in an Armchair*.
Paris, 1941. Zervos XI, 155
1 Page: manuscript writing

**No. 109**
Paper-covered graph-paper
notebook with "Notes" printed
on front
1940
10.5 x 17.5 cm

Front Cover: inscribed "Royan/
10.1.40"
Back Cover: inscribed "Royan/
26.5.40"
4 Pages: pencil drawings after the
painting *Les Femmes d'Alger
dans leur appartement* by Eugène
Delacroix, 1834 (Musée du
Louvre, Paris)
5 Pages: color studies in watercolor, one inscribed "Les femmes
d'Alger par Delacroix"
67 Pages: pencil drawings of
female figures
16 Pages: pencil drawings of
horses
1 Page: ink drawing of an animal
skull, related to the painting
*Still Life with Steer's Skull*. Paris,
1942. Not in Zervos

**No. 110**
Cardboard-covered notebook with
printed "Sennelier" label
1940
16 x 24.5 cm

Front Cover: inscribed "Royan/
31.5.40"
Back Cover: inscribed "Royan
10.8.40"
Inside Front Cover: inscribed
"Royan/31.5.40"
7 Pages: ink drawings of seated
female nudes, related to the
painting *Woman Dressing Her
Hair*. Royan, 1940. Zervos X, 302.
29 Pages: ink drawings of female
figures, eight colored with red
and blue crayon
6 Pages: ink drawings of skulls

**No. 111**
Drawn on the pages of the book
*Picasso* by Jean Cassou
(Editions Hypérion, Paris)
1940
Size undetermined

60 Pages: embellished with ink,
watercolor, and crayon drawings
of male and female figures
47 Pages: inscribed with Picasso's
manuscript additions to the text

**No. 112**
Cardboard-covered notebook with perforated pages
1940–1942
30.5 x 41.5 cm

Inside Front Cover: inscribed "Royan/30.5.40"
10 Pages: pastel, gouache, pencil, and/or ink drawings of female figures, one inscribed with color notations
6 Pages: oil paint and/or ink drawings of compositions with female nudes, two related to the painting *Woman Dressing Her Hair*. Royan, 1940. Zervos X, 302
3 Pages: ink drawings of a standing female nude in a studio with a painting of a head of a woman on an easel
1 Page: ink drawing of a couple making love
1 Page: ink drawing of a male nude
12 Pages: pencil or ink drawings of a head of a woman
2 Pages: gouache drawings of a head of a woman
3 Pages: ink drawings of a head of a man
1 Page: ink drawing of a skull
1 Page: pencil drawing of a reclining dog

**No. 113**
Leather-covered notebook with "AC" printed on front in gold ink
1943
15 x 23 cm

16 Pages: pencil drawings, related to the painting *First Steps*. Paris, 1943. Zervos XIII, 36; including one page with a pencil drawing of the head of the child in the painting, inscribed "17 Août 43"
2 Pages: ink drawings of sheep's heads, related to the sculpture *Man with Sheep*. Paris, 1944. Spies 280
8 Pages: pencil drawings of a rocking chair
1 Page: pencil drawing of the head of a rooster
1 Page: pencil drawing of a skull and a jug, related to the painting *Still Life with Skull, Leek, and Pottery*. Paris, 1945. Zervos XIV, 97
6 Pages: pencil drawings of a seated female figure
7 Pages: pencil drawings of still lifes
3 Pages: pencil drawings of reclining female nudes
3 Pages: nineteenth-century ink drawings (not by Picasso)

**No. 114**
Antique leather-covered notebook
1945–1963
32 x 43.5 cm

Inside Back Cover: six separate sheets, including one with a pencil portrait of Françoise Gilot, related to the paintings *Seated Woman*. Paris, 1946. Zervos XV, 13; and *Woman-Flower*. Paris, 1946. Zervos XIV, 167; and two with an index in crayon of the manuscript portions of the sketchbook
10 Pages: pencil and ink drawings of abstracted female heads
7 Pages: manuscript writing in ink
4 Pages: ink drawings of burning logs, one with a drawing related to the sculpture *La Vénus du Gaz*. 1945. Spies 302A at left
1 Page: ink drawing of a female nude
2 Pages: ink drawings of roosters
2 Pages: ink drawings, related to the painting *The Charnel House*. Paris, 1944–1945. Zervos XIV, 76
3 Pages: ink drawings of skulls
2 Pages: ink drawings of a landscape with human and animal/man figures painting at easels
1 Page: ink portrait of Edgar Allan Poe, inscribed with fourteen lines of poetry
1 Page: ink drawing of a reclining male nude
9 Pages: pencil or gouache portraits of Françoise Gilot, one inscribed "Dimanche 10.6.45."
1 Page: inscribed "Matisse m'a dit cette après- / midi premier janvier / 1947 «hier j'ai eu 77 ans» / 1947 le 15 mai à 1 H ½ après midi / Claude / Boulogne-Billancourt 19 avril 1949 / à 19 Hs 40 Paloma"
8 Pages: ink and/or crayon drawings of a seated female figure, one inscribed with color notations
3 Pages: ink drawings of a stage design (?)

3 Pages: ink and crayon manuscript entitled "Soneto Burlesco"
10 Pages: ink and crayon manuscript entitled "Soneto Heroico"
3 Pages: ink drawings after a painting by Lucas Cranach, one inscribed "le 22.3.49"
1 Page: ink portrait of a woman, inscribed "10.11.53"
3 Pages: ink drawings after a painting by Albrecht Altdorfer, one inscribed "12.11.53"
7 Pages: ink drawings of a composition with female nudes and men and women in seventeenth-century costumes, each inscribed "18.11.53"
1 Page: inscribed "2.3.61 / Vallauris / 7 hs ½" in ink
1 Page: ink drawing of a centaur wearing a hat and holding a spear, inscribed "–Ramon Reventos– / (MONI) / EL CENTAURE / PICADOR"
1 Page: ink drawing of peasant women and children
3 Pages: ink drawings of a centaur with men, one inscribed "9.2.47"
1 Page: ink drawing of a bull's head and an inscription related to a bullfight, inscribed "9.2.47"
1 Page: ink drawing of a seated faun playing pipes, inscribed "9.2.47 le dimanche"
1 Page: ink drawing of the head of a bearded faun, inscribed "Ramon Reventos / (MONI) / EL CREPUSCULE / D'UN FAUNE"
5 Pages: ink manuscript interspersed with ink drawings of fauns, female nudes, and bulls

**No. 115**
Leather-covered notebook with
"Société Maternelle de Rouen /
Exposition 1844" printed on front
in gold ink
1946
30 x 39 cm

Inside Front Cover: pieces of
checkered fabric, tinfoil, and
blue shiny paper
2 Pages: collage and crayon
portraits of Françoise Gilot
2 Pages: collage and crayon self-
portraits by Françoise Gilot
2 Pages: pencil portraits of
Françoise Gilot
2 Pages: manuscript writing,
dated 1844

**No. 116**
Paper-covered notebook with
"Dessin" and a design of a
rooster printed on front
1946
24 x 31 cm

5 Pages: pencil portraits of
Françoise Gilot
2 Pages: pencil self-portraits by
Françoise Gilot, one inscribed
"P. Picasso / 28 Mars / 46"

**No. 117**
Drawn on the first blank page
of the book *Picasso* by Paul
Eluard (Braun & Cie., Paris)
1946
Size undetermined

1 Page: crayon portrait of
Françoise Gilot

**No. 118**
Cardboard-covered notebook with
"Sennelier" label
1947
15.5 x 24.5 cm

43 Pages: crayon, ink, and watercolor drawings, subject matter
undetermined

**No. 119**
Leather-covered notebook with
gold trim
1950–1951
Size undetermined

52 Pages: crayon drawings
of flowers and insects
16 Pages: manuscript writing
in ink
8 Pages: ink line drawings
of interiors
1 Page: purple ink drawing of a
flower, inscribed "Françoise/
Pablo/Claude/Paloma" in the
center
3 Pages: birthday greetings for
Françoise Gilot, each inscribed
"26.11.1951"

**No. 120**
Paper-covered notebook with
"Dessin" printed on front
1951
24 x 32 cm

12 Pages: ink or pencil landscape
drawings, one inscribed "Vallauris
20.9.51"

**No. 121**
Spiral-bound cardboard-covered
notebook
1951
33 x 41.5 cm

Inside Back Cover: inscribed
"Tous les dessins de cet
album / ont été faits le soir
du 10–11 Janvier / 1951"
29 Pages: ink marker drawings
of clowns' heads, related to
the linoleum cut *Le Vieux Roi*.
1963. Block 1152

**No. 122**
Spiral-bound cardboard-covered
notebook
1951
21 x 27 cm

Front Cover: blue ink drawing of
the profile of a head, inscribed
"28.11.51"
31 Pages: blue ink drawings of
male and female heads
4 Pages: blue ink drawings of an
artist at an easel
1 Page: blue ink drawing of an
artist painting a female nude

  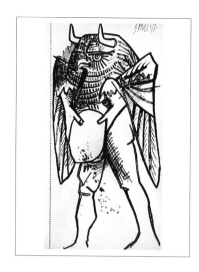 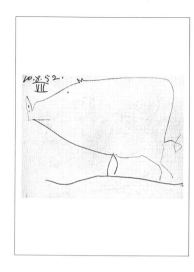

**No. 123**
Cardboard-covered notebook with perforated pages and printed "Sennelier" label
1951
27 x 34 cm

Inside Front Cover: colored ink marker drawing of a clown's head, inscribed "9.1.51"
40 Pages: ink marker drawings of clowns' heads, related to the linoleum cut *Le Vieux Roi*. 1963. Block 1152

**No. 124**
Notebook with perforated pages
1952
15.5 x 24 cm

3 Pages: ink drawings of an owl, one inscribed "PARIS le 28.4.52"
58 Pages: pencil or ink drawings, related to the murals *La Guerre*. 1952. Zervos XV, 196; and *La Paix*. 1952. Zervos XV, 197; subjects include: compositions with an owl in the sky and rain falling on people, bird/man figures, a reclining female nude holding a child, and a composition with dancing children and two standing female nudes with raised arms

**No. 125**
Cardboard-covered notebook with printed "Sennelier" label
1952
13 x 22 cm

12 Pages: ink or pencil drawings of bird/man figures, birds' heads, and women dancing in a circle, related to the murals *La Guerre*. 1952. Zervos XV, 196; and *La Paix*. 1952. Zervos XV, 197

**No. 126**
Paper-covered graph-paper notebook
1952
17 x 22 cm

174 Pages: pencil drawings, many related to the murals *La Guerre*. 1952. Zervos XV, 196; and *La Paix*. 1952. Zervos XV, 197; subjects include: horses, male and female figures, camels, pigs, and skeletons

**No. 127**
Spiral-bound cardboard-covered
notebook with "Croquis/Dessin"
printed on front
1953
Size undetermined

1 Page: black crayon drawing of
a woman
2 Pages: ink drawings of a tiger
attacking a bird, related to the
painting *Cat and Bird*. Le
Tremblay-sur-Mauldre, 1939.
Zervos IX, 297
1 Page: ink drawing of a standing
male figure and a reclining
female nude

**No. 128**
Spiral-bound cardboard-covered
notebook
1953
27 x 35 cm

15 Pages: ink or pencil line
drawings of fallen warriors with
a dove in the sky
6 Pages: pencil caricatures of men
and women

**No. 129**
Spiral-bound cardboard-covered
notebook with "Croquis/Dessin"
printed on front
1953
33 x 42 cm

17 Pages: pencil drawings of
a female head

**No. 130**
Spiral-bound cardboard-covered
notebook
1953–1955
22 x 28 cm

16 Pages: pencil or ink drawings
of a cat attacking a bird, related
to the painting *Cat and Bird*.
Le Tremblay-sur-Mauldre, 1939.
Zervos IX, 297
1 Page: ink drawing of a reclining
nude, inscribed "16.12.53"
1 Page: pencil drawing of a still
life, inscribed "19.10.55"

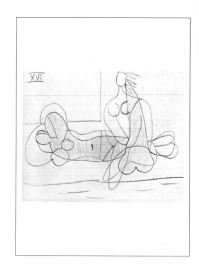

**No. 131**
Paper-covered notebook
1954
21 x 27 cm

Front Cover: inscribed
"PREMIERS dessins / du
déjeuner sur l'herbe / 1954"
Back Cover: inscribed
"PREmiers / dessins / du déjeuner
sur l'herbe"
4 Pages: pencil drawings after the
painting *Le Déjeuner sur l'herbe*
by Edouard Manet, 1863 (Musée
d'Orsay–Louvre, Paris)
1 Page: pencil drawing after the
painting *Self-Portrait* by Eugène
Delacroix, 1839 (Musée du
Louvre, Paris)

**No. 132**
Spiral-bound cardboard-covered
notebook
1954
22 x 28 cm

Front Cover: inscribed
"15.11.54/Paris"
Back Cover: inscribed
"5.12.54/Paris"
4 Pages: ink drawings of an easel
9 Pages: ink drawings of female
nudes
3 Pages: ink drawings of heads
of men and women
1 Page: ink drawing of an artist
at an easel
1 Page: ink drawing of a bearded
man
2 Pages: ink drawings of a man
on a horse
6 Pages: pencil drawings of two
seated female nudes in an
interior
4 Pages: ink portraits of
Jacqueline Roque
1 Page: ink drawing of a horse

**No. 133**
Spiral-bound cardboard-covered
notebook
1955
32 x 43.5 cm

24 Pages: pencil portraits of
Helena Rubenstein

**No. 134**
Blue paper-covered notebook
with lined paper and "Ecole/
Cahier" printed on front
1955
17 x 22 cm

9 Pages: pencil drawings of two
female nudes on a beach

  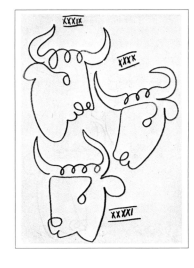

No. 135
Spiral-bound cardboard-covered
notebook
1955
27 x 42 cm

Front Cover: inscribed
"Novembre/1955"
Back Cover: inscribed
"Décembre/1955"
24 Pages: ink and/or crayon
drawings of studio interiors
8 Pages: ink and/or crayon
drawings of a seated woman
in a Turkish costume
1 Page: red crayon drawing of a
firing squad executing prisoners,
inscribed "la commune de Paris
de 70"
5 Pages: ink drawings of male and
female heads after paintings by
Cranach, Holbein, Rembrandt,
and Vermeer
1 Page: pencil drawing of
abstracted figures
Note: produced as a limited-
edition facsimile with an introduction by Georges Boudaille,
*Picasso: Carnet de la Californie*
(Paris: Editions Cercle d'Art,
1959)

No. 136
Spiral-bound cardboard-covered
notebook
1956
33 x 42 cm

Front Cover: inscribed
"La Californie / janvier / 1956 /
22.4.56"
Back Cover: inscribed "janvier/
1956/22.4.56"
27 Pages: pencil and/or ink drawings of a female nude seated on a
patterned floor fixing her hair
4 Pages: ink or charcoal drawings
of female heads, one colored
with gouache
1 Page: ink line drawing of a
figure
12 Pages: ink and crayon drawings of a seated and a reclining
female nude
3 Pages: pencil drawings of an
artist and model
1 Page: ink drawing of four seated
bearded men, inscribed
"22.4.56 / d'après un dessin de
Rembrandt / fait d'après une
miniature / indo-persane / «Salon
des millions» / de Schönbrunn"

No. 137
Spiral-bound cardboard-covered
notebook
1956
33 x 42 cm

Front Cover: inscribed
"La Californie / 19.3.56–17.6.56"
Back Cover: inscribed
"La Californie / 19.3.56–17.6.56"
4 Pages: pencil portraits of
Jacqueline Roque
8 Pages: ink drawings of a figure
in an interior
2 Pages: ink drawings of clasped
hands
2 Pages: ink drawings of plants
6 Pages: ink caricatures of Jaime
Sabartés, one inscribed "Retour
de Bruxelles"

No. 138
Spiral-bound cardboard-covered
notebook with "Esquisses"
printed on front
1956–1957
24 x 32 cm

Front Cover: crayon drawing of
abstract patterns, inscribed
"La Californie / 5.11.56"
14 Pages: blue crayon drawings
of bulls' heads
2 Pages: red and blue crayon
drawings of the head of a
sailor
7 Pages: pencil drawings of stick
figures, related to the sculptures
*The Bathers*. Cannes, 1956. Spies
503–508
4 Pages: pencil or crayon drawings of abstracted figures and
faces, one inscribed "Bernard
Geiser"
16 Pages: crayon drawings
of clowns' heads

**No. 139**
Spiral-bound cardboard-covered
notebook
1956
33 x 42 cm

Front Cover: inscribed
"La Californie / 17.3.56"
Back Cover: inscribed
"La Californie / 17.3.56"
2 Pages: ink drawings of a couple
making love
1 Page: black crayon drawing of
two female nudes on a beach
1 Page: ink drawing of a bull
crushing a toreador
4 Pages: ink drawings of bulls
1 Page: ink drawing of two figures
dancing around a circle and a
female nude
1 Page: pencil portrait
of Jacqueline Roque
4 Pages: ink drawings of vase of
flowers

**No. 140**
Spiral-bound cardboard-covered
notebook
1956
28 x 37 cm

Front Cover: inscribed
"La Californie / 16.9.56"
Back Cover: inscribed
"La Californie / 17.10.56"
1 Page: ink drawing of a head of a
bearded man
13 Pages: ink and crayon
drawings of stick figures, related
to the sculptures *The Bathers*.
Cannes, 1956. Spies 503–508
18 Pages: charcoal line drawings
of abstracted heads
12 Pages: blue, red, and black
crayon drawings of faces
32 Pages: blue and red crayon
portraits of Jacques Prévert,
one inscribed "Jacobus Prevertus,
le 3 octobre 1956"

**No. 141**
Cloth-covered notebook with
printed pattern
1957
6.5 x 9.5 cm

Front Cover: inscribed "PEPE/
ILLO/TAUROMAQUIA"
108 Pages: ink drawings of toreadors, bulls, abstract patterns,
and manuscript writing, one
inscribed "le 24.12. / 1957"
Note: produced as a limited-
edition facsimile with essays
by Gustavo Gili Esteve and
Bernhard Geiser, *El Carnet de
"La Tauromaquia" de Pepe
Illo* (Barcelona: Editorial Gustavo
Gili, 1963)

**No. 142**
Canvas-covered notebook with
printed pattern
1957
6.5 x 9.5 cm

Front Cover: inscribed "Pour /
Duhamel / Marcel / le 18.1.65."
Back Cover: inscribed "monsieur/
marcel/Duhamel"
Inside Front Cover: manuscript
writing
Inside Back Cover: manuscript
writing
26 Pages: ink drawings of male
and female heads
10 Pages: ink drawings of male
and female figures
21 Pages: manuscript writing
48 Pages: ink drawings of abstract
patterns
6 Pages: ink drawings of birds,
insects, and plants
Note: produced as a limited-
edition facsimile, *Le Carnet des
Carnets* (Paris: privately
printed, 1965)

**No. 143**
Binding undetermined
1957–1958
25 x 32.5 cm

Front Cover: inscribed "15.12.57/
UNESCO"
Back Cover: inscribed "4.1.58/
UNESCO
30 Pages: ink and/or crayon
drawings, related to the
fresco design for UNESCO

**No. 144**
Binding undetermined
1958
24 x 31.5 cm

Front Cover: inscribed "4.1.58/
UNESCO"
5 Pages: drawings of undetermined medium, related to the
fresco design for UNESCO

**No. 145**
Spiral-bound cardboard-covered
notebook with "Croquis"
printed on front
1958
27 x 37 cm

Front Cover: inscribed "19.7.58 /
portraits d'Arturo Rubinstein"
Back Cover: inscribed "portraits
d'Arturo Rubinstein / le 19.7.58"
Inside Back Cover: three separate
sheets of crayon drawings of
abstracted faces drawn on the
backs of invitations and one
separate sheet with a crayon
drawing of an abstracted face
inscribed "Portrait très resem-
blant d'Arturo Rubinstein / le
19/7/58"
22 Pages: pencil portraits of
Arturo Rubinstein

**No. 146**
Spiral-bound cardboard-covered
notebook
1958
27 x 37 cm

Front Cover: inscribed "5.5.58/
22.5.58"
Back Cover: inscribed "5.5.58/
22.5.58"
18 Pages: pencil and ink drawings
of bulls
4 Pages: ink caricatures of male
and female figures
1 Page: pencil drawing of a ten-
thousand-franc note, inscribed
"BANQUE DE FRANCE"
11 Pages: pencil drawings of owls
and doves
8 Pages: pencil drawings of architectural designs
6 Pages: pencil drawings of
reclining female figures and
female heads

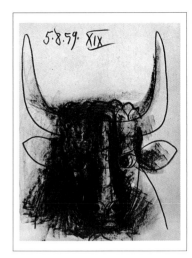

**No. 147**
Paper-covered notebook
1958
24 x 32 cm

Front Cover: inscribed "18.5.58"
Back Cover: inscribed "18.5.58"
26 Pages: pencil drawings of a
woman looking at the bottom
of her foot
3 Pages: pencil drawings of a
reclining figure under a tree
4 Pages: pencil drawings of stick
figures, related to the sculptures
*The Bathers*. Cannes, 1956. Spies
503–508.
19 Pages: pencil drawings of
leaves, one colored with
crayons
10 Pages: pencil drawings of
a figure
4 Pages: pencil drawings of a
composition with four figures
holding hands and a dove holding
a branch

**No. 148**
Spiral-bound cardboard-covered
notebook with "Album à Dessin /
Canson" printed on front
1959–1961
24 x 31 cm

Front Cover: inscribed
"Vauvenargues 11.8.59"
Back Cover: inscribed
"Vauvenargues 11.8.59"
9 Pages: pencil drawings of studio
interiors
3 Pages: pencil line drawings of
a composition with a head and
a dove, one inscribed "Youri
Gagarine"

**No. 149**
Spiral-bound cardboard-covered
notebook with "Esquisse"
printed on front
1959
33 x 42 cm

8 Pages: pencil line drawings of
figures, a table and chair, and
abstract patterns
3 Pages: pencil drawings of a
female figure with a dog
5 Pages: pencil drawings of a
female figure

**No. 150**
Spiral-bound cardboard-covered
notebook with "Esquisse"
printed on front
1959
33 x 42 cm

Front Cover: inscribed
"Vauvenargues le 28.3.59 /
Vauvenargues / 5.8.59"
Back Cover: inscribed
"Vauvenargues le 28.3.59 /
Vauvenargues / 5.8.59"
23 Pages: pencil drawings of an
ornate armoire
16 Pages: crayon designs for the
leg of a toreador's costume
8 Pages: brown and black crayon
drawings of a bull's head
2 Pages: pencil drawings of a bull
and a toreador

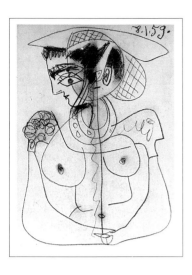  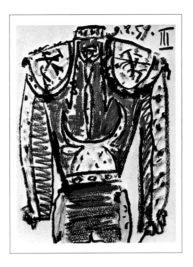 

**No. 151**
Spiral-bound cardboard-covered
notebook
1959
27 x 37 cm

Front Cover: inscribed "8.1.59 /
(*dibujos y escritos*) 19.1.59"
Back Cover: inscribed "8.1.59 /
(*dibujos y escritos*) 19.1.59"
1 Page: charcoal drawing of a
woman
1 Page: charcoal drawing of an
abstracted bull's head
11 Pages: manuscript writing
9 Pages: ink drawings of a reclining female nude and a seated
female nude looking at the
bottom of her foot

**No. 152**
Spiral-bound cardboard-covered
notebook
1959
33 x 42 cm

Front Cover: inscribed "28.4.59"
Back Cover: inscribed "28.4.59"
7 Pages: pencil drawings of a
seated female figure
1 Page: pencil drawing of a dog in
an interior
1 Page: pencil drawing of a naked
painter at his easel holding a
palette with his foot

**No. 153**
Blue paper-covered notebook
1959
17 x 22 cm

Front Cover: inscribed
"Dimanche 9.8.59"
Back Cover: inscribed "Dimanche
9.8.59"
3 Pages: crayon drawings of
studies for a toreador costume

**No. 154**
Spiral-bound cardboard-covered
notebook with "Aquarelle"
printed on front
1960
27 x 37 cm

2 Pages: black crayon drawings of
an owl, related to the sculpture
*Owl*. Cannes, 1961. Spies 574

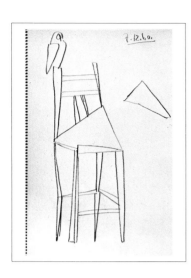

**No. 155**
Spiral-bound cardboard-covered
notebook
1960
27 x 42 cm

1 Page: pencil drawing of a bird
perched on the back of a chair

**No. 156**
Spiral-bound cardboard-covered
notebook
1960
24 x 32 cm

Front Cover: inscribed "10.11.60/
23.11.60"
Back Cover: inscribed "10.11.60/
23.11.60"
18 Pages: pencil drawings of
seated female nudes, three
colored with crayon
2 Pages: ink drawings of faces
1 Page: blue crayon drawing of
a face
11 Pages: pencil drawings of
designs with birds' heads

**No. 157**
Spiral-bound cardboard-covered
notebook
1960
23 x 31.5 cm

37 Pages: pencil drawings of
female nudes, many related
to the painting *Bather with Sand
Shovel*. Vauvenargues, 1960.
Zervos XIX, 236; including a
study after that painting inscribed
"dessin / fait d'après le / tableau /
(et mal fait) / 12.4.60"

**No. 158**
Spiral-bound cardboard-covered
notebook with "Croquis/dessin"
printed on front
1960–1961
Size undetermined

Front Cover: inscribed "21.6.60"
Back Cover: inscribed "21.6.60"
10 Pages: ink drawings of a
building
7 Pages: pencil or ink drawings
of figures

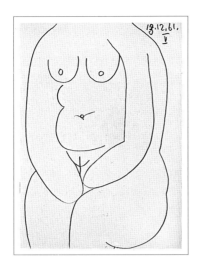

**No. 159**
Paper-covered notebook
1961
24 x 32 cm

Front Cover: inscribed "N.D. de
V. / 20.12.61. / 24.12.61"
Back Cover: inscribed "N.D. de
V. / 20.12.61 / 24.12.61"
5 Pages: pencil drawings of
female heads, three colored with
crayon
2 Pages: pencil drawings of a
reclining female nude, one
colored with crayon

**No. 160**
Paper-covered notebook
1961
24 x 32 cm

Front Cover: inscribed "N.D. de
Vie. / 17.12.61"
Back Cover: inscribed "N.D. de
Vie / 17.12.61"
8 Pages: pencil line drawings of
male and female nudes

**No. 161**
Spiral-bound cardboard-covered
notebook
1962
27 x 42 cm

7 Pages: pencil drawings of two
male and two female figures
in a landscape, related to the
painting *Luncheon on the
Grass, after Manet*. Vauvenargues,
1960. Zervos XIX, 204

**No. 162**
Spiral-bound cardboard-covered
notebook
1962
21 x 27 cm

Front Cover: inscribed "N.D. de
V. / 26.10.62 / 3.11.62"
Back Cover: inscribed "N.D. de
V. / 26.10.62 / 3.11.62"
27 Pages: charcoal, crayon, or
pencil drawings, related to
the painting *Rape of the Sabines*.
1963. Zervos XXIII, 121; subjects include: studies of horses,
a woman crying over a baby,
female heads, and a man chasing
after a woman

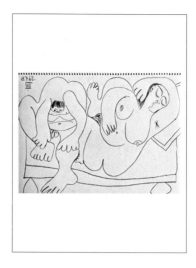

**No. 163**
Spiral-bound cardboard-covered
notebook
1962
26.5 x 35 cm

Front Cover: inscribed "15.6.62/
7.6.62"
Back Cover: inscribed "15.6.62/
7.6.62"
24 Pages: pencil drawings of two
male and two female figures
in a landscape, related to the
painting *Luncheon on the
Grass, after Manet*. Vauvenargues,
1960. Zervos XIX, 204

**No. 164**
Spiral-bound cardboard-covered
notebook
1962
27 x 42 cm

Front Cover: inscribed "N.D.
de V. / 24.10.62 / 25.10.62"
25 Pages: pencil drawings, related
to the painting *Rape of the
Sabines*. 1963. Zervos XXIII, 121;
subjects include: a woman falling
off a bicycle, entangled lovers,
warriors, and a warrior attacking
a running woman and child or
a woman falling off a bicycle

**No. 165**
Spiral-bound cardboard-covered
notebook with "Esquisse"
printed on front
1962
23 x 32 cm

Front Cover: inscribed "17.6.62"
2 Pages: pencil drawings of male
and female figures in a landscape, related to the painting
*Luncheon on the Grass, after
Manet*. Vauvenargues, 1960.
Zervos XIX, 204
1 Page: pencil drawing of an
architectural scene
1 Page: pencil drawing of
abstracted female figures
18 Pages: pencil drawings of a
male and a female nude on a bed
9 Pages: pencil drawings of a
seated and a reclining female
nude on a bed
1 Page: pencil drawing of a
standing figure
9 Pages: pencil drawings of
two couples making love, three
colored with crayon
5 Pages: crayon drawings
of a satyr chasing a woman
3 Pages: crayon drawings
of an abstracted swimmer

**No. 166**
Blue paper-covered staple-bound
notebook with "Dessin" printed
on front
1962
24 x 32 cm

Front Cover: inscribed "N.D. de
V. / le 5.1.62 / 11.12.62"
Back Cover: inscribed "N.D. de
V. / le 5.1.62 / 9.1.62"
6 Pages: crayon drawings of
a head of a woman
2 Pages: crayon drawings of
a reclining female nude

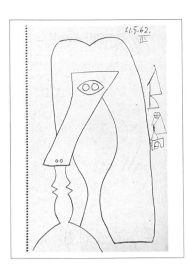

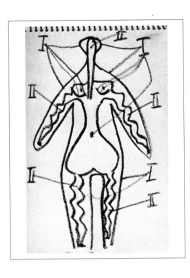

**No. 167**
Spiral-bound cardboard-covered
notebook
1962
27 x 42 cm

Front Cover: inscribed "23.4.62/
8.6.62"
Back Cover: inscribed "23.4.62/
8.6.62"
3 Pages: pencil or crayon drawings, related to the linoleum
cut *Nature morte sous la lampe*.
1962. Block 1101
9 Pages: pencil or crayon drawings of female heads, seven
related to the sculpture *Head of
a Woman*. Mougins, 1964. Spies
643
1 Page: pencil drawing of a seated
female nude
2 Pages: pencil drawings of
female nudes in an interior

**No. 168**
Spiral-bound cardboard-covered
notebook
1962
13.5 x 21 cm

3 Pages: black crayon drawings
of figures

**No. 169**
Cardboard-covered notebook with
perforated pages
1963
14.5 x 28.5 cm

21 Pages: crayon drawings of
female nudes
5 Pages: crayon drawings of two
standing male nudes
1 Page: crayon drawing of a
standing male nude and a seated
female nude
2 Pages: crayon drawings of the
head of a man
9 Pages: pencil and/or crayon
drawings of three laughing
male heads

**No. 170**
Spiral-bound cardboard-covered
notebook
1963
21.5 x 13.5 cm

Front Cover: inscribed "13.10.63 /
N.D. de V. / 28.11.63"
Back Cover: inscribed "13.10.63 /
N.D. de V. / 28.11.63"
5 Pages: crayon drawings
of seated female nudes
6 Pages: black crayon drawings
of male and female heads
14 Pages: pencil line drawings of
a seated old man with a
young girl
1 Page: crayon drawing of an artist at an easel holding a palette
and painting a sculpture bust
on a pedestal

**No. 171**
Spiral-bound cardboard-covered
notebook
1963
21 x 27 cm

Front Cover: inscribed "N.D. de
V. / le 10.2.63 / 21.2.63"
Back Cover: pencil drawing of
a hand inscribed "N.D. de V. /
le 10.2.63 / 21.2.63"
Inside Back Cover: inscribed "La
peinture est / plus forte que
moi / elle me fait faire / ce qu'elle
veut / le 27.3.63"
1 Page: pencil drawing of a seated
female nude with a horse's head
24 Pages: pencil drawings of an
artist at an easel painting a
reclining, seated, or standing
female nude, a seated male nude,
or a seated baboon, nine colored
with crayon
1 Page: pencil drawing of the
head of an old man wearing
a hat
3 Pages: crayon drawings of a
seated artist holding a palette
and painting a sculpture bust

**No. 172**
Spiral-bound cardboard-covered
notebook
1964
11 x 17.5 cm

Front Cover: inscribed "30.1.64/
7.3.64"
Back Cover: inscribed "30.1.64/
7.3.64"
13 Pages: pencil drawings of the
head of a reclining woman
with her arms clasped above her
head
13 Pages: pencil drawings of the
head of a baboon
3 Pages: pencil drawings of heads
of men
1 Page: pencil drawing of an interior with an artist and a baboon
each painting the other
7 Pages: pencil drawings of a
reclining nude
1 Page: pencil drawing of a
baboon painting a man

**No. 173**
Spiral-bound cardboard-covered
notebook
1964
13.5 x 21 cm

Front Cover: inscribed "17.1.64/
23.1.64"
Back Cover: inscribed "17.1.64/
23.1.64"
1 Page: pencil and crayon drawing
of a painter at an easel
14 Pages: pencil drawings of an
artist at an easel painting a
reclining female nude, two
colored with crayon
9 Pages: pencil drawings of a trip-
tych of interiors with a reclining
female nude
5 Pages: pencil drawings of
reclining female nudes
1 Page: pencil drawing, related to
the sculpture *Head of a Woman.*
Mougins, 1964. Spies 643.
2 Pages: pencil drawings of an
abstracted chair

**No. 174**
Spiral-bound cardboard-covered
notebook with "Lavis/Aquarelle"
printed on front
1964–1965
17 x 35.5 cm

Front Cover: inscribed "17.1.64"
Back Cover: inscribed "17.1.64"
5 Pages: pencil or crayon drawings of a bearded artist at an
easel painting a reclining female
nude
12 Pages: pencil drawings of
reclining female nudes, two
colored with crayon
1 Page: crayon drawing of the
head of a woman with her
hands raised over her head

**No. 175**
Binding undetermined
1967
8 x 11 cm

Front Cover: signed and inscribed
"Pour Jacqueline ma femme /
3.12.67"
10 Pages: medium and subject
matter undetermined

*References*

Bloch, Georges. *Pablo Picasso:
Catalogue de l'oeuvre gravé et
lithographie, 1904–1969.* 2 vols.
Bern: Kornfeld and Klipstein,
1968–1971.

Geiser, Bernhard. *Picasso,
peintre-graveur: Catalogue
illustré de l'oeuvre gravé et
lithographie, 1899–1931.* 2 vols.
Vol. 1 published in Bern by the
author, 1933; Vol. 2 published in
Bern by Kornfeld and Klipstein,
1968.

Zervos, Christian. *Pablo Picasso.*
33 vols. Paris: Cahiers d'Art,
1932–1978.

The following list, keyed to page numbers, applies to photographs for which a separate acknowledgement is due:

Bill Jacobson Studio, New York: 11 bottom left, 12 top left, 12 right, 13 left, 15, 20–50, 62–79, 86, 87, 88 left, 89 right, 92–111, 115 left, 124–139, 152–177, 180 bottom left, 185 right, 186, 190–209, 215, 216, 235–247, 249–261, 263–265, 268–273, 278–280, 282–289, 292–299, 305 far right, 310 far right, 312 near left, 313 near right, 338 near right, 338 far right. Museo Picasso, Barcelona: 303, 304, 305 far left, 305 near left, 306, 307 far left, 307 near right. National Gallery of Art, Washington: 9. Galerie Louise Leiris, Paris: 13 right. The Museum of Modern Art Photo Archive, New York: 141, 142. Dennis H. Powers Collection/Light Gallery, New York (copyright 1986, Juliet Man Ray, Paris): 140. ©Succession Picasso: 8, 18, 52, 54, 59, 80–82, 112–114, 115 right, 117 left, 178, 180 right, 181–184, 214, 217–234, 248, 262, 266, 267, 274–277, 281, 290, 291, 305 near right, 307 near left, 307 far right, 308, 309, 310 near left, 310 far left, 311, 312 far left, 312 near right, 312 far right, 313 far left, 313 near left, 313 far right, 314–337, 338 far left, 338 near left, 339–346; S.P.A.D.E.M., Paris, is the exclusive French agent for such reproduction rights, and V.A.G.A., New York, the exclusive United States agent for S.P.A.D.E.M.

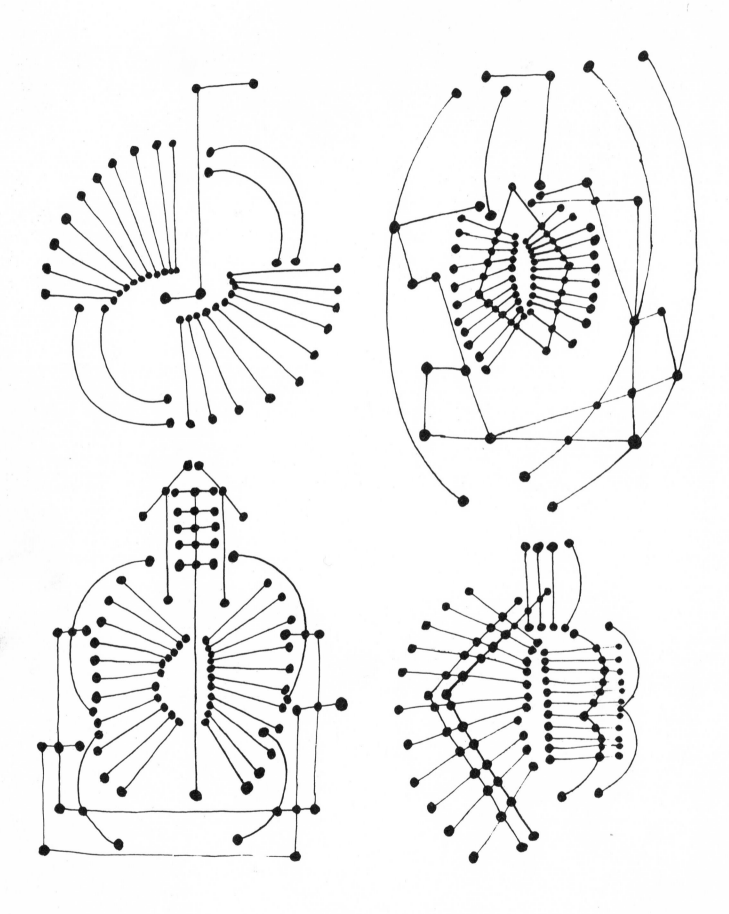